MALAYSIAN
CHINESE

MALAYSIAN CHINESE

Recent Developments and Prospects

EDITED BY

LEE HOCK GUAN • LEO SURYADINATA

ISEAS

INSTITUTE OF SOUTHEAST ASIAN STUDIES
Singapore

First published in Singapore in 2012 by ISEAS Publishing
Institute of Southeast Asian Studies
30 Heng Mui Keng Terrace
Pasir Panjang
Singapore 119614

E-mail: publish@iseas.edu.sg
Website: <http://bookshop.iseas.edu.sg>

The responsibility for facts and opinions in this publication rests exclusively with the authors and their interpretations do not necessarily reflect the views or the policy of the publisher or its supporters.

ISEAS Library Cataloguing-in-Publication Data

Malaysian Chinese: recent developments and prospects / edited by Lee Hock Guan and Leo Suryadinata.
   1.   Chinese—Malaysia.
   I.   Lee, Hock Guan.
   II.   Suryadinata, Leo, 1941–
DS595.2 C5M232   2012

ISBN 978-981-4345-08-8 (soft cover)
ISBN 978-981-4345-09-5 (E-book PDF)

Typeset by International Typesetters Pte Ltd
Printed in Singapore by Markono Print Media Pte Ltd

CONTENTS

PREFACE

On 10 July 2008, the Institute of Southeast Asian Studies (ISEAS) and Chinese Heritage Centre (CHC) jointly organized an international seminar on the Chinese in Malaysia. It was the second one in the series on "Ethnic Chinese Communities in Southeast Asia".

The first joint seminar was held in 2007 on "The Ethnic Chinese in Indonesia in the Era of Globalization". In this second seminar, we chose the topic, Malaysian Chinese, as there had been new developments in Malaysia, especially after the momentous outcome of the March 2008 general election, when the ruling coalition lost its two thirds parliamentary majority for the first time since Malaysia attained Independence. This seminar, therefore, was topical and timely. We invited leading scholars on Malaysia to discuss "Malaysian Chinese: Recent Developments and Prospects". We selected most of the papers from the seminar and put them together as a book so that they can reach a wider audience. We would like to take this opportunity to express our sincere thanks to the writers for their kind cooperation in revising their papers for publication.

Lee Hock Guan, ISEAS
Leo Suryadinata, CHC

CONTRIBUTORS

Beh Chun Chee is Lecturer at the Faculty of Creative Industries, Department of Mass Communication, Universiti Tunku Abdul Rahman, Malaysia.

James Chin is Professor of Political Science and Head of the School of Arts and Social Sciences, Monash University, Sunway Campus, Malaysia.

Ho Khai Leong is Professor and Dean of the Institute of Chinese Studies, Universiti Tunku Abdul Rahman, Malaysia.

Khor Yoke Lim is Associate Professor and Head of the Persuasive Section of the School of Communication, Universiti Sains Malaysia.

Lee Hock Guan is Senior Fellow at the Institute of Southeast Asian Studies, Singapore.

Lee Kam Hing is Senior Research Fellow at the Institute of China Studies, University of Malaya.

Lim Lai Hoon is Lecturer at the School of Social Science and Humanities Courses, Tunku Abdul Rahman College, Penang.

Rosey Ma is Research Fellow at the Department of Islamic History and Civilization, Academy of Islamic Studies, University of Malaya, 50603 Kuala Lumpur, Malaysia.

Leo Suryadinata is Professor and Director of the Chinese Heritage Centre, Singapore.

Tan Chee-Beng is Professor of Anthropology at The Chinese University of Hong Kong.

Toh Kin Woon was a former leader of the Parti Gerakan Rakyat Malaysia — the Malaysian People's Movement Party — and former Senator, Malaysian Upper Chamber of Parliament.

Wong Chin Huat is Lecturer in Journalism at the School of Arts and Social Sciences, Monash University, Sunway, Malaysia.

GLOSSARY

BA	Barisan Alternatif (Alternative Front)
BCIC	Bumiputra Commercial and Industrial Community
BERSIH	Coalition for Clean and Fair Elections
BN	Barisan Nasional (National Front)
CMS	Cahaya Mata Sarawak
CPI	Corruption Perception Index
DAP	Democratic Action Party
EC	Election Commission
FDI	foreign direct investments
GCC	Group of Concerned Citizens
Gerakan	Parti Gerakan Malaysia
GM	*Guang Ming*
HINDRAF	Hindu Rights Action Force
ICSS	Independent Chinese Secondary Schools
IMP	Independence of Malaya Party
INSAP	Institute of Strategic Analysis and Policy Research
IPTA	public institutions of higher learning
IPTS	private institutions of higher learning
ISA	Internal Security Act
JAWI	Federal Territory Department of Religious Affairs
KEADILAN	Parti Keadilan Nasional
KLSCAH	Selangor Chinese Assembly Hall
KOSATU	Koperasi Belia Bersatu
KTHCF	Kudat Thean Hou Charitable Foundation
LDP	Liberal Democratic Party
MAFREL	Malaysians for Free and Fair Elections
MCA	Malaysian Chinese Association
MCKK	Malay College Kuala Kangsar
MIC	Malaysian Indian Congress
MIMOS	Malaysian Institute of Microelectronic Systems
MK	*Malaysiakini*

MMM	Malay/Melanau/Muslims
MR	*Merdekareview*
NDP	National Development Policy
NEA	New Economic Agenda
NEP	New Economic Policy
NGO	Non-governmental Organization
NHEFC	National Higher Education Fund Corporation
NMB	Non-Muslim Bumiputra
NOC	National Operations Council
NSTP	New Straits Times Press
NUS	National University of Singapore
NVP	National Vision Policy
OEM	Original Equipment Manufacturer
OSA	Official Secrets Act
PAS	Parti Islam Semalaysia (Pan-Malaysian Islamic Party)
PBB	Parti Pesaka Bumiputera Bersatu
PBS	Parti Bersatu Sabah
PGCC	Penang Global City Centre
PGRM	Parti Gerakan Rakyat Malaysia
PKR	Parti Keadilan Rakyat
PPPA	Printing Presses and Publications Act
PR	Pakatan Rakyat (People's Pact or People's Alliance)
PRS	Parti Rakyat Sarawak
ROS	Registrar of Societies
SAPP	Sabah Progressive Party
SC	*Sin Chew*
SDC	Special Delegates Conference
SEAPA	Southeast Asian Press Alliance
SELCAT	Select Committee on Competency, Accountability and Transparency
SIB	Sidang Injil Borneo
SJKCs	Sekolah Kebangsaan Jenis Cina
SMEs	small and medium enterprises
SPDP	Sarawak Progressive Democratic Party
SPM	Sijil Pelajaran Malaysia
STPM	*Sijil Tinggi Persekolahan Malaysia* (Malaysian Higher School Certificate)
SUPP	Sarawak United People's Party
UEC	United Examinations Certificate

UM	University of Malaya
UMNO	United Malays National Organisation
UPSR	*Ujian Pencapaian Sekolah Rendah* (Primary School Evaluation Test)
Y4C	Youth for Change

INTRODUCTION

The results of the 8 March 2008 election stunned both the ruling coalition and opposition parties (Ooi et al. 2008). The Barisan Nasional were denied a two-third majority in parliament, and five states — Penang, Kedah, Perak, Selangor and Kelantan — were won by the opposition parties. Overwhelmed by the unexpected outcome, some observers characterized the election results as a "political tsunami" and extrapolated that the political landscape of Malaysia has completely changed. Of course, with the benefit of hindsight observers have become more cautious in their assessments of the impact of the March 2008 election. Nevertheless, the momentous March 2008 event is worth further examining, especially its impact on the Malaysian Chinese.

This collection of ten papers, including this introduction, attempts to assess the state of the art in the study of the Chinese community in Malaysia. It examines the nature of Malaysian multi-ethnic society and the position of the ethnic Chinese, the conflation between ethnicity and religion, the 8 March 2008 election and its impact on the community, the similarities and dissimilarities of the Chinese positions in East and West Malaysia, the new developments in the economy, and the media and education in the past few decades under the New Economic Policy that have had major bearings on the 8 March 2008 election, and the post-election Malaysian Chinese community.

NATION BUILDING AND THE POLITICS OF ETHNICITY AND IDENTITY

Since Independence in 1957, nation building in Malaysia has been bedevilled by the question of how to construct a common nationality that will have

Malay culture as its core and is also inclusive of, and fair to, the non-Malay cultures. Most Chinese naturally prefer an inclusive national identity that embodies the multicultural foundation of Malaysian society. In contrast, most Malays insisted that their language, religion, and culture should be granted a privileged position in the common national identity. Indeed there are Malay leaders who would conflate Malaysian nationalism with Malay nationalism and favour using the term *Melayu* nationality. In the 1960s, because ethnic-bounded identity was omnipotent, the prevailing sentiment was that "the Malay is first of all a Malay, then Muslim and then a Malayan; and the Chinese first of all a Chinese then a Buddhist or Christian if he is religious and then possibly a Malayan ... " (Wang 1992, p. 192). Consequently, after the May 1969 ethnic riots, the UMNO-Malay dominated nation essentially abandoned multiracial Malayan nationalism for a largely Malay-defined common nationality.

In his chapter Tan Chee-Beng argues that nation building in Malaysia has come to be shaped mainly by the politics of ethnicity, which has resulted in entrenching a communal world view and created a nation that is communally divided.[1] UMNO Malay elites aggressively set about creating a Malaysian nation that is Malay in cultural characteristics and Islamic in identity. Indeed, two mechanisms that have further communalized the polity and polarized the communities are the *Ketuanan Melayu* ideology and the New Economic Policy (NEP).

Initially, it was argued that the NEP was needed in order to alleviate the Malay economic handicap, and create a level playing field, and that it would only be for twenty years — from 1971 to 1990. But, over the years, the justification for the continuation of the NEP has increasingly been linked to Article 153, which stipulates the safeguarding of the special position of the *Bumiputra* through a system of quotas. Article 153 was initially meant to be a temporary measure implicitly agreed to by the Alliance elites, but since the 1980s, UMNO leaders have insisted on Article 153 being a timeless "social contract" which endows the Malays with "special rights". The special rights position, Tan argues, has, in fact become a "political and administrative weapon to promote the interest of the Malays under the Bumiputera ideology". With the implementation of the NEP, Malaysian society gradually became more ethnically divided, with the Chinese seeing themselves as being discriminated against, while the Malays as a whole are protected and the recipients of state favours.

The NEP and *Bumiputra* ideology have communalized society to the extent that many issues in the country have invariably become interpreted, problematized, and debated in ethnic terms. In the 1970s and 1980s, the centre of controversy was in the cultural and language arenas, with UMNO Malay nationalists pushing aggressively to expand and entrench Malay culture and language, and the Chinese resisting firmly to defend their cultural and linguistic space. With Islamic resurgence and the increasing Islamization of the Malay identity and the seizure of PAS by Islamists in the mid-1980s, championing Islam became the focal point of the UMNO-PAS political competition. In part to win the Malay Muslims' support, the UMNO-dominated country promoted an Islamization policy which, among other things, resulted in the expanding presence of Islam in the public sector, as well as the bureaucratization of Islam. For example, school curricula and public educational institutions became increasingly Islamized. Tan points out that the increasing Islamization of national schools indeed pushed the Peranakan Chinese of Terengganu to enrol their children in the Chinese schools in town increasingly instead of enrolling them in neighbourhood national schools. Based on his research on the Peranakan Chinese of Trengganu and other studies he has conducted, Tan observes that race and religion were not contentious issues in the past as Malaysians were generally sensitive towards and tolerant of one another's cultural practices and religious beliefs. Race and religion only became problematic issues when they were mobilized to gain the support of the Malay Muslim population. Referring to the political competition between PAS and UMNO, Tan argues that "it is not the presence of diverse religions that causes social tensions; it is the use of religious symbols in communal politics that causes this".

Tan concludes that the Malaysian experience shows how ethnic-based politics and nation building cannot create an inclusive society, but, instead, causes polarization among the ethnic groups. Accordingly, he argues that to redress the economic disparities between ethnic groups, affirmative action policy should be need based rather than ethnic based. Ethnic based affirmative action should only be for small minorities and not for the majority group in a society such as Malaysia. More generally, Tan proposes that the Malaysian nation building project should move away from UMNO's narrow ethnic based vision towards a non-racial policy that is consistent with the multi-ethnic composition and character of the society. The authoritarian statist approach to managing ethnic issues and relations have, Tan claims, worsened ethnic relations in Malaysia in part because UMNO monopolized the definition and interpretation of the ethnic problem by banning alternative non-racial versions. Moreover, UMNO and the bureaucratic elites have manipulated the *Bumiputra* ideology to further their vested interests. Tan insists that a democratic state would enable oppositional views to be debated in society and thus expose the ordinary Malaysians to alternative ways of managing ethnic relation and nation building. The March 2008 election which has resulted in a two-coalition party system can potentially democratize political space and provide promising possibilities of a Malay-led, but non-racial, or, perhaps, a less racial, model.

Because of the politics of ethnicity and identity in Malaysia, Chinese Muslims find that their multiple and fluid identities are largely ignored by the Malay-Muslim dominated state on the one side, and the Chinese community on the other. Rosey Ma's chapter captures succinctly the identity dilemma of Chinese Muslims, especially converts, who have become a casualty of the Malay-Chinese political rivalry. In particular, Ma points out, Chinese converts encounter a "general belief that being Malay is equivalent to being Muslim, as defined in the Constitution, a notion endorsed by the authorities and accepted by the public at large" so much so that it is difficult to position the identity of Chinese who are Muslims. In Malaysia, "where ethnicity and religion are so entwined in one's social and official identity, the Chinese Muslims are of the ethnicity of one community — the Chinese, while professing the religion of another community — the Malays. In the Malaysian context, this group is reduced to a double-minority: minority Muslim among the majority non-Muslim Chinese, and minority Chinese among the overwhelmingly Malay Muslims". Hence for Chinese converts the "redefining and construction of the new identity takes place within two dimensions, religious and ethnic/cultural".

The conflation of ethnicity and religion in Malaysia in the context of the strained ethnic relations between the Malays and Chinese has deleterious effects on Chinese Muslims such that it is difficult for the latter to maintain both their Chineseness and faith separately. They indeed find that they are not welcomed by either community. On the one hand, many Malays expect Chinese Muslim converts to leave their Chineseness behind as much as possible and adopt the Malay way of life; indeed they should *masuk Melayu* or become Malay — implying complete assimilation. In this sense, the Malays are emphasizing Malay characteristics to manifest their religious identification. If Chinese converts do not *masuk Melayu*, the Malays may suspect that they have become Muslims so as to become *Bumiputra* in order to gain access to all the privileges and perks that come with being *Bumiputra*. Thus becoming Malay is an indication that converts have not just left behind their Chineseness, but also that they now identify, and their loyalty is, with the Malays. On the other hand, Chinese converts find rejection and hostility from families of their ethnic community, who frequently equate their conversion with their becoming Malay. Here the "religious identity of the convert overshadows his cultural and ethnic identity in the eyes of other Chinese". Because of the frayed relationship with the Malays, many Chinese would equate becoming Muslim with effectively becoming Malay and thus view such conversion as betraying one's family and race, and bringing shame to the community.

More generally then, Ma argues that "a Chinese who has become Muslim ... has stepped out of his ethnic boundaries to cross over to the other one". For both communities, it is difficult to place being Malaysian Chinese and being Muslim in the same identity space. This is because in the Malaysian context,

> [o]ne does not cross ethnic boundaries: if you are born Malay or Chinese, you remain Malay or Chinese. One may cross religious boundaries, but officially and subjectively, only by leaving the former religion before stepping onto the other one. [In] Malaysia where one's religion and ethnicity are spelled in the same breath, how does one cross the religious boundaries when the attached ethnic part bounces back from the other sphere?

Fortunately, in recent years things have started to become better for Chinese Muslims in Malaysia. A major contributing factor is that Malaysians are now more educated and are thus becoming more aware of the two separate identities: Chinese and Muslim. The opening up of Malaysia's relations with China, and, also, greater exposure to the outside world, have helped to improve the situation for Chinese Muslims in Malaysia. Lastly, Chinese Muslims have mobilized their community to struggle for their space and rights in society.

THE CHINESE IN MALAYSIAN POLITICS AND ELECTIONS

In his interesting chapter (Chapter 3), Lee Kam Hing proposes to use Wang Gungwu's quadrilateral model of Malaysian politics to frame and account for the recent political developments in Malaysia.[2] Bearing in mind the complex social and ethnic stratification in Malaysia, Wang posited that there are four major sources of power in Peninsula Malaysia, namely: the Malay rulers, Islam, Malay nationalism, and the plural society, which refers to the non-Malay communities, especially the Chinese. The Malaysian political structure can thus be depicted as a quadrilateral shape with the four sources of power constituting the "legs" which anchor politics in the country. For that reason, if the "legs or four institutions become seriously out of proportion in relation to one another, then the stability of the table or Malaysian politics is threatened".

The nature and significance of each of the four sources of power and their relation to one another have obviously changed from colonial times to the present. In particular, Lee claims that since Independence the influence and power of Malay nationalism, or *Bumiputra* nationalism, and Islam have greatly expanded. After the 1969 ethnic riots, the UMNO-led Malay nationalists used the tragedy to entrench Malay hegemony or supremacy — *Ketuanan Melayu* in Malay — in the political, sociocultural, and educational fields, and the state apparatus. Official preferential policies and strategies were implemented to expand Malay participation in various sectors, and also ownership of the economy. At the same time, Islam has also become more influential as a result of the resurgence of Islam since the 1970s, the emergence of Muslim civil society groups, and the Islamists' control of PAS since the mid-1980s. With the Islamists in control of PAS, the growing intensive UMNO-PAS political competition for Malay-Muslim support became circumscribed by each party trying to outdo one another in championing Islam.

In contrast, Lee argues that the Malay rulers and Chinese "legs" of the quadrilateral model have lost significant influence and powers since Independence. During the Mahathir administration, the Malay rulers' powers were to some extent clipped by two successive constitutional amendments in 1983 and 1993 that deprived the rulers of some of their legal immunity. He however pointed out that since the "Malay rulers have largely retained their powers as defined by the 1957 constitution", it is possible that "in a situation where the ruling coalition and opposition are more evenly balanced, they can play a critical role". In the aftermath of the March 2008 election where UMNO political dominance was considerably weakened, Malay rulers, especially in Kedah, Perak, and Selangor, have tried to regain some of their powers.

For Lee, the most important political development, since Independence, has been the greatly diminished power of plural society, especially the Chinese and Indians. Several factors have contributed to the weakening of the non-Malay communities' political position, such as: non-Malay elites' acceptance of "constitutional compromises which conceded political pre-eminence to bumiputra nationalism"; and "a relative decline of the Chinese in the total population because of lower birth rate, and consequently [a] decreasing number of Chinese-majority seats in parliament". Among the Chinese, their influence and power were further weakened by deep divisions "between those in opposition and in government", within the ruling coalition between Gerakan and MCA", and "intra-party splits that occur at regular intervals such as those in the MCA and these sap the energy and resources of the largest Chinese-based party".

Until the March 2008 election results, power was concentrated around Malay nationalism and Islam, with the Chinese politically marginalized. To make matters worse, the Chinese are "increasingly sandwiched between a Malay nationalism [that] has been usurped by UMNO's *Ketuanan Melayu*, and [a version of] Islam [shaped] by PAS's conservative Islamic state outlook". In the past, because the Chinese fear a PAS's Islamic state more than UMNO's *Ketuanan Melayu*, UMNO could count on winning a majority of the Chinese support. In the March 2008 election, the opposition won more than a third of the parliamentary seats in part because when PAS downplayed its Islamic state goal, it led a large number of Chinese to reject UMNO's *Ketuanan Melayu* and vote especially for the DAP and PKR. Does March 2008 mark "a temporary setback for the UMNO brand of Malay nationalism or [does it] mark the emergence of an alternative Malay nationalism led by PKR and a moderate leadership faction from PAS"? If the Malay constituency remains fragmented, then winning Chinese support will be critical to both the BN and PR. And for PR to maintain its advantage over BN in winning a majority of the Chinese, PAS must restrain its Islamic state demands. Thus for now UMNO's Malay nationalism has lost considerable credibility while the "emergence of a two-party system in the parliament has given the Malay rulers and, to an extent, non-bumiputra a chance to return to a situation resembling the old quadrilateral model" before the ascendance of Malay nationalism and Islam. In a succession of by-elections since March 2008, UMNO remained incapable of regaining the support of the majority of the Chinese (see Chapter 5) who continue to support the opposition coalition.

Ho Khai Leong's chapter focuses on the pattern of the Chinese vote in, and the implications for Chinese-based parties after, the March 2008 election. While most analysts predicted correctly that Indian and Chinese votes would swing in favour of the opposition, none anticipated the huge size of the swing; more than 70 per cent of the Chinese and 60 per cent of the Indians voted for the opposition. Combined that with a more fragmented Malay vote, the BN lost its two-third parliamentary majority and as well as five state governments to the opposition coalition PR. The MCA, the largest Chinese-based party in the BN, lost half of the thirty-one parliamentary seats it won in the 2004 election. Gerakan, another Chinese-based party in BN, fared even worse, losing eight out of the ten parliament seats it won in the 2004 election, as well as the Penang state government. In contrast, the DAP increased the number of seats it won from twelve in the 2004 to twenty-eight in 2008. The best performance was recorded by the PKR which bolstered its one parliamentary seat won in 2004 to thirty-one seats in 2008. The performance of the DAP and PKR, and to some extent PAS, would indicate that there was cross-ethnic voting in their favour.

What prompted the Chinese to vote overwhelmingly for the opposition, especially the DAP and PKR? Several factors, according to Ho, contributed to the general vote swing against the BN, such as the negative impact on the local economy of the American sub prime crisis and the rising cost of living, corruption and cronyism, the worsening crime and security situation, election fraud and gerrymandering, and various forms of power abuse by the BN government. UMNO's racist posturing and its demands not just to continue the NEP, but to claim an even larger share of the economic pie further alienated the non-Malay voters. The Anwar Ibrahim factor also played a key contributing factor to the excellent performance of the opposition. Finally, another factor was the important role played by the alternative media in providing the opposition with the means to broadcast its message to the voting public and thus counter the pro-BN mainstream media's monopoly of the news.

Chinese voters were disillusioned with the MCA and Gerakan because the two parties had failed to speak out, defend, and advance their interests. Indeed, they were perceived as weak and dominated by the UMNO-Malay party in the BN coalition. In addition, the MCA was also considered to be rife with corruption, with the party, especially its leaders, viewed as being more interested in looking after its own vested interests than the interest of the community it allegedly stands and fights for. It also did not help that the MCA was driven by intraparty factional fighting, not over principles, but over the spoils of the incumbent. In the case of Gerakan, it lost the Chinese support in Penang because the Chief Minister of Penang, Koh Tsu Koon, and the Penang Gerakan leaders were generally perceived as weak, and had given in to UMNO in the administration of the state. In contrast, the DAP was outspoken and stood up in many instances for the Chinese and thus won over their support, especially among the younger Chinese voters. The PKR also attracted much support from the Chinese community as its New Economic Agenda advocates moving away from a race-based to a more need-based policy.

Can the Chinese-based parties in the BN, MCA, and Gerakan, remain relevant? What are the implications of the March 2008 election results for the Chinese, the Chinese-based parties in the BN and, more generally, for ethnic-based politics? Because of the fragmented Malay vote, and if this situation were to persist, winning the majority of Chinese votes would be necessary in order to win in ethnically mixed constituencies. Thus a fragmented Malay vote would empower the Chinese and Indians. The future of Chinese-based parties in the BN, MCA and Gerakan, will very much depend on UMNO. If UMNO persists in playing up race-based politics and fails to address the various issues that have alienated the Chinese, then the MCA's and Gerakan's support among the Chinese will continue to diminish. On the other hand, Chinese support for the DAP and PKR will also be negatively impacted if the more conservative elements in PAS and PKR were to succumb to the urge to play up ethnic and religious politics. Hence, for Ho, whether the two-coalition party system and more democratic politics will consolidate depends on many tangible and intangible factors.

Wong Chin Huat observes that Malaysian politics has shifted from being "United Malays vs Divided Chinese" towards a new situation of "Divided Malays vs United Chinese". In a nutshell, while the overwhelming Malay vote used to support the BN, in the March 2008 election there was a significant Malay vote swing to the opposition, especially for PAS and PKR, which means that the Malay bloc is now divided. Meanwhile, the March 2008 election saw an almost wholesale Chinese vote swing in favour of the opposition, so much so that one can conclude that the Chinese bloc is now united in its opposition to the UMNO-led BN. The fundamental question here is whether this "Chinese united against the UMNO" pattern is here to stay. Wong attempts to answer this question by looking at the factors that led to the Chinese voting *en masse* for the opposition, and whether those factors have been reinforced or weakened since the March 2008 election.

In strategic terms, the Chinese are caught between a politics of negotiation through representation within the government and a politics of pressure through voting for the opposition. Up until the March 2008 election, the Chinese bloc was divided between the negotiation and pressure camps. However, the failure of the Chinese-based parties in the ruling coalition to obtain concessions from the BN government gradually withered Chinese support for the BN to the extent that in the March 2008 election a huge majority of Chinese rejected the BN and voted in unison for the opposition. In uniting behind the opposition, the Chinese appear to have overcome their three traditional fears, namely; fear of ethnic violence, fear of losing representation in the government, and fear of instability or uncertainty. In the states of Penang, Perak, and Selangor, Wong provides empirical evidence and explanations to show how the Chinese in those states overcame the three fears and voted for the opposition in droves.

The intriguing question then is whether Chinese voters have consigned to history their fear of ethnic violence, losing representation in the government, and instability or uncertainty since the March 2008 election. For the two years since the March 2008 election, UMNO and its various affiliated groups have tried to raise the spectre of ethnic violence, but thus far they have not managed to terrify Malaysians, especially the Chinese, "to bow to violence and modify their political preferences". Instead, their playing up of racial and religious issues was roundly condemned and delegitimized by civil society and opposition parties, especially Malay Muslims. The MCA and Gerakan claim that, if the Chinese do not strongly support them, the community will be marginalized in the government, has lost credibility since the DAP and Chinese PKR politicians were not only allocated places in the Penang, Selangor and Perak state governments, but, in fact, appear to have more parity in their relationships with their Malay counterparts. Moreover, the Chinese are no longer constrained by their fear of instability or uncertainty, given the stability — despite the occasional intra and interparty bickering — of the state governments of Penang, Selangor and Perak (before UMNO's usurped control of it). As such, Wong concludes that for the BN to make gains in the next general election, it would have to depend on Malay votes.

To what extent is Chinese politics in Sabah and Sarawak similar and different from that in Peninsular Malaysia? James Chin's chapter provides a succinct picture of Chinese politics in the East Malaysian states and shows the limited applicability of Wang's quadrilateral model to those states. While Chinese politics in East Malaysia has also undergone increasing marginalization, especial in electoral politics, there is however a "key difference between Chinese politics in the peninsula and East Malaysia [with] the continued pre-eminence of the local-based parties in Sabah and Sarawak".

The majority of Sarawakian Chinese have consistently voted for the Sarawak United People's Party (SUPP), a party in the Sarawak BN, and that has not changed even up to the most recent state election in 2006. The main argument that the SUPP has used to win Chinese support is that the latter need representation in the local government to look after the community's interests. This argument, in spite of the pro-*Bumiputra* federal policies, has convinced a majority of the Sarawakian Chinese to throw their support behind the SUPP. However, over the years, gerrymandering and malapportionment in the delineation of constituencies have drastically reduced the proportion of Chinese majority seats to far below their demographic percentage. As such, the Chinese vote has been gradually marginalized electorally while Malay-Muslim majority seats have increased faster than their population growth. Nevertheless, Chin argues that a growing number of Chinese, especially those of the younger generation, have become disillusioned with SUPP for failing to protect and advance the community's interests. The increasing abuse of power by and corrupt practices of Chief Minister Abdul Taib Mahmud and his family have also alienated the Chinese community. Intraparty squabbles in the SUPP have also caused splits within the party, with many former SUPP members and supporters switching their support to the opposition. That more Chinese are now willing to vote for the opposition, which, in Sarawak, means largely the DAP, was clearly demonstrated in the Sibu parliamentary by-election in 2010 where the DAP defeated the SUPP in what was traditionally a SUPP stronghold. Chin's chapter did not discuss the 2011 election as it was written in 2008. But in his recent notes to the editors of this volume, Chin wrote that "Taib decided to call for a snap state election in April 2011. The election results confirmed the 2008 voting trend. The Chinese voters abandoned SUPP completely. With the exception of Batu Lintang and Bawang Assan constituencies, the DAP won all the Chinese majority seats. Batu Lintang was won by a Chinese candidate from PKR, DAP's alliance partner. In Bawang Assan, DAP won in all the urban, Chinese voting streams. Wong Soon Koh (of the SUPP) was only able to win Bawang Assan because he won heavily in native areas in the constituencies." Chin went on to argue that, "The depth of SUPP's losses can be seen by the defeat of the SUPP president, George Chan, by an unknown first time DAP candidate. Two SUPP deputy ministers were also defeated. The Chinese were simply fed-up with SUPP's inability to represent them and more importantly, were particularly incensed with allegations of Taib's corruption."

Unlike in Sarawak where Chinese politics is largely represented by SUPP, in Sabah the Chinese bloc is fragmented as there are several Chinese-based parties in the BN. Over the years, the already divided Chinese vote also experienced political marginalization similar to that in Sarawak. Specifically, their diminished electoral strength was due to the pro-Malay Muslims' biased delineation of constituencies, as well as to the government systemically enlarging the Malay Muslim population by granting citizenship to Muslim immigrants from the the Southern Philippines and Indonesia. All the same, recently a number of developments have negatively impacted Sabahan Chinese support for the BN. Firstly, the mass granting of citizenship status to Muslim immigrants from the Southern Philippines has triggered a backlash from the Chinese and Kadazans. Secondly, because the federal government has not honoured the 20-Point Agreement over the years, it has led to a rising Sabahan nationalism among both the Kadazans and Chinese. Thirdly, discriminatory actions against non-Muslim faiths such as that illustrated in the controversy over Malay-language bibles and the usage of the word "Allah" among Christians, and the refusal of the government to permit the construction of Mazu, a deity important to the Chinese, have also alienated the Chinese and Kadazans. Hence, the March 2008 election showed an increase in support for the DAP and PKR but the two parties did not do as well as they should have precisely because they failed to agree on an electoral pact and ended up splitting the Chinese vote between them in constituencies where both contested.

Chin concludes that while both in Sabah and Sarawak the Chinese have lost the role of "kingmaker" because of the electoral marginalization of the community, it "would [still be] unpalatable not to include them in any government". In Sabah, the Chinese vote will remain fragmented with support divided among several Chinese-based parties in the BN and the DAP and PKR in the opposition. For Sarawakian Chinese, while their current choice is either the Chinese-based party, SUPP, in the BN, or the DAP from the opposition, it is possible that the MCA and Gerakan may decide to expand into Sarawak sometime in the future.

ECONOMY, EDUCATION, AND MEDIA

The Malaysian NEP is perhaps one of the most comprehensive ethnic-based preferential policy in Asia, if not the world. Officially, it has two objectives: one, to eradicate poverty regardless of ethnicity; and two, to restructure society so as to eliminate ethnicity with economic functions, or more generally, to reduce the economic inequality gap between the Malays and Chinese. State elites have always emphasized with the eradication of poverty via raising the productivity and income levels of the poor, but they did not pay any attention to narrowing the gap between the rich and poor within and across ethnic groups. The narrowing of economic inequality was framed in ethnic terms and the emphasis was on closing the gap between the Malays and Chinese. To a large extent, the state has successfully enhanced Malay participation in the occupational structure of the modern and productive economic sectors by the 1990s. Beginning with the Mahathir administration in the early 1980s, the government became engrossed with establishing a Bumiputra Commercial and Industrial Community (BCIC), and indeed devoted huge resources, as well as used a privatization strategy to build a Malay capitalist and corporate elite.

While the various government policies and programmes have greatly lowered the poverty rates, as well as narrowed the ethnic economic inequality in the country, there has, however, been a widening intraracial income inequality gap, especially among the Malays. Thus the NEP has contributed to "enhancing the life chances of many bumiputras through affirmative action policies". It has, however, also nurtured a state-dependent class of rentiers who are closely linked to the BN, and UMNO in particular. The special preferential treatment given to the politically well connected rentiers have created market distortions, such as the inefficient allocation of resources, waste, and declining competiveness. Moreover, in recent years the debate over the NEP has been hijacked by those with vested interests, and has focused on the NEP target of increasing *Bumiputra* equity ownership to 30 per cent. Although critics have challenged the claim that the 30 per cent target has yet to be achieved, the state and UMNO have continued to use the 30 per cent figure to frame economic policies. The problem here is that the 30 per cent-equity ownership issue essentially involves only the upper strata of Malaysian society and, as such, has little or no bearing on the rest of society. Toh argues that UMNO authoritarianism and arrogance, and the party's corruption and cronyism partially contributed to the alienation of a significant number of the Malay middle-class who voted for the opposition in the March 2008 election.

The New Economic Agenda (NEA) proposed by Anwar Ibrahim and the PKR, with varying levels of support from the DAP and PAS, promised to move away from the narrow, ethnic-based NEP to a more inclusive, need-based policy orientation. The central rationale is that, with the current level of economic development and the success of NEP in creating a sizeable Malay middle-class, it is time to introduce an affirmative action policy that is more need-based. Even with a need-based affirmative action policy, the NEA argues the *Bumiputra* would be the main beneficiary of the NEA as they constitute the majority of the poor. Linked to the NEA need-based affirmative action policy is also the emphasis on *Ketuanan Rakyat* (People's Supremacy) instead of UMNO's *Ketuanan Melayu* (Malay Supremacy). NEA's *Ketuanan Rakyat* would be more inclusive and promises a new type of Malay leadership which would not marginalize the non-Malays. Indeed, in terms of Wang Gungwu's quadrilateral model, the NEA proposes to harmonize Malay nationalism with the non-Malays' position. And in terms of governance, the NEA promises a clean, transparent, and merit-based system of administration. With an open tendering process, government procurement and projects would be free of crony-style business dealings, which characterized previous UMNO-dominated administrations. Lastly, the NEA would introduce more competition and meritocracy in the education system to improve the quality of human capital in the country.

Since coming into power the state governments of PR-controlled Selangor, Penang, and Perak (before UMNO usurped control of it) have initiated a number of policies that are consistent with NEA's principles. The Penang administration introduced its Clean, Accountable, and Transparent governance, including an open tendering process for government projects and procurement. On its part, the Selangor administration has introduced a Committee on Competency, Accountability & Transparency (SELCAT) and passed the Freedom of Information Bill 2010. The short-lived PR state administration of Perak addressed the various problems encountered by the lower income groups, regardless of their ethnicity, such as land titles. In all three state governments, Chinese and Tamil schools were granted financial assistance, as well as land for their expansion needs. However, these opposition-controlled state governments very quickly discovered the limits as to what they could do precisely because over the years power has been vested in the central government, leaving the local governments with limited jurisdiction and financial capacities.

However, various moves by the opposition-controlled state governments to introduce a more ethnic-blind policy received much resistance from within the coalition and especially virulent criticisms from UMNO, Malay business groups, and various Malay non-governmental organizations (NGOs). The virulent reaction to the opposition attempt to move towards need-based affirmative action is best illustrated by the new Malay "non-governmental group", PERKASA. It embodies the worst aspects of *Ketuanan Melayu*, which insist on Malays having entitlements derived from their indigenous status. In this, they usually refer to Article 153, which stipulates that Malays have a special position because of their indigenous status and that safeguards were introduced to protect their special position. Interestingly, during the Constitution negotiations the Reid Commission had proposed this Article as a temporary measure to be removed later on. This is because the Constitution should uphold the equality of every citizen, regardless of ethnicity, and the Commission was afraid that Article 153 could be used to justify discrimination of citizens based on ethnicity. PERKASA, whose members mostly also belong to UMNO, have fanned Malay fears of losing their special rights and more frighteningly the political dominance to the Chinese. As such, they have manufactured a climate that has negatively impacted ethnic relations in the country. Nevertheless, PAS, Malay members of the PKR, and various Malay individuals and groups have come out to criticize PERKASA and UMNO for playing race politics in the country.

Like the rest of the Malaysian media, the development and function of the Chinese media was radically affected by expanding state intervention and regulation of the sector in the aftermath of the May 1969 ethnic riots. Constitutional amendments to Article 10 and the Sensitive Act constrained and stunted the development of the freedom of speech while the Printing Presses and Publications Act (PPPA) forced the transfer of any foreign ownership of newspapers to local owners, especially to the government-funded PERNAS and the UMNO-funded Fleet Group. Subsequently, the MCA and MIC also through party-funded companies, acquired the other mainstream newspapers as well. Thus, PERNAS became the majority owner of *Nanyang Siang Pau*, the leading Chinese newspaper, and the MCA-funded HUAREN acquired *Malayan Thung Bao*.

During the Mahathir administration, state intervention and the regulation of the media were further strengthened through more amendments to the Constitution and as well as changes to the PPPA. Three successive factors — the economic and financial conditions in the 1980s, the implementation of privatization, and the political crisis triggered by the Mahathir-Anwar fallout in 1998 — contributed to the downsizing of the number of newspapers published, and to increasing ownership concentration of the Chinese media. In addition, intraparty rivalry in the MCA also spilled over to rival interests vying for control of the Chinese newspapers. Thus by 2006, Tiong Hiew King, a Sarawakian businessman who used to be close to Ling Liong Sik president of the MCA from 1986–2003, has control over all four major Chinese dailies, comprising about 85 per cent of the Chinese newspaper market.

With the increased ownership concentration of the mainstream Chinese media, alternative and critical voices had to turn to other avenues to reach out to the Malaysian public. The main avenue turns out to be the Internet where two Chinese web-based newspapers, *Malaysiakini* (Chinese version) and *Merdekareview*, were launched in 2005. *Malaysiakini* started out as an online English news daily in 1995 by "activists cum entrepreneurs", with a grant from SEAPA (Southeast Asian Press Alliance), which felt there is a need for alternative and critical voices to be heard and read as a counter-measure to the mainstream media. *Merdekareview*, on the other hand, was founded by journalists from the mainstream Chinese newspapers taken over by the MCA, or Tong, with financial backing from some Chinese businessmen. One distinct advantage that the online newspapers have over their print counterpart is that they are not subject to the PPPA. Initially, since the online media still have to abide by the Sensitive Act, OSA (Official Secrets Act) and ISA (Internal Security Act), the government tried to regulate and stifle the online media through periodic application of the various relevant regulations, and also by refusing to issue Press ID cards to their journalists. Nevertheless, in the aftermath of the March 2008 election, the BN government control over the online newspapers has weakened as opposition-controlled state governments have freely allowed online media access to information, press briefings, and other state functions.

Commercially, because sale of the mainstream newspapers has fallen, or even plummeted in some instances, and this is partly due to readers turning to the free and more vocal online media, mainstream journalists are pushing for more freedom of expression.

An examination of how the Chinese print and online media covered the March 2008 election demonstrates major "differing interpretation of news values" between the various newspapers, and between the print and online media. The mainstream Chinese newspaper, *Sin Chew*, tended to focus more on the "official" coverage and version of news, while *Guang Ming* "as [a] regional newspaper gave prominence to issues in Penang and the DAP state government". Much of its "news was straightforward reporting of day-to-day issues such as crime prevention, distribution of rice to the needy, and land issues". In contrast, both *Merdekareview* and *Malaysiakini* focused primarily "on the controversial issues, presenting views from diverse groups, including the opposition parties and non-government organizations". This way, *Merdekareview* and *Malaysiakini* came across as critical of the BN government as they provided the opposition parties and civil society groups with a medium to articulate their views.

It is clear that the "ownership pattern of Chinese newspapers in Malaysia has shifted from personal ownership, where control is in the hands of the founding family or group, to state control in the Eighties, and finally to concentration in the hands of a conglomerate with strong connections with the power centre". Thus parallel to the concentration of ownership is the increasing control of the media "through a combination of repressive laws, shareholdings, direct nominees and close political relationships". Thus *Merdekareview* and *Malaysiakini*, and the Internet in general, have reintroduced media diversity, as well as the flourishing of critical independent points of views and analyses. In this sense, the Internet has played a crucial role in enabling opposition parties to disseminate information and their views to the electorate, and thus indirectly assisting the PR to achieve its outstanding results in the 2008 election. If the UMNO-dominated administration continues to stand by its cyber laws, then it will be difficult for the ruling coalition to control what Malaysians read — and how they should think.

Language and education issues have generated much heated debates in Malaysia even before the country was granted Independence in 1957. Indeed the importance of language and education issues resulted in three major reports being carried out in succession a few years before 1957, namely, the Barnes Report (1950), Fenn-Wu Report (1951), and Razak Report (1956). The key problem encountered was how to transform the decentralized, multilingual, colonial education system into a centralized, national education that privileges Malay as the sole national and official language, while also respecting the language rights of the minority groups. In post-colonial Malaysia, due to the UMNO-Malay dominated nation's aggressive attempts to use education as a means to create a Malay-centric nation and advance Malay socio-economic interests, language and education have remained contentious issues, with the Chinese community struggling to protect and advance their community's educational opportunities and mother tongue education. This is especially the case since the Chinese put a lot of emphasis on education as a stepping stone to socio-economic success, and a means to transmit and preserve their language and culture.

In the education sector, because the Malaysian state has allocated large investments to expanding the sector, the country has made impressive educational gains since Independence. The Malaysian Chinese have also benefited from state educational investments: illiteracy is almost negligible in the community, younger generation of Chinese are better educated, there are better educational opportunities for most Chinese, and the ethnic preferential policy has narrowed inter-ethnic educational inequalities. With the increasing privatization of the higher education sector since the 1990s, qualified Chinese students can acquire a local tertiary education without much problem — provided they can afford to pay for it. Changing societal and community attitudes towards women acquiring higher education qualifications, and also changing familial and economic structures, have enabled Chinese women to make impressive gains in educational attainment, especially at the higher education levels. Nevertheless, there is still discrimination when it comes to women employment opportunities.

With regard to education medium, Lee argues that the preference of most Chinese is to enrol their children in Chinese primary schools and then national secondary schools. While most Chinese are satisfied with this educational compromise, the UMNO-Malay dominated nation for many years harboured the idea of establishing a single Malay-stream education for all. The nature of ethnic politics in the country, however, prevented UMNO Malay nationalists from eliminating the Chinese primary schools. This has not stopped the state from marginalizing Chinese education in terms of public financial allocations, land for the expansion of existing schools, and the granting of licences for building new schools. Moreover, the increasing discrimination against Chinese students in the national primary schools has resulted in more than 90 per cent of the Chinese students enrolling in Chinese schools since the 1990s. With the overwhelming majority of Chinese students enrolled in Chinese schools, several problems have arisen, including, among other things, overcrowding in and shortage of Chinese schools. Until the March 2008 election, the Chinese community encountered strong resistance from the UMNO-controlled administrations in getting land for extending schools, and licences to build new schools. That has changed since the March 8 2008 election, especially in states controlled by the opposition-coalition, PR. This in turn has influenced the UMNO-controlled federal government to be more accommodating to the Chinese community's application of land and new licences for schools.

When the UMNO-dominated state implemented a wide-ranging, ethnic-quota higher education admission policy from 1971 onward to increase Malay enrolment, it dramatically decimated the higher educational opportunities for qualified Chinese students in the country. This was because higher education opportunities in the country were limited and this remained so until the privatization of higher education and the expansion of public higher education, especially from the 1990s. The privatization of higher education came about with the influence of the then neoliberal pro-market ideology and the sector underwent a huge expansion especially in the aftermath of the 1997 Asian financial crisis. The privatization of higher education shifted the burden of financing higher education to families, in particular, Chinese families. It also partially helped to increase the "production" of tertiary educated Malaysian students for the government objective of moving the economy up the value chain. However, the privatization of higher education, coupled with the state continuing with its pro-Malay admission policy, has resulted in the ethnic segmentation of higher education, with the Malays identified with the public higher education, and the Chinese with the private higher education.

The UMNO-dominated state marginalization of Chinese primary schools and the discrimination against Chinese students in the admission into local public higher education had the most adverse impact on the lower-income segment of the Chinese community, especially the more than one million Chinese New Village residents. Chinese schools in the New Villages are more dependent on state financial allocation because they cannot expect to receive much funding from the generally lower-income Chinese families who constitute the majority in the villages. Indeed a lack of financial resources has led to Chinese schools in many New Villages having facilities in need of repairs, as well as a shortage of teaching staff. In addition, school dropout rates are much higher among Chinese students from the New Villages because of the lower quality of instruction, their weak command of the Malay language, the cost of attending secondary schools, which are usually located in towns, the need for these students to work to supplement family incomes, and so on. Unsurprisingly, the privatization of education has not helped to enhance the higher education opportunities for Chinese students from lower-income families as they are frequently priced beyond their families' financial means. Chinese students from lower-income homes then largely have to depend on gaining admission into the local public higher education institutions.

CONCLUSION

Malaysia under the long and dynamic Mahathir Administration underwent a number of major political, socio-economic, and cultural changes. In a sense, the results of the 2008 election reflect the changes in the country under the Mahathir administration. UMNO obtained fewer Malay votes and both the MCA and Gerakan — Chinese parties in the ruling coalition — were seriously challenged by the DAP, giving rise to questions of their future development, if not viability. Nevertheless, the significance of the changes in the political landscape since the March 2008 election is still limited and perhaps even tentative. Malay power has been undermined somewhat as the Malays have become divided while the Chinese have become more united, but Malay dominance in the political system remains entrenched and the ideology of the indigenous state, or *Ketuanan Melayu*, continues to prevail as the UMNO-dominated Barisan Nasional still dominates politically and ideologically.

Globalization and the rise of China have had major impact on Malaysia in general, and the Chinese population in particular. Because globalization releases economic forces which do not recognize state and ethnic boundaries, the economic rise of China has provided more opportunities for Malaysian Chinese businesses and has thus contributed to their economic dominance in Malaysia. Globalization has also changed the landscape of the Chinese mass media in Malaysia, where a multinational Chinese conglomerate, which is close to the state elite, now has control over the main Chinese newspapers in the country, but, at the same time, the worldwide web has given rise to an alternative mass media. The impact of new media on Malaysian Chinese politics is tremendous as reflected in the March 2008 election. Chinese education has also experienced new developments, with more concessions to Chinese-medium education made, and more private educational institutions set up, making the ethnic division in the educational field more conspicuous: the Malays concentrate in public tertiary institutions, while the Chinese dominate private tertiary institutions.

As ethnic size matters in an ethnic-based political system, the fact that the Chinese population in Malaysia has been declining in terms of percentage, though not in absolute numbers, will undoubtedly affect the future political landscape of Malaysia. In all probability, unless a fragmentation of the Malay community materializes, the political influence of Malaysian Chinese will continue to weaken in line with their shrinking percentage in the total population.

Notes

1 Tan prefers to use the word "communal" instead of "ethnic".
2 Wang introduced his quadrilateral model in his seminal essay, *Reflections on Malaysian Elites* (1986).

References

Ooi Kee Beng, Johan Saravanamuttu and Lee Hock Guan. *March 8: Eclipsing May 13*. Singapore: Institute of Southeast Asian Studies, 2008.

Wang Gungwu. "Reflections on Malaysian Elites". In *Community and Nation: China, Southeast Asia and Australia*. 2nd ed. New South Wales, Australia: Asian Studies Association of Australia and Allen & Unwin, 1992.

1

MALAYSIA: ETHNICITY, NATIONALISM, AND NATION BUILDING

Tan Chee-Beng

On 31 August 2007, Malaysia celebrated her fifty years of Independence from British rule.[1] While Malaysians and non-Malaysians may hold differing views of Malaysia, both would, however, agree that there has been considerable economic achievement and visible modernity as symbolized by the famous Petronas Twin Towers and modern highways. But in recent years, there is a mounting general dissatisfaction among Malaysians over a number of developments, such as the increase in crime mainly in urban areas and scandals involving the police whose professionalism is questioned, as well as the perception of more corruption, and doubts about judicial independence. Above all, there is also agreement among researchers and observers, and even the general public, that Malaysia has become more racially divided. What has gone wrong?

This chapter[2] will discuss ethnicity, nationalism, and nation building in Malaysia and see what we can learn from the Malaysian case. It will show that nation building in Malaysia has been shaped by the politics of ethnicity, which has fostered a communal world view and created a nation that is communally divided. In other words, not only Malaysians of different ethnic groups would imagine[3] the Malaysian nation differently; but the nation itself has also become highly polarized. Because politicians of different ethnic groups have articulated along ethnic lines, the revival of Malay nationalism after 1969 and non-Malay reaction pushed the country to become a highly polarized nation. Malay nationalism here refers to the nationalistic ideology of the Malay elite who pursue a Malaysian nation that is Malay in cultural characteristics and Islamic in identity. It is communal nationalism or ethnic nationalism, that is, nationalism that is articulated by an ethnic group within a multi-ethnic state for the group's interest and to project the cultural nationalism aspired to by the group, or the cultural view of the nation as imagined by the group. This kind of nationalism is common in new states such as Malaysia and Indonesia, where the indigenous elite, faced with the presence of an influential minority such as the Chinese, seeks to have a greater share of the economy and to dominate the cultural conception of nationhood. But in practice, this nationalistic articulation serves to promote the economic and political interests of the indigenous elite. The communal nationalism we are concerned with here is, of course, not separatist nationalism, which seeks to form a separate state.

A significant change in Malaysian politics occurred with the March 2008 national election, which saw the opposition parties winning control over a few state governments. Did it signal the decline of communal politics, and will the government pay attention to the complaints of non-Malays and the socio-economic needs of the people, irrespective of their ethnic background? The rejection of the ruling coalition, despite its clinging to power, provided much food for thought. It was a rejection of the politics of fear, which the UMNO-led coalition had used effectively to rally the support of Malays by exploiting their fear of Chinese economic dominance and of losing Malay cultural characteristics in nation building. The UMNO-led government has also used the politics of fear to rally the support of non-Malays — however reluctantly — by exploiting their fear of an Islamic state led by the PAS, as well as their fear of racial riots. This politics of fear perpetuates the communal political process in Malaysia.

Does the 2008 general election mark the beginning of the end of the politics of fear in Malaysia? The result of this election no doubt provides much room for reflection about ethnicity, nationalism, and nation building, and indeed democracy, too. David Brown (1994) has written about ethnicity, nationalism, and democracy in Southeast Asia, and I shall use the Malaysian case to reflect on this issue and on nation building. I argue that the politics of ethnicity is perpetuated through the politics of fear using ethnicity and religion, and that both a reduction in communal politics and an improvement in democracy are favourable for the promotion of ethnic harmony or national unity. The deterioration of democracy will only lead to more oppression of the minorities and more polarized communal politics, in turn leading to more ethnic disharmony.

I use the term "communal" to mean "racial". This is the English term that is commonly used in the British Commonwealth, and it has the advantage of not being confused with race and racial in the biological sense. It is ethnic in the cultural and political sense. Nation building is also a common term for "new nations" such as Malaysia and Indonesia, new states created after Independence from colonial rule. These states find it necessary to bring their people together and promote unity to foster a united nation. In the context of Malaysia, nation building has meant the building of a prosperous and harmonious nation where economic development and ethnic harmony are emphasized.

According to the 2000 census, the population of Malaysia was about 22 million. Of these 65.1 per cent were *Bumiputra* (predominantly Malays), 26 per cent Chinese, and 7.7 per cent Indians. About 60 per cent of the population are Muslims, 22 per cent Buddhists and followers of Chinese popular religion, 9 per cent Christians, 6 per cent Hindus, and 3 per cent others or have no religion. The Malays, Chinese, and Indians are the major ethnic groups in Peninsular Malaysia. In East Malaysia, the major ethnic groups in Sarawak are Ibans (30.1 per cent of the state's Malaysian citizens), Chinese (26.7 per cent), and Malays (23 per cent), and in Sabah the major ethnic groups are Kadazan/Dusun (18.4 per cent), Bajau (17.3 per cent), Malays (15.3 per cent), and Chinese.[4] As expected, the proportion of Malays and non-Malays in the population is a sensitive matter, particularly as the official use of the term *Bumiputra* to group together Malays and non-Malay "indigenous" people, has the effect of "enlarging" the Malay population since the term *Bumiputra* is very much associated with Malays. In Sabah, the term *pribumi*, which also refers to the "indigenous" populations as opposed to citizens of Chinese and Indian origins, was used in the 1980 census to group together all the "indigenous" members of the population so that they appear to be an overwhelming majority. In the 2000 census official figures for the main ethnic groups in Sabah did not even mention the Chinese. In contrast, the 1991 census indicated that the largest ethnic group in Sabah was the Kadazan/Dusun (25 per cent of the state's 1.4 million people), followed by the Chinese (15.6 per cent), Bajau (15.2 per cent), Malays (8.9 per cent), Murut (3.9 per cent), other indigenous peoples (19.3 per cent), and others (12.7 per cent) (cf. Tan 2005, p. 781).

Generally, while ethnic relations between ethnic groups in East Malaysia are better than in West Malaysia, as there is more interaction and less communal tension between members of different ethnic groups, the communal politics of Peninsular Malaysia has nevertheless infected East Malaysia too in recent years. The main rivalry in Malaysia's communal politics is mainly between the Malays and non-Malays (usually the Chinese and Indians), and to avoid generalization, this chapter will focus on these two categories when referring to ethnicity and the communal process in Malaysia.

FROM COLONIAL PLURAL SOCIETY TO CONSOCIATIONAL DEMOCRACY?

Malaysia, like Burma, was often described as a plural society under British colonial rule. The colonial scholar, J.S. Furnivall, who introduced the term, described a plural society as follows:

> It is in the strict sense a medley, for they mix but do not combine. Each group holds by its own religion, its own culture and language, its own idea and ways. As individuals they meet, but only in the market place, in buying and selling. There is a plural society, with different sections of the community living side by side, but separately, within the same political unit. Even in the economic sphere there is a division of labor along racial lines (Furnivall 1948, p. 304).

Furnivall was perceptive in his analysis and observed that colonial relations were predominantly economic and that colonial policy was framed with reference to the interest of the colonial power (Furnivall 1948, pp. 5–8). He was, however, wrong in assuming that the lack of "common social will" made it necessary for the colonial power to hold a plural society together (Furnivall 1948, pp. 307–08). Rather, it was precisely the colonial power that created the "plural society" and made sure the different ethnic populations were kept separate for its rule and economic exploitation. In Malaya, the demand for Independence by Chinese, Indian, Malay, and other elites showed the common will for self-determination and nation building. Today there is no doubt that Malaysian citizens of different ethnic background see themselves as Malaysian and belonging to Malaysia. Besides the articulation of leaders of the different ethnic communities, the national education no doubt plays an important part in forging this common recognition of being Malaysian.

It was convenience that led leaders of the main political parties of the three major ethnic communities in Malaya, namely the Chinese, Indians, and Malays, to form an alliance to run for election and subsequently form the Alliance government, which led to the development of a form of consociationalism in Malaya (Chee 1991). For the ruling party, this model which involved the coalition between leaders of the major ethnic political parties was so successful that in the 1970s the Alliance was expanded to include more political parties to form the National Front (Barisan Nasional, BN). Except for the racial riots in May 1969, Malaysia has been a new nation that has remained politically stable. With its economic achievements in the 1980s and 1990s, Malaysia was seen as a successful model of nation building, that is, for those who emphasize political stability and economic development over the deterioration of democracy and human rights.

Yet on its fiftieth Independence celebration in 2007, many observers, including well known Malaysian journalists and scholars, lamented that the younger generation of Malaysians was racially more polarized. As someone who was active in a social reform non-government organization, *Aliran*, in Malaysia in the 1980s, which advocates a non-racial approach to nation building, but who has been out of the country since 1996, I am amazed — or more accurately, disappointed — that there are still the similar kinds of racial issues which seem to have become worse, and there are more religious issues that further reinforce racial polarization. There is, for instance, the debate on whether Malaysia is a secular or an Islamic state, and I will comment on this afterwards.

Let us first note that the so-called consociationalism of Malaysia has become increasingly more communal in the implementation of national policies, and there is no equal sharing in decision making as UMNO leaders have dominated the coalition and Malaysian politics since 1969. Although Malaysia practises parliamentary democracy, the consociationalism in Malaysia is really not consociational democracy as defined by Arend Lijphart. According to Lijphart (1977, p. 25), the most important element of a consociational democracy is "government by a grand coalition of the political leaders of all significant segments of the plural society". The other three elements include mutual veto in decision making; "proportionality as the principal standard of political representation, civil service appointments, and allocation of public funds"; and "a high degree of autonomy for each segment to run its own internal affair" (Lijphart 1977, p. 25). The functioning of a consociational democracy thus depends very much on mutually agreed power sharing and the functioning of democracy beyond holding national elections.

As events developed since the 1969 racial riots have shown,[5] the criteria for consociational democracy were violated as UMNO assumed political dominance and ignored the principle of proportionality. The erosion of democracy further made it impossible to realize the consociational model and this has serious implications on ethnic relations and nation building. Lijphart himself doubted Malaysia's democracy and consociationalism after

1969 because of the growing "limitation of the freedom of expression and the increasing political and economic discrimination in favor of the Malays" (Lijphart 1977, p. 153). The UMNO-dominated government's support and pursuit of the Malay nationalist vision of nationhood put an end to consociationalism while racializing nation building. Instead of consociational democracy, Malaysia has an UMNO-dominated coalition rule that has become authoritarian. BN is a coalition for sharing ministerial posts; the distribution of ministerial posts to persons of different ethnic origins serves as a symbol of political participation by different ethnic groups, but the influential ones are held by UMNO politicians. Other than grouping together to ensure success in the general election, there is neither consociationalism nor the concern for democracy. The relevant issue here with regard to the 2008 election is whether democracy will be restored and reinforced as a result of the ruling coalition's reaction and attempt to regain the support of most Malays and non-Malays; or if the opposition coalition comes to power, whether it will restore democracy and adopt a non-racial approach to nation building.

Ethnicity and Nation Building

In Malaysia, political mobilization along ethnic lines has the effect of reinforcing ethnicity. This has become worse after the introduction of the New Economic Policy (NEP) following the May 1969 racial riots. While the aim of the government, as outlined in the Second Malaysia Plan (1971–75), has been to eradicate poverty and restructure the economy so that it does not identify with "race", its approach has been racial because of its assumption of the Malays and other indigenous peoples as the "have-nots", and the non-Malays as the "haves". The Malay special position is made full use of to formulate policies in favour of the *Bumiputra* who are often read as being "Malays". The term *Bumiputra* refers to the Malays and other "indigenous" peoples and serves to put the Chinese and Indians, whose migrant ancestors came from outside the Malay Archipelago, as a sort of permanent aliens or citizens who are not natives. It distinguishes a category of citizens as indigenous and another category as non-indigenous even though many of the latter have a history of settlement in the country for a few generations.

The affirmative action policy for the Malays and other natives[6] has its legal provision in Clause 2 of Article 153 in the Malaysian Constitution, which states:

> … the Yang di-Pertuan Agong shall exercise his functions under this Constitution and federal law in such a manner as may be necessary to

safeguard the special position of the Malays and natives of any of the states of Sabah and Sarawak and to ensure the reservation for Malays and natives of any of the states of Sabah and Sarawak of such proportion as he may deem reasonable of positions in the public service (other than the public service of a State) and of scholarships, exhibitions and other similar educational or training privileges or special facilities given or accorded by the Federal Government and, when any permit or license for the operation of any trade or business is required by federal law, then, subject to the provisions of that law and this Article, of such permits and licenses.

The Yang di-Pertuan Agong is a constitutional monarch elected every five years by and from among the nine Malay sultans. This provision in the Constitution was included as a compromise between the Malay and non-Malay political leaders who formed the Alliance, with the tacit understanding that it would be reviewed. With the dominance of UMNO in Malaysian politics after the 1969 racial riots, the "special rights" position has become a political and administrative weapon used to promote Malay interest under the *Bumiputra* ideology. Unlike first Prime Minister Tunku Abdul Rahman, who represented the Malay aristocratic class, the new UMNO leaders represent the professional (teachers, doctors, lawyers, etc.) and the emergent business class.

The NEP was implemented in ways that further polarized the Malays and non-Malays. The Chinese, for example, see themselves as being discriminated against, while the Malays as a whole are protected and given favours by the state, although, in actual fact, the majority of poor Malays have remained poor. Although children of poor Malays are entitled to government scholarships reserved for *Bumiputra*, they need to compete with well off and politically connected Malays. Again, while many Malays see the Chinese as being generally well off, there are actually a large number of Chinese who are in the lower-income group. Nevertheless, their urban concentration and their businesses (as symbolized by business signboards) make the Chinese very visible in the country. With strong government intervention, there are now rich and politically influential Malays who are high officials and directors of business corporations. In fact, an "achievement" of the NEP is that all government and statutory bodies are dominated by *Bumiputra*. Hence, measured by the UMNO-dominated government's aim to create a class of rich Malays, the NEP has been fairly successful.

To a great extent, Malaysian society has become racialized by the *Bumiputra* ideology and NEP. For example, in the 1980s there were many racial problems, the most prominent of which was the national culture debate.

The Malay elite pushed for a concept of national culture that is based on
Malay culture and Islam, while the non-Malays reacted with their vision of
a national culture in which non-Malay cultures have equal place with Malay
culture. In a way, the post-1969 period was characterized by the resurgence
of Malay nationalism,[7] which had emerged in the twentieth century in
reaction to both colonialism and the increasing presence of the Chinese.
The Malay fear of Chinese economic dominance and the Chinese fear of
Malay political dominance have their root in the pre-Independence period.[8]
In fact, the preference for the Malays has its root in Malay nationalism and
the colonial patronizing attitude favouring Malays in response to the rise of
Malay nationalism. Even the *Bumiputra* ideology is a revival of the "sons of
the soil" slogan in the 1930s. The *Straits Chinese* newspaper in Malacca in
its editorial of an issue in 1932, for instance, opines that:

> The cry of Malaya for the Malays is carried out too far, and the local-
> born citizens, who have contributed towards the material prosperity of
> the country, have reason to resent this agitation for depriving them of
> their legitimate rights....[9]

With independence, Malay nationalists realized that their vision of a
Malay state had to be compromised by sharing political power with the
non-Malays. The dominance of Malay political power in the UMNO-led
BN government in post-1969 Malaysia provided Malay nationalists with a
chance to push for a more Islamic and Malay-oriented Malaysia. In schools,
the history of Malaysia was rewritten to give it a Malay emphasis. Even the
teaching of the English language suffered in the face of the strong rhetoric
for the use of Malay as the national language.[10] While the NEP has achieved
significant results in increasing Malay participation in the private sectors
(such as through the government policy of requiring firms to employ 30 per
cent of *Bumiputra*) and in dominating the public sector, this has disastrous
effects on Malaysian tertiary institutions. In government funded universities
and colleges, it has become an unwritten rule that the vice-chancellors,
deans, and, in most cases, department heads, too, have to be Malay. The
promotion of academicians to higher positions and higher academic ranks
when they do not have the requisite international standard of scholarship,
as well as the disillusion of many serious academics, has caused Malaysian
universities to decline drastically in academic standards and to lose respect in
the international academic world.[11] At the same time, it is an insult to good
Malay academics to be seen as having attained their achievements because
of their Malay ethnicity.

What is perhaps more serious is the racializing of Malaysians' world view. One can talk of a more racial NEP generation, namely the young people born after 1969. It is worth noting that eminent Malaysian historian Khoo Kay Kim made the following remarks on Malaysia's marking of fifty years of Independence:

> Over the years, our politics has been so communal and that has been reflected in our education system. It produces a generation of parents who instills the same thing in their children. My generation may have had their hang-ups, but the walls are much higher today (Ng 2007).

My own research on the *Baba* (this term is loosely used to refer to Malay-speaking Chinese) in Malacca in 1977 backs Khoo's view as my older informants told me about the good relationship between the *Baba* and Malays, and how before Independence, it was possible for some Chinese to marry Malay women and even bring them into the Chinese (that is, *Baba*) families as family members. Today this would be an emotional communal issue, as would be the rare conversion of Malay individuals to Christianity or Buddhism. While Malaysians share common national institutions, interpersonal interaction between Malays and Chinese outside the workplace and some sports (such as soccer) is rather limited. Children acquire communal views from their parents and peer. For example, Chinese parents often remind their children that they have to study hard because it will be more difficult for them than for their Malay classmates to gain admission to a public university in Malaysia. As these children grow up they find their ethnic sentiment reinforced as they encounter what they perceive as discrimination when they fail to get a scholarship or an admission to a public tertiary institution. While Furnivall may be criticized for his view that colonial power was necessary to hold the plural society together, his observation that different groups meet, but live separately, is in many respects still valid. This is despite the fact that, contrary to Furnivall's assumption, there was social interaction outside of the market. Today there are shared public institutions, and there is identification with Malaysia as a nation, but socially Malaysians remain plural.

However, the interaction between the Malays and non-Malays appears to be cordial. There is, in fact, a culture of avoidance. It has become a norm that when the non-Malays interact with the Malays, sensitive topics, including the issue of Malay special rights and non-Malay grievances of discriminatory policies, are avoided, so the Chinese-Malay interpersonal interaction appears cordial. But there is much accumulated tension between ethnic groups and this is expressed in the nation's communal political process. A Malay

politician (often a highly educated person) may call for a certain political
action which the non-Malays see as being against their interest or their ethnic
honour, and non-Malay politicians and leaders will then speak up against
it, and vice versa. The communal process ensures that the country remains
communally divided.

RELIGION AND ETHNICITY

Malaysia is also a multireligious society in which Malays are Muslims and
Chinese are mainly followers of Chinese popular religion and the rest are
Christians, Muslims and followers of other faiths. Islam is the official religion,
while the freedom to practise other faiths is guaranteed by the Constitution.
Muslims and non-Muslims got on well in the past, and I learned this from
my interviews with old informants in Malacca, Kelantan, and Terengganu. It
is actually in modern-day Malaysia that religion, namely Islam, has become
an ethnic issue. This has to do with Islamic resurgence since the 1980s and
the mobilization of Islamic symbols in communal politics, both among the
Malays and between the Malays and non-Malays. Among the Malays, the
main challenge to UMNO comes from PAS, the Islamic party that seeks
to turn Malaysia into an Islamic state. UMNO politicians portray PAS as
radical and anti-progress, while PAS portrays UMNO as less Islamic. As long
as Malaysia practises democratic election, there is little chance of a party
that calls for an Islamic state coming to power at the national level since the
non-Muslims, as well as many Muslims, do not support the idea. However,
in some predominantly Malay states the Islamic party may be elected to run
the state government, as has been the case in Kelantan and Terengganu.[12] An
Islamic state is not possible without changing the Malaysian Constitution, and
so even when PAS comes to power at the state level, while it can implement
more stringent control of gambling, Karaoke bars, and prostitution, it cannot
introduce policies that violate the national Constitution.

However, in competing to be seen as more Islamic, and in response to
the Islamic resurgence in the 1980s, the UMNO-led government introduced
Islamization policies which caused concern to the non-Muslims. In actual
fact this comes in the form of using more Islamic symbols, which the
non-Muslims see as Malay cultural domination. For example, it is now
the norm to have a Muslim prayer before a major government function,
even in universities. The non-Muslims are free to practise their faiths, but
since the 1980s non-Muslim religious leaders have complained that it has
become more bureaucratic and difficult for non-Muslims to be allocated land
to build churches and temples. Still, non-Muslims continue to get partial

financial allocation from the government via the non-Malay parties in the ruling coalition to build some temples and churches. Islam as a state religion allows mosques to be built from government funds. This is actually not an issue, but the institutional discrimination arising from Malay nationalism and Malay control of the public sector (that is, domination in decision making) have caused unhappiness among the non-Muslims. Even in Sarawak and Sabah, where ethnic relations are much better than in the Peninsula, the ban, official and unofficial, on the importation of Malay Bibles from Indonesia caused unhappiness among the non-Malay indigenous people, many of whom are Christians.

In Terengganu where the Peranakan-type Chinese (that is, acculturated Chinese) villagers and Malays interacted closely in the past — some of my older Chinese informants even told me about their childhood days when they waited outside the village Islamic schools for their Malay friends to finish their Islamic study to go and play together — there was unhappiness in the 1980s because the daughters of the Chinese were teased by some of their Muslim classmates for not wearing the head scarf, which by then had become a common attire for Muslim women in Malaysia. Now the rural Chinese send their children to a Chinese primary school in town rather than to a nearby Malay school in the village, as they did in the past. In Terengganu Town, the urban Chinese were not happy because Malay squatters built houses over graves in the Chinese graveyards, and some squatters even had the political connections to get electricity supply (cf. Tan 2002, pp. 129–43). The lack of swift response to Chinese complaints caused unhappiness in a region of Malaysia where Chinese-Malay relations had been very good.

The point is that religious diversity was not a problem in the creation of a Malaysian nation, as the people have learned to respect one another's faith, and the non-Muslims have basic knowledge about Muslim sensitivities and are careful about these. Religion becomes an issue as a result of the communal politics of the 1980s and since. A most recent example is the clarification of then Deputy Prime Minister Najib Razak that Malaysia is an Islamic state, a view declared by Prime Minister Mahathir Mohamad in 2000. While this was a form of reaction to the PAS's call for an Islamic state, it upset the non-Muslims. Eventually then Prime Minister Abdullah Badawi stepped in to clarify that Malaysia is neither a secular state nor an Islamic state like Iran and Pakistan; it is a country that practises parliamentary democracy.[13] In actual fact, the Constitution is quite clear that Malaysia is not an Islamic state although Islam is recognized as the religion of the Federation, and Malaysians generally have no quarrel over this. Leading Malaysian human rights activist and Islamic scholar Chandra Muzaffar (2007) points out that it is misleading to cast Malaysia as either a secular or Islamic state. It is not an Islamic state since its governance is not based on the *Qur'an* and *Sunnah* (the way of the Prophet), but it is also not secular either since Islam is the official religion and Muslims benefit from the government in building mosques and Islamic schools. The debate over whether Malaysia is a secular or an Islamic state, and the rhetoric that Malaysia is already an Islamic state, have caused more polarization between Muslims and non-Muslims. It is not the presence of diverse religions that causes social tension; it is the use of religious symbols in communal politics that causes this.

ETHNICITY AND DEMOCRACY

The racialization of the Malaysian nation coincided with the erosion of democracy in Malaysia. Malaysia began with a very hopeful democracy, with a clear separation of power between the Executive, the Parliament and the Judiciary. After the ascendance of UMNO power since 1970, and especially under the prime ministership of Mahathir Mohamed from 1981 to 2003, democracy was eroded bit by bit, with business people supporting Mahathir for economic achievement — until the financial crisis in the late 1990s. After the 1969 racial riots, public rallies were banned although government politicians continue to hold them. Government politicians often evoked the threat of racial riots to warn voters not to vote for the opposition (cf. Tan 1991). Laws were enacted to ban the public discussion of so-called sensitive issues, including the special privileges for the Malays. Throughout the Mahathir period, there was increasing restriction on the freedom of speech, especially when his power was also challenged from within UMNO.[14] Newspapers have to apply for licence renewal every year, and so self censorship was inevitable. The use of the police to curb the opposition inevitably eroded police professionalism, vividly symbolized by the infamous beating of Anwar Ibrahim while being handcuffed and blindfolded in police detention by the Inspector General of Police Rahim Noor. Anwar Ibrahim was the deputy prime minister and minister for finance before Prime Minister Mahathir sacked him and ordered his arrest following their split and Anwar's open challenge against him. Frequent reports since the 1980s about police brutality or unprofessional conduct also point to the erosion of police professionalism.

The most serious threat to Malaysian democracy was the sacking of Tun Salleh Abas, lord president of the Supreme Court, in 1998, as he was about to rule on the legality of UMNO, following an internal fight within the party still headed by Mahathir Mohamad.[15] The incident marked the end of the independence of Malaysia's judiciary, which until then was respected internationally. Since then there has been a deterioration of public confidence in the judiciary.

The increase in the power of the Executive under the authoritarian leadership of Mahathir, the control of the parliament via the coalition's control of the two-third majority which allows the ruling elite to amend the Constitution in its favour, and, finally, the control of the judiciary by the Executive, led to the erosion of democracy in Malaysia. This, together with the growth of Malay communal nationalism and the related Islamization policy, polarized Malaysian society seriously. On the other hand, the erosion of democracy and human rights aroused concerned individuals of different ethnic backgrounds to work together for a more democratic nation. In 2007 more than 100,000 Malaysians, including writers, film producers, and human rights lawyers petitioned online to urge the king, whose duties are ceremonial, to intervene to help promote humans rights and judiciary integrity.[16] This unprecedented event came about because, as a lawyer put it, "People have lost confidence in the media, judiciary, police and the universities...." (Kuppusamy 2007*b*). A consoling trend as a result of the increasing authoritarianism and communal split is the emergence of a small group of concerned citizens of different ethnic backgrounds to strive for democracy and an alternative voice. There is thus an increasing interest among these Malaysians of different ethnic origins in the *Malaysiakini* website (<http://www.malaysiakini.com>), which is critical of the government.

Indeed the use of websites by opposition politicians and government critics to bypass the government-controlled mainstream newspapers (especially during the election campaigning period) contributed much to the success of opposition politicians. This is an interesting and significant trend when young people are involved in the national election.[17] In the Malaysian election held on 8 March 2008, five states in Peninsular Malaysia were won by opposition parties, unlike in previous elections where only the predominantly Malay states of Kelantan and Terengganu would be won by PAS. This time, other than Kelantan, Kedah, Penang, Perak and Selangor were won by the opposition parties, which formed an alliance among themselves.[18] Other than Kelantan and Kedah, which are predominantly Malay in population, the other three states are quite multi-ethnic, with a strong Chinese and Indian presence. The BN loss of the four states (that is, other than Kelantan which was expected) which it had always controlled since Independence showed that a significant number of Malays and non-Malays had turned away from UMNO, MCA, MIC, and Gerakan. While this indicates hope for multi-ethnic politics, one should note that ethnicity remains important in Malaysian politics; more specifically the Malay factor remains significant. The Anwar factor is obviously significant not only in bringing about the difficult cooperation between PAS and DAP, but also in putting aside the Malay fear of non-Malay dominance in national politics.

The injustice suffered by Anwar symbolized to many Malays and non-Malays the injustice of Mahathir's rule. While Mahathir and his supporters blamed then Prime Minister Abdullah Badawi for the National Front's poor performance, it was in fact Mahathir's policies that had caused the desertion of many non-Malay voters from the MCA, Gerakan and MIC, and Malay voters to turn against UMNO. With such a blow to the BN, there could be a racial reaction if UMNO leaders played up the Malay fear of non-Malay dominance. To the credit of the Abdullah government, this did not happen. In fact Chief Minister of Penang Koh Tsu Koon set a moderate tone when he graciously accepted defeat and congratulated the DAP on its success. While former Prime Minister Mahathir Mohamad unfortunately tried to stir up the Malay fear, telling his Malay audience that the Chinese and Indians had gained politically at their expense and that Malays would not be "masters in our own country" if this continued (Kuppusamy 2008), he was, fortunately, unsuccessful.

The government's loss of the two-third majority is actually good for democracy in Malaysia as the BN government cannot amend the Constitution to enhance the authoritarian rule that marked the Mahathir government. Nevertheless, it remains to be seen if the politics of fear, on which I shall expand, will be eradicated. The formation of the opposition alliance can be seen as a good development for a political process that is more democratic and less communal, as this will act as a check on the BN. Voters will have the choice of a government which they perceive to be less communal and more democratic. However the opposition is very fragile, depending very much on the charisma and mobilizing ability of Anwar Ibrahim. The distrust between the PAS and DAP remains very serious, especially the DAP and non-Malay distrust of PAS's Islamic agenda in nation building. Thus Anwar and the party led by his wife, Parti Keadilan Rakyat (PKR), play a crucial role in bridging the PAS and DAP.

NO ALTERNATIVE TO RACIAL NATION BUILDING?

An increasing number of Malaysians are aware of the seriousness of racial division. In 2007 there was a request that the largely communally based political parties in the BN be merged to form a multiracial party as a way to reduce racial politics. The prime minister, who is the leader of the National

Front, rejected the suggestion (see *South China Morning Post* 2007). As for the racial approach in the implementation of the NEP, there are even some non-Malays who have conceded that it was necessary. Ye Lin-Sheng, in his controversial book, argues that the NEP has saved Malaysia from the racial riots that happened in Indonesia in 1998 (Ye 2003). In actual fact, Malaysian nation building could have been non-racial and, at the same time, corrected the ethnic polarization along ethnic lines. Instead of a racial quota, affirmative action policies could have been based on socio-economic needs. For example, instead of the racial bloc approach, students from rural areas with poor educational facilities could have been given additional points for university admission. Since most of the Malays and other "indigenous peoples" live in the rural areas, they will benefit most without the policy being seen as racial.

This non-racial approach to affirmative policy is possible in Malaysia since many members from the majority ethnic group also need special assistance. It also ensures that disadvantaged non-Malays are not neglected and marginalized. Not only are there poor Chinese, there are many more Indians who are poor and need assistance. In November 2007 more than 10,000 Indians protested publicly to demand a fair share of the country's resources and an end to discrimination.[19] This followed the mass protest two weeks before that by poor Malaysians who were mostly Malays (Kuppusamy 2007e). A further rally in Kuala Lumpur by some 300 Indians in February 2008 was broken up by the police and some people were arrested (Agence France-Presse 2008). The protests showed the failure of the racial approach to restructure the ethnically polarized economy. Unlike the United States or China where the affirmative action policy is for the marginalized minorities, that in Malaysia is for the majority population and mainly serves the interests of the middle class and rich Malays while the marginalized indigenous minorities remain neglected.

There are alternatives to development via the *Bumiputera* policy, and some Malay scholars are not happy either with the racial and state patronage approach to development for the Malays. Ahmad Fauzi Abdul Hamid (2004), for example, used the example of a grass roots Islamic movement, Darul Arqam, which was led by Ashaari Muhammad, to show that it is possible for *Bumiputera* "to assume middle class credentials without relying on state patronage". Furthermore the NEP fails "to build a social and cultural capital that would advance the Malays to be on par with the Chinese" (Maznah Mohamad 2004, p. 172). That the NEP helps to prevent racial riots is merely an assumption, and as Maznah Mohamad (2004, p. 175) has pointed out, the "successes of Malaysia's ability to achieve economic growth and ethnic peace are actually spuriously correlated with its adoption of the NEP". It is misleading to argue that without a particular economic approach, Malaysia would not have achieved the level of economic development and political stability in the 1980s. Racial riots are politically staged by a certain interested party of a society, and its occurrence needs to be studied in relation to the agitation of that particular group or gang, police professionalism, and so on. It can occur even in a state with mature democracy, such as the United States.

A comparison with Indonesia is interesting as the country is often perceived by foreigners as having more racial trouble than say, Malaysia. In actual fact, there has always been close interaction between the Chinese and native Indonesians. With democratization and the correction of racial policy since 1998, Indonesia is in fact on the way to becoming not only a more democratic and liberal society than Malaysia, but also one that is less racial. In fact, the Indonesian Government has abolished the classification of citizens as indigenous (*pribumi*) and non-indigenous.[20] In Malaysia, the grouping of citizens into *Bumiputra* and non-*Bumiputra* remains administratively important and socially divisive, even after the NEP officially ended in 1990 and was followed by the National Development Policy (NDP, 1991–2000) and the National Vision Policy (NVP, 2001–20). Thus unless Malaysia changes its communal approach to nation building, communal tension will not decrease, and as democracy erodes, social harmony cannot be assured. Even if there is no obvert racial violence, the quarrel over racial quotas in businesses will have long-term negative effects on the country's economic dynamism.[21]

LESSONS FROM MALAYSIA

There are some lessons we can learn from Malaysia.

1. National unity in communally polarized societies such as Malaysia, that is, post-colonial societies that remain plural, cannot be achieved by using a racial policy to correct ethnic imbalances between the major ethnic groups. In other words, racial imbalances in these societies cannot be corrected by racial policies. The application of the *Bumiputra* and non-*Bumiputra* distinction in the implementation of government policies reinforces and worsens polarization along ethnic lines. While education and the sharing of national institutions have helped create a sense of identification with the Malaysian nation, socially, the people of the different ethnic groups, especially the Malays and non-Malays

in Peninsular Malaysia, have become more separate. In other words, while there is identification with Malaysia as a nation, different ethnic groups imagine the nation differently. The nationalistic Malays envision a nation that has the stamp of Malay culture and Islam. For the Chinese and Indians, Malaysia should be a nation where all citizens enjoy equal treatment and no one ethnic culture dominates over the others. The current communal policy can only encourage communal imagination of nationhood.

2. Marked socio-economic imbalances between ethnic groups can be and need to be corrected via policies that address the socio-economic needs of the people. An affirmative action policy in Malaysia can be introduced in a non-racial way by allocating quotas based on socio-economic needs. An ethnicity based affirmative action policy can be justifiably introduced only for small marginalized communities (mainly indigenous peoples) and if its implementation will help improve relations between these marginalized minorities and mainstream society, and to ensure that the minorities have a better chance of participation in the national society.

3. Increasing polarization along ethnic lines cultivates ethnic tension which hinders the achievement of social harmony. This is worsened by the erosion of democratic institutions and the professionalism of security forces. We have noted that communal issues need be dealt with quickly and professionally. The delay and unprofessional treatment of sensitive ethnic issues or conflicts will only give the impression that the government is favouring a particular ethnic or religious group, and this will worsen ethnic tension or conflict.

4. Religious diversity is not a cause of social disharmony. It is the encapsulation[22] of religion in communal politics that is the problem. People in Malaysia have sufficient knowledge of the dos and don'ts of different religious traditions, and at the local level, they have developed what I call intergroup norms on social interaction (Tan 1979) to respect one another's religious practices, such as the rural Baba in Malacca giving New Year cakes to their Malay neighbours a day before they hold their Chinese New Year worship at home; or the rural Chinese in Kelantan not smoking or eating in front of the Malays during the Muslim fasting month.

5. Democracy is needed for a non-racial approach to nation building. In fact, despite the erosion of democracy, the presence of minimum democracy, in the form of the right to vote in the national election, has helped to check more serious racial discrimination and political

oppression. This is because the government in power has to be concerned that it has to face the people in national election. It has been the politics of fear that has allowed the government to get away with the erosion of democracy and its racial policies. The 2008 election served to remind the government that there is a limit to its racial politics and assault on democracy. While democracy has the potential danger of becoming the tyranny of the majority (Tocqueville 1945), true democracy must have freedom of speech, which helps to expose lies and rhetoric that create fear. Nevertheless the politics of fear can be used to rally political support in times of insecurity as was the case of United States under President George W. Bush. Barack Obama campaigned against this politics of fear and lies and his election as the new American president can be seen as a rejection of this kind of politics.

CONCLUSION

The Malaysian case shows how consociational democracy fails. While a major reason for the failure appears to be the deterioration of democracy following the 1969 racial riots and the domination of one section over the others in the coalition, the racial arrangement of nation building had sown the seeds for communal politics which polarizes the society along ethnic lines. The deterioration of democracy and communal politics resulted in polarization and social tension. With the Malay section in the ruling coalition becoming more dominant, the use of religion and Malay communalism by UMNO resulted in the implementation of Malay nationalist causes. As the UMNO-led government was able to push through various Malay nationalist policies, this widened the communal gap between the Malays and non-Malays even though non-Malay politicians also used communal issues.

Viewed from another perspective, the Malaysian case shows the loss of an opportunity to bring about a harmonious and democratic society. Following Independence, there were the democratic institutions following the British model of parliamentary democracy, and there was the ideal among different sections of the population to build a non-communal nation. Even in the years before Independence, there were Chinese writers who expressed their patriotism for a non-communal Malaya (cf. Goh 1989). There was also the non-communal party, the Independence of Malaya Party (IMP), led by the prominent Malay leader, Dato' Onn bin Ja'afar. The attempts at a non-communal approach to nation building did not succeed, and, in fact, as Ratnam (1965, p. 215) points out, the decision to form the Alliance was very much due to UMNO's and MCA leaders' distrust of the IMP. UMNO and the MCA wanted the communal approach and they are very much responsible for the communal approach to nation building. If a non-racial approach to nation building had been adopted, and imbalances between ethic groups corrected via non-racial policies, Malaysia could have been a model of democracy that manages ethnicity well. As it is, unless things are remedied, Malaysia looks set to slide from being one of the more democratic and developed countries in Southeast Asia to being one of the less democratic and developed countries, while Indonesia, for instance, firmly establishes its democracy and revives its economy.

In the above analysis I have referred to some social science theories. Indeed the Malaysian case illustrates some theories on ethnicity, and I should like to end this chapter by reflecting on these. I have mentioned the plural society theory and the consociational democracy model, and I have shown that the deterioration of democracy and communal politics have resulted in more social tension. On reducing ethnic tension, Rabushka (1974) is of the opinion that "racial tensions and conflict are kept to a minimum under conditions of voluntary exchange in free markets". I have argued elsewhere that this is not realistic without a policy to address the identification of ethnicity with economic functions as existed in Malaya at the time of Independence (Tan 2004). In discussing the problem of the new states, Clifford Geertz (1963) was of the opinion that "the new states are abnormally susceptible to serious disaffection based on primordial attachments". The Malaysian case shows that it is the communal politics and the mobilization along communal lines that are the underlying causes. The communal politics and UMNO-Malay-centric version of nationhood can only lead to a communally divided nation rather than one to which all Malaysians share a civic belonging. But Geertz's concern about primordial attachment is legitimate in that in the new states, primordial sentiments can easily be mobilized to stir up racial sentiments for political support. However, primordial sentiments by themselves do not cause ethnic polarization; they are divisive only when they are mobilized for political purposes.

Communal politics plays up symbolic politics and affirmation of ethnic status, as Horowitz (1985) has shown. In doing so, in the case of the Malays, Chandra Muzaffar has argued that UMNO is able to portray itself as the Malays' protector. We can argue that "protecting" Malay interest through the racial application of affirmative action further makes the Malay masses feel dependent on the UMNO-dominated government. And this is a serious challenge to freeing Malaysia from the communal approach to nation building. Non-Malay populations, especially those of the younger generation, yearn for a more egalitarian cultural citizenship, and their aspiration cannot be ignored without it leading to more tension. In fact, the non-Malays have generally accepted the basic Malay characteristics of the Malaysian nation as defined in the Constitution, namely the use of Malay as the national language and the status of Islam as the religion of the Federation. There is thus a cultural basis for building a common Malaysian nation. Letting communal nationalism go beyond the consensus on cultural nationhood will only push Malaysia towards a bleak future. There is hope as shown in the 2007 annual general assembly of UMNO where UMNO leaders called for its members not to indulge in anti-Chinese rhetoric (Kuppusamy 2007*d*). In other words, while the UMNO elite has been vocal in pushing for Malay nationalism, if political leaders have the will, they can pave the way for at least a less racial political process. The main aim of Vision 2020 is to create a *Bangsa Malaysa* or Malaysian Nation. There is already a Malaysian nation, but it is a plural nation; perhaps when the political process is less communal, a more harmonious nation can be brought about.

Lastly, the lesson of the 2008 election is that Malaysians should continue to resist the politics of fear to transcend ethnicity and nationalism, and support a democracy that favours a non-racial approach to nation building. That the politics of fear is a great threat to democracy is becoming more recognized. Gore (2008) has shown clearly how the politics of fear in the United States under President George W. Bush has eroded American democracy and rational decision making. Fear of terrorism is used in the United States for rallying political support for the Bush government. In Malaysia it is ethnicity fear — fear of the Malays of non-Malays, and vice versa with regard to their mutual ethnic interests, as well as fear of racial riots. The 2008 election, which saw for the first time so many Malaysians using their right to vote to reject the BN, is a testimony to the rejection of fear of political instability and racial trouble if the BN is not in power. This is a major psychological breakthrough. No doubt there will be politicians who will still exploit ethnicity fears, but if Malaysians can reject these fears, there is hope for democracy and a more common imagination of nationhood, which will be better for nation building and the achievement of the nation's full potential for economic and social development. The future is still uncertain, for if the weakened BN especially UMNO, decides to take undemocratic measures and stir up ethnic fear to weaken the opposition, Malaysia will still be encapsulated in communalism and disharmony. Only the will of the people to reject the politics of fear will free the country from this kind of encapsulation, and enable it to become a free, harmonious, and developed nation.

Notes

1   In this writing about Malaysia, Malaya refers to the Federation of Malaya created in 1957 when the Peninsula (now referred to as West Malaysia) attained Independence from the British. In 1963, Sarawak, Sabah, and Singapore joined the Federation of Malaya to form the Federation of Malaysia. In 1965, Singapore left the federation to become an independent island state. East Malaysia refers to Sarawak and Sabah. There are altogether eleven states in Peninsular Malaysia and two states in East Malaysia. In addition, there are three federal territories, namely, Kuala Lumpur and Putrajaya in Peninsular Malaysia and Labuan in East Malaysia.

2   Previous versions of this chapter had been presented at the seminar on Malaysian Chinese: Recent Developments and Prospects (organized by the Institute of Southeast Asian Studies and Chinese Herirtage Centre, Singapore, 10 July 2008) and at the Beijing Forum 2007: The Harmony of Civilization and Prosperity for All — Diversity in the Development of Human Civilization (organized by Peking University, 2–4 November 2007).

3   This is, of course, inspired by Anderson's concept of nation as "imagined". See Anderson (1991, p. 6).

4   See <http://www.statistics.gov.my/english/census/pressdemo.htm>.

5   Malaysia was in effect ruled by the National Operations Council (NOC), headed by Tun Abdul Razak, who replaced Tunku Abdul Rahman to become the second prime minister of Malaysia from 1970 to 1976. UMNO supremacy in the ruling coalition really began with the NOC and the rule of Tun Razak.

6   For a description on affirmative action policy in Malaysia, see Ariffin Omar (2004).

7   This was already pointed out by K.J. Ratnam in his classic work on communalism and the political process in Malaya. See Ratnam (1965, p. 23). Malay nationalism here refers to Malay ethnic nationalism, which articulates for a nation with Malay characteristics.

8   For a good study of Chinese-Malay relations before Independence, see Khoo (1981).

9   See *Malacca Guardian* 1932. This is discussed in Tan (1988, p. 225).

10   While teaching at the University of Malaya in the 1980s, I witnessed at the Faculty of Social Science meetings the call to teach English literature in the English Department in Malay.

11   The contrast is obvious when one compares the present University of Malaya (UM) in Kuala Lumpur with the National University of Singapore (NUS), both of which branched off from the original University of Malaya established in Singapore in 1949. While UM has declined in standard and international respectability, the NUS has performed well and gained international respect. Partly in response to complaints by non-Malays and the low rating by the

Times Higher Educational Supplement-Quacquarelli Symonds survey, which lists the University of Malaya at 246, four non-Malays were appointed to be deputy vice-chancellors in 2007 (cf. *Yazhou Zhoukan*, 11 November 2007, pp. 18–19).

[12] After the March 2008 election, PAS continued to govern Kelantan, while Barisan Nasional retook Terengganu from PAS.

[13] See Malaysian Chinese paper *Nanyang Siang Pau*'s front page report, 5 August 2007.

[14] For an analysis of the authoritarian trends in post-1969 Malaysia, see Crouch (1992).

[15] For an account of the event, see Salleh Abas with K. Das (1989).

[16] An explosive issue in September 2007 was about a video clip that allegedly showed a well connected lawyer brokering the appointment of top judges with a leading judge of the country. See Kuppusamy (2007*a*).

[17] In Malaysia during the March 2008 national election, SMS messages also played a part in influencing voting. Some church members told me that many church members sent messages to other church members urging them to vote for opposition candidates.

[18] In this election, the DAP (28 parliamentary seats, 73 state seats) did very well compared with MCA (15 parliamentary seats, 32 state seats) the main Chinese political party, and Lim Guan Eng of the DAP became the chief minister of Penang. The DAP is the main Chinese-based, multi-ethnic opposition party. It is the main rival of the Chinese party, MCA, and the Chinese-based, multi-ethnic party, Gerakan, in the National Front, just as the PAS is the main Malay-based, opposition party to UMNO of the National Front. The PKR or the People's Justice Party, which was formed in 2003 from the merger of the National Justice Party (led by Anwar's wife) and the older Malaysian People's Party, also performed very well compared with their respective past record, winning 31 parliamentary seats and 40 state seats. Its good performance in the 2008 Election shows that it has emerged as another influential Malay-based party. The PAS won 23 parliamentary seats and 83 state seats, while UMNO won 79 parliamentary seats and 239 state seats. See "Malaysia Decides 2008: General Election Results", updated on 10 March 2008, at <http://thestar.com.my/election/results.html>.

[19] The protest was organized by the Hindu Rights Action Force (HINDRAF) which was established in 2006 in response to the destruction of Hindu temples by the National Front government (cf. Govindasamy 2008). That HINDRAF was able to gather so much support shows the frustration of many ordinary Indians about their marginality.

[20] On the new promulgation of laws related to citizenship, see *Undang-undang Republik Indonesia No. 23 Tahun 2006 tentang Administrasi Kependudukan* (Promulgation of Law No. 23/2006 Re: Civil Registration), and *Undang-undang*

Republik Indonesia No. 12 Tahun 2006 tentang Kewarganegaraan Republik Indonesia (Promulgation of Law No. 12/2006 Re: Citizenship), etc.

[21] The recent government ruling that requires publicly listed companies to declare the ethnic background of their employees has caused unhappiness among the Chinese in Malaysia. See Kuppusamy (2007*c*).

[22] The use of the word "encapsulation" is inspired by Strauch (1981, p. 7).

References

Agence France-Presse. "Malay Police Fire Tear Gas on Indian Rally". *Sunday Morning Post*, 17 February 2008, p. 8.

Ahmad Fauzi Abdul Hamid. "The *Taqwa* versus *Quwwah* Dichotomy: An Islamic Critique of Development via the Malaysian *Bumiputera* Policy". In *The 'Bumiputera Policy': Dynamics and Dilemmas*, edited by Richard Mason and Ariffin S.M. Omar. Special issue of *Kajian Malaysia (Journal of Malaysia Studies)* 21, nos. 1–2 (2004): 123–62.

Anderson, Benedict. *Imagined Communities: Reflections on the Origin and Spread of Nationalism*. London: Verso, 1991. First published in 1983.

Ariffin Omar. "Origins and Development of the Affirmative Policy in Malaya and Malaysia: A Historical Overview". In *The 'Bumiputera Policy': Dynamics and Dilemmas*, edited by Richard Mason and Ariffin S.M. Omar. Special issue of *Kajian Malaysia (Journal of Malaysia Studies)* 21, nos. 1–2 (2004): 13–29.

Brown, David. *The State and Ethnic Politics in Southeast Asia*. London: Routledge, 1994.

Chandra Muzaffar. *Protector*. Penang: Aliran, 1979.

———. "A Secular State or an Islamic State: International Movement for a Just World Statement", 19 July 2007. <http://www.Just-international.org/article.cfm?newsid+20002396>.

Chee, Stephen. "Consociational Political Leadership and Conflict Regulation in Malaysia". In *Leadership and Security in Southeast Asia: Institutional Aspects*, edited by Stephen Chee. Singapore: Institute of Southeast Asian Studies, 1991.

Crouch, Harold. "Authoritarian Trends, the UMNO Split and the Limits to State Power". In *Fragmented Vision: Culture and Politics in Contemporary Malaysia*, edited by Joel S. Kahn and Francis Loh Kok Wah. North Sydney: Allen & Unwin Pty Ltd., 1992.

Furnivall, J.S. *Colonial Policy and Practice: A Comparative Study of Burma and Netherlands India*. Cambridge: Cambridge University Press, 1948. 1956 edition by New York University Press.

Geertz, Clifford. "The Integrative Revolution". In *Old Societies and New States*, edited by Clifford Geertz. New York: Free Press, 1963.

Goh Then Chye. "Modern Chinese Malaysian Literature: Past, Present and Future". In *Social Change and Southeast Asian Chinese Literature*, edited by

T.C. Carino. Manila: China Studies Program, De La Salle University and Philippine Association for Chinese Studies, 1989.

Gore, Al. *The Assault on Reason*. London: Bloomsbury Publishing Plc., 2008.

Govindasamy, Anatha Rahman. "Hindu Rights or Indian Rights? The Secular Origins of Malaysia's Hindu Rights Action Force". Paper presented at the conference on Globalising Religions & Cultures in the Asia Pacific, organized by the Australian Research Council Asia-Pacific Futures Research Network, University of Adelaide, 1–5 December 2008.

Horowitz, Donald. *Ethnic Groups and Conflict*. Berkeley and Los Angeles: University of California Press, 1985.

Khoo Kay Kim. "Sino-Malay Relations in Peninsular Malaysia before 1942". *Journal of Southeast Asian Studies* 12, no. 1 (1981): 93–117.

Kuppusamy, Baradan. "Inquiry Call after Video Suggests Collusion in High Legal Circles". *South China Morning Post*, 21 September 2007*a*, p. A16.

———. "Malaysians Look to their King to Put Things Right". *South China Morning Post*, 2 October 2007*b*, p. A10.

———. "Malaysian Firms told to List Staff by Race". *South China Morning Post*, 15 September 2007*c*, p. A9.

———. "UMNO Assembly Seeks to Heal Racial Wounds". *South China Morning Post*, 5 November 2007*d*, p. A10.

———. "Leaders Urge Return to Moderation after Protests in Malaysia". *South China Morning Post*, 27 November 2007*e*, p. A10.

———. "Mahathir Revives Racial Doctrine". *South China Morning Post*, 27 May 2008, p. A11.

Lijphart, Arend. *Democracy in Plural Societies*. New Haven: Yale University Press, 1977.

Malacca Guardian. "Malaya for the Malays". 25 April 1932, p. 6.

Maznah Mohamad. "Bumiputera, Malays and Islam in the Politicization of the New Economic Policy". In *The 'Bumiputera Policy': Dynamics and Dilemmas*, edited by Richard Mason and Ariffin S.M. Omar. Special issue of *Kajian Malaysia (Journal of Malaysia Studies)* 21, nos. 1–2 (2004): 163–76.

Ng, Eugene. "Remembering '57: Four Malaysians Tell Us What Merdeka means to them". *Going Places* (Malaysia Airlines magazine), August 2007.

Rabushka, Alvin. *A Theory of Racial Harmony*. Studies in International Affairs, no. 11. Columbia (South Carolina): University of South Carolina Press, for the Institute of International Studies, University of South Carolina, Durham, D.C., 1974.

Ratnam, K.J. *Communalism and the Political Process in Malaysia*. Kuala Lumpur: University of Malaya Press, 1965.

Salleh Abas, Tun with K. Das. *May Day for Justice: The Lord President's Version*. Kuala Lumpur: Magnus Books, 1989.

South China Morning Post. "Abdullah Vetoes Plan to Merge Top Parties". 9 October 2007, p. A11.

Strauch, Judith. *Chinese Village Politics in the Malaysian State*. Cambridge, Mass.: Harvard University Press, 1981.

Tan Chee-Beng. "Baba Chinese, Non-Baba Chinese and Malays: A Note on Ethnic Interaction in Malacca". *Southeast Asian Journal of Social Science* 7, nos. 1–2 (1979): 20–29.

———. *The Baba of Melaka: Culture and Identity of a Chinese Peranakan Commuity in Malaysia*. Petaling Jaya (Malaysia): Pelanduk Publications, 1988.

———. "Resorting to Ethnic Games (Again)". *Aliran Monthly* 11, no. 1 (1991): 20–24.

———. *Chinese Minority in a Malay State: The Case of Terengganu in Malaysia*. Singapore: Eastern University Press, 2002.

———. *Chinese Overseas: Comparative Cultural Issues*. Hong Kong: Hong Kong University Press, 2004.

———. "Malaysia". In *Encyclopedia of the World's Minorities*, vol. 2, edited by Carl Skutch. New York: Routledge, 2005.

Tocqueville, Alexis de. *Democracy in America*. New York: Random House, Inc., 1981. First published by Alfred A. Knopf, Inc. in 1945.

Ye Lin-Sheng. *The Chinese Dilemma*. Kingsford, New South Wales: East West Publishing Pty Ltd., 2003.

2

BEING MUSLIM AND CHINESE IN MALAYSIA

Rosey Ma

INTRODUCTION

It has been a general view that being Muslim and Chinese in Malaysia must be something out of the ordinary, or an issue that is problematic. This chapter focuses on the identity dilemma faced by the Chinese Muslims in Malaysia and offers a general look at the reasons behind this and the consequences of this perceived dichotomy, for a better understanding of the issue.

There is a limited number of previous publications on the subject. References include studies on Chinese Muslims in Malaysia, ethnic relations, social identity and a few published or unpublished theses on Chinese-Malay mixed marriages, Chinese converts, religion, and ethnicity. A major part of this chapter is based on observations, interviews, informal surveys, and oral history compiled in the course of the writer's voluntary work as a counsellor to Chinese Muslims in Malaysia over more than a decade. The writer's own experience as a Chinese and Muslim living in Malaysia adds to a better understanding and analysis of the subject. Not written in the vein of a conventional academic study, this chapter is mainly an account voicing the identity dilemma of the many Chinese Muslims in Malaysia trying to live, and for the challenge they face to be acknowledged, in their multiple and fluid identities.

ISLAM AND CHINESE MUSLIMS IN MALAYSIA

Malaysia is well known as a multi-ethnic, multicultural, and multireligious country, and anybody who has lived here even for a short while quickly becomes aware of the intimate relationship between ethnicity, culture, and religion in everyday life. Due to the country's unique political and social history, a person's official and social identities are usually defined according to his ethnic background which is closely related to his religion. It is hard to distinguish the thin line between the religious and cultural traditions of the various ethnic communities, especially where the Malays and Muslims are concerned.

Islam, the religion of the Malays, is also the official religion. People of other ethnic descents share a diversity of religions. The Constitution grants and protects the non-Muslims' right and freedom to religious beliefs and practice. The Chinese in Malaysia may be Buddhist, Christian, Taoist, or ancestor worshippers, etc; and there are also many who are not affiliated to any religion. Only less than one per cent of the Malaysian Chinese is Muslim. In China there are about 30 million Muslims, according to the officially stated figure, or about 50 to 60 million as claimed by the Muslims themselves — a number that surpasses the population of many Muslim nations in the Middle East, a fact that is not generally well known.

Islam, being a way of life, also incorporates in its practice the customs, language, values, superstitions, and other cultural aspects of the people concerned. Religion is embedded in the Muslim traditional culture. As in most Muslim communities, the Malay Muslims also perceive themselves as an integrated whole community that combines religion with all aspects of their lifestyle. For most Malaysians, it is not apparent that a person, who does not look, speak, dress, or act Malay, might be a Muslim.

Chinese Muslims have had a presence in Malaysia since the fifteenth century (Muljana 1968; Lombard & Salmon 2001; Tan 2003; The 1993).[1] There have also been Chinese Muslim labourers during colonial times (Djinghiz 1911), and sporadic migrants towards the end of nineteenth century.[2] Since China opened its doors, Malaysia in the last three decades has been a choice destination for *Hui* (Chinese Muslim) students and businessmen who find ways of staying in the country for many years. These latter and a handful of other *Hui* families form the small group of original Chinese Muslims in Malaysia today. The big majority of the nearly 60,000 Chinese Muslims[3] in the country are converts. In Malaysia, a Chinese, first of all, does not look Muslim; if it is ascertained that she/he is Muslim, the subsequent thought that comes to mind is that she/he is a convert.

Chinese Muslims form a very distinct and unorthodox group in Malaysian society. Because of the general belief that being Malay is equivalent to being Muslim, as defined in the Constitution — a notion endorsed by the authorities and accepted by the public at large — it becomes difficult to define the identity of the Chinese who are Muslim. In this country where ethnicity and religion are so entwined in one's social and official identity, the Chinese Muslims are of the ethnicity of one community, the Chinese, while professing the religion of another community, the Malays. In the Malaysian social context, this group is reduced to a double-minority: minority Muslim among the majority non-Muslim Chinese, and minority Chinese among the overwhelming Malay Muslims.

History has shown that among the original Chinese Muslim migrants, many have eventually assimilated with the Malays and lost their ethnic features (Tan 1988; Ma 2005), while some have moved towards their Chinese counterparts and left their religion (Ma 2005). To discuss the issue of identity dilemma, this chapter focuses on the Chinese Muslim converts. Unless it is specified otherwise, the term "convert" in this chapter points to a Malaysian Chinese who embraces Islam at an adult age.

Starting with interracial marriages some forty, fifty, years ago, there has been a steady stream of Chinese who have embraced Islam for various reasons. The most common deciding factor is marrying a Muslim partner, usually a Malay. Other reasons may include convenience because they live in a Muslim-majority nation, being influenced by close association with Malay neighbours or friends, and in rare cases, to get some economic or political mileage (Kasimin 1985; Fadzilah 1987; Khairuman 1991; Ma 1996). There is also an increasing number of people who have come into the religion because of conviction through reading or a better knowledge about Islam. In Malaysia a convert to Islam is also called *muallaf*, or *saudara baru* (new brother/sister).[4]

Conversion is not just a simple, straightforward transition from one spiritual belief to another. At the very least, it is a major change of the core identity of an individual that involves a redefinition of self-identity. For the Chinese convert in Malaysia, it is observed that it is not just Islam that he is undertaking to embrace, but to some extent, also the Malayness that comes with it. Therefore the redefining and construction of the new identity takes place within two dimensions: religious and ethnic/cultural. The process is different from the identity reconstruction of the *Hui* who assimilated with the Malays (without a change in religious identity), and those who chose to get out of Islam (without changing their Chinese ethnic identity). The extent of the change the convert undergoes and the adaptation he engages in depends on many factors, including family background, previous beliefs or religion, motives for the conversion, educational and professional background, level of previous knowledge of Islam and the process of learning the religion, and his socio-economic standing.

As was said earlier, for the Malays who do not make much distinction between their religious and cultural boundaries, it is desirable that other Muslims amidst them also live within the same kind of socio-cultural confines. The convert himself soon realizes that to be fully accepted by the Malays as Muslim, it is not enough for him just to accept and learn a new religion, but also to learn a new way of life that he has to internalize. Raghavan's (1977, p. 454) observation thirty years ago is still valid today to some extent: "It should be borne in mind that ... to be fully accepted and assimilated into the Malay community, one has to go beyond the mere stage of conversion into the Islamic faith and attend the Malay technique du corps. The candidate must live within the new social environment and successfully internalize the new way of life he has chosen."

This situation is clear to the Chinese community; and both sides often identify conversion to Islam as "*masuk Melayu*", a phrase that literally means "enter Malay" or "become Malay", thus emphasizing the blanket ethnicization of Islam in the country. This notion has an implication for the Chinese Muslim and puts a question mark on his identity. When one embraces Islam, how much of Chineseness may he retain, and how much of Malayness should he adopt? What does he write in the box asking for *bangsa* (race), which figures in all forms, official and unofficial? He cannot and does not write Malay, because he is not; but if he writes Chinese, it is assumed he is not Muslim.[5]

It is common among minority communities anywhere in the world, when faced with a sense of not belonging, to strive for recognition from the majority population. The Chinese Muslim in Malaysia, by virtue of his conversion to Islam, becomes a minority Muslim within his former Chinese "in-group";[6] at the same time, from having been in the "out-group" of the Malay Muslim community, he steps into the group by becoming Muslim. On both sides he is a minority, and has to strive for recognition on two fronts: to be accepted into the Malay Muslim fraternity, he has to prove to the Malays that he is Muslim enough by adopting not just a Muslim, but also a Malay way of life to a certain degree. At the same time, so as not to be ostracized by the Chinese community, he has to show them that he is still Chinese by exhibiting characteristic cultural features of his Chineseness. In the process of reconstructing this identity, it may happen that he becomes neither this nor that — not fully accepted by one, and snubbed by the other, if both communities tend to see in the convert "what he is not" rather than "what he is", and look for "how he is different from us" rather than "how he is like us". In which way does a Muslim Chinese in Malaysia construct a social identity that encompasses his religion, ethnicity, and culture without compromising his religious values and his ethnic cultural feelings, when the prevalent social reality points to the mutual exclusiveness of Chinese and Muslim?

Muslims in Malaysia who are non-Malay ethnically, such as Indians, Pakistanis, Arabs, Yemenis, Europeans, Orang Asli, and the people of East Malaysian tribes, find their place amid the Muslim fraternity. Somehow this inclusiveness is not easily or always extended to embody the Chinese. The problem then is not simply the exclusivity of Malays as Muslim, but rather the non-inclusiveness of Chinese as such. Looking at the reasons behind, first of all, we cannot deny that historically there has been a mutual resentment and divisiveness between the two ethnic groups, brought about by, among other factors, government policies, preceded by the colonial policy, and economic disparity. Secondly, some Malays erroneously believe that the Chinese who convert to Islam are automatically granted the status of *Bumiputra*; they suspect that the motive for their conversion is to benefit from some incentives, such as to get certain land titles, be entitled to a kind of charity payment, and be accorded licences to run certain businesses designated for Muslims only.[7] There is also a defensiveness of the Malays towards their religion. In the process of Malaysianization — especially after Bahasa Malaysia became the official and education language — Islam, for the Malays, came to be the only remaining characteristic on which the Chinese cannot, and will not be allowed to encroach (Chandra, Shamsul). One interviewee said she was made to feel that "they — Malay officers at the religious institution — do not seem to like us to become Muslim; they want to keep the religion to themselves" (Interview 1994, Kuala Lumpur).

CONFUSION BETWEEN ETHNIC AND RELIGIOUS IDENTITIES IN MALAYSIA

Being Chinese is an ethnic and cultural characterization; being Muslim is a religious identification; yet these two identities of different spheres are regarded as being incompatible, sometimes, for the Malays, to the extent of their not being willing to acknowledge a Chinese as Muslim. In my personal experience I have many times encountered no response to my *salam*,[8] once, even at the washing area in a mosque. Similar accounts have been recounted by my counselees. Like many of them, my family members and I have also been stopped by the guard on entering the prayer hall in a mosque when it is not the regular prayer time: "What do you want? Non-Muslims cannot enter here." When I say I want to go in to pray, the next question is: "Are you Muslim?" Not a question likely to be asked of a person entering the prayer hall in a mosque. Once my young son heard the boys who had inched next to him during prayers whisper: "*Orang cina tak boleh sembayang sini, tau?*" (Chinese cannot pray here, you know). It is the doubt in the Malay mind about a Chinese being Muslim, and a practising one too. It is the Chinese face that elicits this attitude; the uncertainty that asks "Is this Chinese a Muslim?"

Even though the first thought that comes to the mind of a Muslim when meeting a Chinese Muslim is that he/she is a convert, when it is known that he/she is an original Muslim — a Muslim *asal* — from China, reactions change. Since the mid-1990s articles in newspapers, magazines, exhibitions, and academic seminars on Islam in China started to be seen on many fronts. A few television documentary series, both local and foreign, have screened informative programmes on the Muslims in China. Special travel packages featuring historical Islamic attractions in China have contributed to more knowledge of the long existence of Chinese Muslims. All this has played a positive role in introducing knowledge about Muslims in China, to the Malays and Chinese. Now quite a big section of informed people in Malaysia respond positively when they meet a Muslim from China. The Chinese feel proud that Islam in China has preceded the religion in this part of the world by a few hundred years. The Malays also acknowledge that the Chinese Muslims outnumber Malays by three times, and that they are devout Muslims. It is observed that this cordial reaction is not always shown in the same manner to a convert. In actual fact very often a convert proves to have devoted enormous effort and time to learning Islam, and is conscientious in its practice. Quite a number of them have furthered their studies in Islamic knowledge in higher learning institutions locally and abroad. There are many who are respected for their sound religious knowledge, and are invited to give speeches or hold teaching sessions to a regular following, including Malays. It should also be noted that these speeches and teaching sessions are usually conducted in the Malay language, and only occasionally in English.

In the religious sense Muslims should welcome a convert, and the majority of Malays do display an accepting attitude towards the Chinese convert in their families or community; extreme cases of total non-acceptance are rare.[9] However, for many Malays this acceptance comes with the wish to see the convert leave as much of his Chineseness behind as possible. Many think that the Chinese who embrace Islam, but do not take on the rest of the "package", for example, Malay culture and customs, cannot be sincere in their conversion, as one religious officer expressed: "She still wants to remain Chinese",[10] implying that "She is not totally committed to become Muslim." Therefore they just stop short of requesting — but encourage — the new Muslim to adopt the Malay way of life, with its customs and culture, food, clothing, language, and even a new name. This has been and still is one way to be better accepted by the Malay family and community at large, and this is what the majority of Chinese Muslims tend to do. In reality, they are using the cultural expressions of Malay characteristics to manifest their religious identification.

The reason Chinese Muslims strive for acceptance by the Malays may be found in the fact that often, once they become Muslim, they are not well viewed by their own Chinese community. There are lucky ones who are blessed by family understanding and acceptance.[11] But a large number of converts face family opposition of varying degrees, ranging from resentful tolerance to total rejection. Disagreements about the conversion of a family member leave both sides emotionally scarred. Many said they were rejected by friends and relatives. This kind of hostile reaction does not only come from family members. There are cases where converts working with Chinese bosses lost their jobs because they became Muslim. It is ironic that the reasons for this hostility are the same as those causing the Malay feeling of animosity towards a convert: the historical resentment between the two ethnic groups, discriminating economic policies, suspicion about the person's motive for conversion. That the convert has to acculturate to some degree with the Malay community might be a natural development, especially if the spouse is Malay, but this alienates him/her from the Chinese. It does not make them less Chinese, but this is how it is perceived. The more they exhibit characteristics recognizable as Muslim (or a Malay identity in the eyes of Chinese), the more irritating, or even offensive it is to some of their fellow Chinese. Here, the religious identity of the convert overshadows his cultural and ethnic identity in the eyes of other Chinese.

At the root of this lies the identification of a Muslim as Malay. Many Chinese in Malaysia still refer to Islam as *Malay jiao* — the Malay religion, believing that becoming Muslim is equivalent to becoming Malay. A large number of Chinese only have scant or misleading knowledge about Islam,[12] and they are not curious or interested to get to know what this religion is really about. In their limited knowledge about the religion, it is common for them to judge Muslims from the behaviour of the Malays. Any less respectable behaviour, any negative attitude, is translated as bad Muslim behaviour and bad Muslim attitude. Stereotyping and prejudice against the Malays, the bane in any ethnic relationship, is extended unreservedly to Muslims, including the converts. The Chinese feel that a person who becomes Muslim betrays his or her family and race, and brings shame to the community, by effectively — even if seemingly — becoming Malay.

A few issues stemming from the behaviour of some Malays and the conversion procedures add to the opposition of the Chinese towards any family member wanting to embrace Islam. The most quoted among these are: parents are concerned that their daughters' Malay husbands will marry more wives; their son will not carry the family surname;[13] that they (the Malays) are not very motivated to advance in their careers; the exclusion of non-Muslim relatives, even parents, from the Muslim's inheritance, and vice versa.

Because of all this, it may be inconceivable to many Chinese why one amongst them would consent to become Muslim. Just as we discussed the Malays not easily accepting Muslims of Chinese descent as a non-inclusiveness of the Chinese in the Muslim community, we also observe mirroring this the Chinese non-inclusiveness of the Muslims in the Chinese community. While in general they do not[14] disapprove or ostracize other Chinese who are of Buddhist, Christian, or other non-traditional Chinese religions, many Chinese fail to show the same tolerance to one who is Muslim. The first time I experienced this was in Kota Kinabalu in 1973: I was buying a chicken from a Chinese chicken seller at a wet market; the seller was joyously bantering with me in Chinese. When I requested that the Malay boy (whose job is to slaughter for Muslim customers) slaughter the chicken for me, the attitude of the seller changed. Shoutings. "What? You've become one of them!", he refused to sell me the chicken. Never mind that I spoke better Chinese than he did, and probably had stronger Chinese culture ingrained in me. On account of my exhibiting a trait particular to Muslims (in his thinking, Malay), he just single-mindedly excluded me from my own ethnic community, throwing me to the other side of the ethnic fence.

The blurring of the defining line between religion and ethnicity, religious culture and ethnic culture, is constantly, consciously or unconsciously, demonstrated by both the Malays and Chinese. Lay people, as well as Muslim religious authorities, have no qualms using double standards in the issues of religion and ethnic and cultural expressions when they deal with the Malays and Chinese. If a Muslim individual is Malay, there is a deliberate attempt to tie his religious affiliation with ethnic identity, notwithstanding the person's outward religious and cultural expressions. A Malay who does not perform the religious rituals, who does not engage in any communal religious activity, whose sense of dress may be far from decently conservative, who may not be proficient in Bahasa Malaysia, preferring English as his/her intimate language, in short, one who does not exhibit characteristic Malay-Muslim behaviour, is still regarded as Muslim. It is a crime if he openly denies his Islamic affiliation if he wishes to do so. The Muslim identity of a Malay is an identity vested in his ethnicity, regardless of his religious feelings or expressions. On the other hand, in the case of a Chinese, religious affiliation and devotion, apart from the practice of prayers and fasting and other religious injunctions, is also measured against the person's Malay cultural identification: such as wearing Malay costume, speaking the Malay language, preferring Malay food, frequenting Muslim social circles, practising and taking on Malay customs. The more the person adapts to Malay culture, the better a Muslim he is assumed to be; and the more Chinese culture he exhibits, the more his Muslim piety will be questioned.[15]

DISTINCTIONS BETWEEN CHINESE MUSLIMS AND MALAYS

Being Chinese is an ethnic and cultural characterization, being Muslim is a religious identification; yet somehow, these two identities are thought of as being conflicting; and this general assumption is quite pervasive in both communities. My reason for getting converts to discuss the identity dilemma of being Chinese and Muslim in Malaysia in this chapter is that I believe this issue is more than the simple matter of a Chinese and Muslim dichotomy. The real problem is that of "the Malaysian Chinese who has become Muslim" — the convert, the *saudara baru*, the new brother/sister who has stepped out of his/her ethnic boundaries to cross over to the other one. Years of observation, personal experience, and interviews confirm this argument. For both the Malays and Chinese, it is being "Malaysian Chinese and also Muslim in Malaysia" that is difficult to place in the same identity sphere. One does not cross ethnic boundaries: if you are born a Malay or Chinese, you remain a Malay or Chinese. One may cross religious boundaries, but officially and subjectively, only by leaving the former religion before stepping into the other one. In a country such as Malaysia, where one's religion and ethnicity are spelled out in the same breath, how does one cross the religious boundary when the attached ethnic part bounces back from the other sphere? Presented in mathematical diagrams, this is an unsolvable problem. Nagata (1978, pp. 102–13) had described this state of the Chinese Muslim in Malaysia with the words "a social anomaly that exists in an ethnic limbo". He is put into one specific categorization of the state, under an official label, which in turn will dictate his cultural expressions. The gross error, in the sense that the boundaries that are forcefully made to collide are from two very different spheres — one religious, the other one ethnic — is often overlooked.

The way this confounding of religion and culture is exercised by authority figures can be quite damaging to all concerned. Not only does it confuse the new Muslim, but it also gives the wrong image of what Islam the religion is about, as illustrated by the following examples.

- A new convert's mother staged a wedding lunch for the newlyweds. They also invited the *ustaz* (religious teacher) who had converted her. When the *ustaz* saw the red tablecloths, he disapproved, and insisted that they be replaced, because "using red tablecloths is [a] Chinese custom, and it is haram[16] to follow [it]".
- The religious teacher in my daughter's school asked her if we use chopsticks at home. When she said yes, she was told to inform us, the parents, that for Muslims, eating with chopsticks is *haram*. For many uninitiated Malay, it seems like anything Chinese is *haram*.
- A lady in Terengganu forbade her Chinese daughter-in-law to speak Chinese, not even to the grocer, and did not allow her to have Chinese friends, because "it will impede your being a good Muslim".[17] She found solace in an understanding husband, but had to abide by her mother-in-law's wishes.

The offspring in an interethnic marriage between a Malay and Chinese may have a self-perceived ethnic identity that does not coincide with the state-defined identity. In one such family, the convert father, Jaafar Lim bin Abdullah,[18] wanting to keep their surname and ethnic descent, registers his son as *cina* with the name Adam Lim. Adam takes his looks from his Malay mother, is looked after by his maternal grandparents, and is brought up within the Islamic and Malay sociocultural environment; he feels Malay and is seen as such by his friends; yet in the eyes of the state, he is Chinese; and may not be eligible, for example, to get into a state residential school reserved for *Bumiputra* only. In another interethnic marriage, the child is registered as Malay, with the name Faridah binti Rashid. The mother is Malay, the father is a convert, Rashid Teoh bin Abdullah. Faridah has physically inherited a big portion of her Chinese parent's genes, with very Chinese looks; she is sent to a Chinese school for practical reasons. She speaks fluent and better Chinese than Malay. She is naturally comfortable among her Chinese friends and feels a part of them. People around her see and treat her as Chinese. Her identity card shows she is *Melayu*, and when she enters a national high school, she is not allowed to take Chinese as a "pupil's own language" class. (These classes are usually scheduled at the same time as the religious class.) These are two examples that show the incompatibility of the state-defined identity and the subjective identification of a Chinese Muslim and his offspring.

After all that has been said, it is rather hard to make a generalization about the feeling of being Muslim and Chinese in Malaysia, just as the identity reconstruction process is complex and varies with each individual convert. Feeling a bit alien among both the Chinese and Malays might be rather common. Some choose to be acculturized with the Malays to the extent of being assimilated, some wish to take on certain characteristics of the Malay culture; yet others accept only the religion and resist any approach towards Malay culture. The process is multidimensional; individual redefinition of identity is diverse, resulting in many levels of identity reconstruction for each convert. The relearning process in the formation of this new identity comprises many areas, including religious knowledge, language, food, social skills, expectations, and responsibilities that are all interrelated. For example, learning the new religion also involves learning a new language — Arabic (for the recitation of *Qur'anic* verses during ritual prayers); it also requires an increased fluency and understanding of the Malay language in which all religious matters are conducted. And it involves a new way of more modest dressing, for some women it may necessitate the covering of their hair. Meal times is another area where this change is most obvious, from the change of eating venues (*halal* restaurants) to the crowd the person now mingles with at meal times. The festive occasions to mark are also different. In many other aspects, some patently apparent, some more emotionally discreet, some imposed upon, some actively sought, the convert goes through a lengthy, multidimensional, and multilevel process of reconstructing a new social identity while at the same time negotiating some features of the former identity. How the reconstructed identity is perceived by society is as important as how it is self-perceived and felt by the individual. In the end, it is a matter of securing a good relationship with the group to which the individual belongs, in the case of the Chinese Muslim, both the Chinese and Malay Muslim communities.

It must be recognized that the status of Chinese Muslim converts in Malaysia and their relationship with the Chinese and Malay communities have slowly evolved in a positive way in tandem with the economic, educational, and social developments in Malaysia. The betterment of the education level in Malaysia has given Malaysians a heightened global awareness on many matters, including the universal Islamic world. Encounters with Muslims of various races and countries have become more common. Higher levels of education, exposure to the world, and increased travel overseas have made one section of Malaysians, Malays, and Chinese more open-minded and accepting of others to a certain extent.

As economic and social equity among ethnic groups in Malaysia was gradually achieved through the implementation of the National Economic Policy, a Malay commercial and industrial community was created in a short time, elevating the economic and social status of the Malays. With the educational, professional, economic, and social gap narrowed, many urban Malays and Chinese now study and work in the same environment and move in common social circles, leading to lessened stereotyped prejudices, increased socialization and cooperation, as well as more intermarriage between people of similar educational, professional, and social backgrounds, even if they are from different ethnic groups. It is observed that the distinction between religious identity and ethnic and cultural identification is now more openly discussed in a civilized manner. Awareness of the long historic presence of Muslims in China has played a key role in the acceptance of the Chinese as Muslim, both within the Malay and Chinese communities. With the spate of publicity featuring Muslims in China, the educated Malaysians, both Malays and Chinese, now realize that the way they used to put being Chinese and Muslim at opposite ends of a pole does not reflect the truth. This is one positive step towards better acceptance of a fellow Chinese who chooses to become Muslim.

THE RISE OF THE MALAYSIAN CHINESE MUSLIM IDENTITY

The increase in the number of Muslims among the Malaysian Chinese, with a more mature age group, along with their elevated educational, professional, economic, and social status, have also played a significant role in the better acceptance. Most are willing to get to know the religion before they commit themselves. The more informed ones show increasing confidence in practising the religion within their own permitted cultural environment. The formation of the Malaysian Chinese Muslim Association (MACMA), now recognized as an entity that represents the Chinese Muslims in Malaysia nationwide and internationally, has provided them with — albeit just to a certain extent and only to a rather limited number — a faint sense of belonging, in addition to courses and counselling. For many of them, the old pattern of having or trying to become Malay becomes one of individual preference and is very much according to circumstances.

In this country where it is so easy to live naturally with a mix of cultures even when one is of full blood from any ethnic group, it would be regretful if the Chinese who become Muslim feel, or are made to feel, that they have to make the choice to be part of only one group; and often this choice is to eventually become Malay. It may be added that this may not be the choice that brings the most joy, but one that is based more on practicality, living in a majority-Malay Muslim community, and the wish for the children to benefit (or not to be marginalized) from a pro-*Bumiputra* policy. In the process, much of the Chinese culture is lost; whereas had things been made easier for them, the fusion of two cultures within the practice of Islam, could have greatly benefited the individuals, their families, society, and the nation at large.

For the Chinese Muslim in Malaysia, acquiring a natural, flexible, and fluid identity by internalizing the religion in the multiple cultural identities would be one way to overcome the identity dilemma. It looks like the educated, religiously well informed Chinese Muslims who are also confident about their Chineseness, are more inclined to do this. For the moment, it is up to each individual Muslim Chinese to find his/her own unique identity within Islam, and a fusion of Malay-Chinese or Malaysian culture in a way most suited to him, his family, and his social circle.

The Chinese Muslims in Malaysia have come a long way since many decades ago when Chinese conversions were rare and isolated, and, for some, a family secret not to be revealed. It cannot be denied that even today there are individuals who cause great distress to their families and are chastised in their own community because of their conversion to Islam; there are also many others who feel disappointed with the lukewarm reception they get from the local Muslims. But in general, the altered positive sentiment is here to stay because the long accepted conventional notion of "Chineseness and Islam are mutually exclusive" is now being challenged. Malaysians are now more disposed to look at Chinese Muslims in a spirit of pluralism and integration, not total assimilation.

Just as promising progress is being made, a new kind of polarization between Malay and Chinese can be observed due to new, global political and economic factors and the institutionalization of Islam in the country, which is also a reflection of a worldwide tide of Islamic radicalization that influences the Chinese Muslims. Gradual and increasing radicalization of Islam in Malaysia is one factor that is driving the Chinese Muslim (and non-Muslim Chinese) to keep their distance from the Malays. Jacobsen (2003) observed this of Islam in both Indonesia and Malaysia: "From being a flexible, co-optive, and tolerant religion that acted as a facilitator between different cultures and peoples, it changed towards a more orthodox religion that excluded the very same people it previously encompassed."

Apart from political and institutionalized Islamization, intense revivalism of Islam is also prevalent in the social context. Many Malays have changed their religious outlook and the dimension of their social contact with the Chinese, and this puzzles the Chinese who suddenly find an imbalance in their usual lifestyle when socializing with Malay friends.[19] One Chinese husband told me how he was feeling alienated now from his wife of many years: "She started to wear the tudung; she never did before, and my family is not used to see[ing] her in this way, sometimes it is embarrassing as I don't know how to explain [it]. And now she does not allow our children to eat at my parents' home, and will not allow them to sleep over, which causes big distress to my family. She wasn't like this before."

The debates on the implementation of *hudud* or Muslim family law, peer pressure in certain quarters on Muslim women to wear the scarf, the big publicity on the case of a Muslim's fight to renounce the religion, the intrusion of the so-called "moral police" in people's intimate lives, the recent *fatwa* on the ban of yoga, have all created a general sense of apprehension towards the religion among a big section of Malaysians, including the Muslims.

The few racial incidences where many Malay politicians have exploited the religion as a political means further pushes the Chinese Muslim to not want to be part of "this kind of Islam". I have encountered a few Chinese who are interested in Islam, who have been regulars in group meetings to learn the tafsir of the *Qur'an*; who have fasted the whole month during Ramadan for many years, but are wary of coming into the religion because of the overeagerness of some Malays to "convert" them. One of them said: "Once I officially embrace Islam, I know they will not let go of me. There're a lot of things I like in Islam but I don't want to be like them (Malays)."

One other factor is that as China becomes an economic superpower, Chinese communities in countries outside China are reverting back to learning the Chinese language, feel proud about their ethnic origin, and proactively defy marginalization. In the context of this chapter, we may cite the controversy about building a Chinese mosque in Malaysia that made headlines in January 2007. The *mufti* of Perlis, Dr Mohd. Asri Zainul Abidin, initiated the issue with a statement urging the religious affairs departments to allow the Chinese Muslims to build their own mosques in all states. The statement sparked a heated debate in the newspapers and forums with various opinions. Some state religious department heads responded negatively, stating that Islam is for everybody and mosques should not be built for any specific communities; some others said that in Malaysia, being Muslim is being Malay, and there should be no communal compromise; a couple of others stated that they would allow the Chinese Muslims in their respective states to build a Chinese mosque and conduct sermons in Chinese.[20] The Chinese Muslims expressed their request for a Chinese mosque, and received the support of a portion of Malays and the mainstream non-Muslim Chinese community. It is seen that as one section of Malays is inching towards further radicalization, and the government is increasingly institutionalizing Islam (in education, politics, and the economy), Chinese Muslims feel pressured to keep the cultural distance wider. They wish to be openly recognized as Chinese.

CONCLUSION

In the current political climate, the existence and recognition of a Chinese Muslim community, with shared cultural traditions and religious fraternity with both the Chinese and Malays, could very well be a positive catalyst in the path of nation building. For this to happen, the Chinese Muslims in Malaysia first have to start being proactive in trying to overcome their own identity dilemma. This they can do by being knowledgeable and confident about both their Chinese ethnic heritage and their Muslim religious acquirement, complemented by the Malaysian pluralistic national characteristics. When they have a recognizable Chinese Muslim identity they can then assert themselves as the bridge between the Chinese and Malays within the Malaysian social context.

Notes

[1]   See Rosey Ma, "Chinese Muslims in Malaysia: Their History and Development", 2003, for a more detailed account of the early presence of the Chinese Muslims in Malaysia.

[2]   Ma in "Shifting Identities: Chinese Muslims in Malaysia", 2005 writes that upon arriving in Malaysia, these Chinese Muslims, finding themselves overwhelmed between a majority, non-Chinese Muslim community and a majority, non-Muslim Chinese community, have, for survival purposes or by political design, rather quickly assimilated into one group or the other.

[3]   National Census 2000 gives the number as 57,221.

[4]   "I am a convert" is the self-referent term often used by somebody who embraced Islam, as well as an accepted social label, usually with no derogatory connotation.

[5]   This may create unanticipated difficulties, also for the original Chinese Muslims. My children, who went to different states for competitions as members (all Chinese) of the Kuala Lumpur state swimming team, filled in

"Chinese" in the *bangsa* (race) box. When they would not eat at the pre-booked non-*halal* Chinese restaurants catering for the swimmers, they were chastised for not having made clear to the organizers that they were "Malay".

6   The term is borrowed from Henri Tafler (1974): "People have an inbuilt tendency to categorize themselves into one or more ingroups building a part of their identity on the basis of membership of that group and enforcing boundaries with other groups."

7   It is true that decades ago, there were indeed promises of certain kind of benefits to encourage Chinese to become Muslim, and it is also true that there have been people who tried to take advantage of this, without any sincerity towards the religion, but these incentives have largely stopped a long time ago. However, suspicion and despise still remain to some extent.

8   An Islamic greeting, which, in full, is "*Assalamualaikum*", meaning "peace upon you", and the response to which is "*Walaikum salam*", "and peace to you too". I grew up with the teaching and habit of always responding likewise to anybody who gives me *salam*, whether the person is Muslim or not, contrary to the announcement and debate that took place in Malaysia a few years ago on whether one should answer to a *salam* from a non-Muslim, and also whether it is lawful for a non-Muslim to utter the Islamic greeting.

9   Such as the Malay mother-in-law who did not even wish to see or get to know the Chinese wife her son married, and rejected her outright because she is Chinese. When they went to visit her with the first baby, the baby was taken into the house with much love, but the mother was not invited in.

10   This was the comment of a religious officer in Kuala Lumpur about a convert who was experiencing some difficulties with some members of her Malay family-in-law.

11   Ma (1996) records that in families with higher education and better socio-economic conditions, the level of acceptance is higher, alleviating the problem of adaptation. For a detailed account, see Rosey Ma (1996), "Difficulties Faced by Chinese Muslim Converts in Malaysia", thesis med.

12   A random unofficial survey (Ma 2002) among students in a Chinese high school revealed that their average common knowledge on Islam amounted to: it is the Malays' religion; they cannot eat pork, cannot drink, and are forbidden to gamble; they celebrate Hari Raya; they can marry four wives, and if a Chinese wants to marry a Malay, he/she has to become Muslim/Malay.

13   The name change policy for converts has seen many modifications over the years. Even though it is not an Islamic requirement, it is common practice to ask a convert in Malaysia to take on a Muslim name, with the addition of *bin/binti Abdullah* at the end, meaning son/daughter of Abdullah (servant of Allah). He may or may not keep his Chinese name and surname. The request for a change of name is one big issue that many families converts' face with acrimony. The surname is a strong cultural trait for the Chinese who

wish to keep their long genealogical history. It is an important part of their
essence and their personal and family identity. They feel that being given the
name bin/binti Abdullah is tantamount to denying their ancestry, and having
"a fictitious father" imposed on them, thus forcing them to lose an important
part of their Chinese identity.

14 I say in general because there are also many instances where offspring who
convert to Christianity are rejected by their families, but in the Chinese
community these religions are not looked upon as un-Chinese.

15 Tan Chee-Beng finds a similar attitude about the Chinese language *vis-à-vis*
nationality: the more Chinese the person speaks, the more his patriotism will
be questioned (Tan 2003, pp. 38–63).

16 *Haram* means unlawful in Islam, anything that is not permissible by the religion.

17 This case was especially sad because the girl had been chased out by her
parents after she converted and married, and was told not to go back. When
after a few years she plucked up the courage to visit her parents with her two
little children, she found out that her family had moved away without telling
the neighbours where they had gone. She had lost her family. It would have
been a consolation to find comfort in her husband's family, but that was
not accorded to her; the enormity of her sacrifice was not recognized. When
I met and interviewed this lady, she was in her sixties. She said her children
grew up totally Malay, but now that her mother-in-law had passed away, she
was teaching her grandchildren the Chinese language, and was happy to see
them becoming bicultural.

18 All the names used are fictitious.

19 Many Malays when they visit a Chinese home now, refrain from drinking from
the cups served to them. The Chinese host has to serve them packet drinks
(commented many times).

20 The writer's personal opinion is: if the term "Chinese mosque", refers to a mosque
with Chinese architecture, like the centuries-old ancient mosques in China, it
would be good, as it would depict the ethnic variety of Muslims in the country.
But if it means that it is a mosque for the Chinese Muslims, where the sermon
is delivered in Chinese, this demand may not be quite appropriate. A mosque is
built when there are at least forty Muslim families in a community. There isn't
any area in any state in Malaysia where there can be found forty Chinese families
in a congregation. Apart from that, language would be a problem, given the
heterogeneity of the Chinese population in Malaysia. In which Chinese dialect
would the sermon be read? Mandarin? Cantonese? Hokkien? In the end it would
still have to be in Bahasa Malaysia, which is the common language with which
the Chinese here are familiar within the religious context. A good idea at this
moment would be to plan for Chinese Muslim cultural centres that would also
house a prayer hall — place where knowledge about Islam in general, and as a
religion, and information about Islam in China, can be accessible to the general
public. This would be far more useful than a "Chinese mosque".

References

Amran Kasimin. *Saudara baru Cina di Wilayah dan Selangor*. Bangi: Universiti Kebangsaan Malaysia, 1985.

Djinguiz Mohammed. "L'Islam aux Straits-Settlements". *Revue du Monde Musulman* 4 (1911): 34–44.

Edmonds, Juliet. "Religion, Intermarriage and Assimilation: The Chinese in Malaya". *Race* 10, no. 1 (July 1968): 57–67.

Fadzilah binte Mustapa. "Saudara baru keturunan Cina di Wilayah Persekutuan dan sekitarnya: Satu kajian mengenai masalah masalah yang dihadapi dan penyelesaiannya". Kuala Lumpur: University Malaya, 1987.

Haja Mohideen bin Mohamed. "Muslim Converts in Malaysia: Do we make them feel comfortable?" *Islamic Herald* 15, no. 1 (February 1994): 19–20.

Hassan bin Tahir. "Perubahan sosio-budaya di kalangan orang-orang Cina yang baru memeluk agama Islam di Negeri Johor: Satu tinjauan kritis". Bangi: Universiti Kebangsaan Malaysia, 1980.

Jacobsen, Michael. "Chinese Muslims in Indonesia: Politics, Economy, Faith and Expediency". Working Paper Series. Hong Kong: Southeast Asia Resource Centre, City University of Hong Kong, 2003.

Jahja H. Junus. "Indonesian Moslems of Chinese Descent". Speech delivered at the symposium "Islam and Development". RISEAP (Regional Islamic Da'wah Council of Southeast Asia and the Pacific), Kuching, Sarawak, 1988.

Khairuman bin Hamim. "Kedudukan muallaf di dalam Islam: Satu kajian menurut enakmen Negeri Selangor". Petaling Jaya: Fakulti Syariah Akademi Islam, Universiti Malaya, 1991.

Lam, Joy Y. "Religious Conversion and Reconstruction of Identities: The Case of Chinese Muslim Converts in Malaysia". Working Papers Series, No. 74. Hong Kong: City University of Hong Kong, 2004.

Lee How Lan. "Perkahwinan campur Melayu Cina". Petalng Jaya: University Malaya, 1989.

Lim Hin Fui. "Pengislaman orang, Cina di Kelang: Satu kajian kes integrasi nasional". Latihan Ilmiah (academic exercises). Jabatan Antropologi dan Sosiologi, Universiti Kebangsaan Malaysia, 1977.

Lombard, Denys and Claudine Salmon. "Islam and Chineseness". In *The Propagation of Islam in the Indonesian Malay Archipelago*, edited by Alijah Gordon. Malaysia: Malaysian Sociological Research Institute, 2001.

Ma, Rosey Wang. "Difficulties faced by Chinese Muslim Converts in Malaysia and the Need to go through Education and Counseling to Overcome the Problems". Thesis presented to the Postgraduate Centre of International Islamic University Malaysia for the degree of Master in Education, 1995.

———. "Chinese Muslims in Malaysia: Their History and Development". In *Chinese Studies of the Malay World: A Comparative Approach*, edited by Ding Choo Ming and Ooi Kee Beng. Singapore: Eastern Universities Press, 2003.

————. "Shifting Identities: Chinese Muslims in Malaysia". *Asian Ethnicity* 6, no. 2 (July 2005): 89–107.

Muhd Zuki Pileh. "Perlunya identity Cina-Islam". *MASSA* 29 (2000): 30.

Muljana, Skamet. *Runtuhnya Keradjaan Hindu Djawa dan Timbulnja Negara-Negara Islam di Nusantara.* Djakarta, 1968.

Muna Othman. "Masalah dan cabaran yang dihadapi oleh mereka yang dipanggil Muslim converts". Seminar on "Dakwah saudara saudara Baru". Kuala Lumpur, 1982.

Muzaffar, Chandra. "Islam in Malaysia: Resurgence and Response". In *Islam in South and Southeast Asia*, edited by Ashgar Ali Engineer. Delhi: Ajanta Publications, 1985.

————. "Islam and Confucianism: Significance for Ethnic Relations in Malaysia". Paper presented at the International Seminar on Islam and Confucianism. Kuala Lumpur, 1995.

Nagata, Judith. "The Chinese Muslims of Malaysia: New Malays or New Associates? A Problem of Religion and Ethnicity". In *The Past in Southeast Asia's Present*, edited by Gordon P. Means. Ottawa, Ontario: Secretariat, Canadian Society for Asian Studies, 1978.

Salleh bin hj. Ahmad. "Orang-orang Cina Islam: satu kajian kes di Kluang". Bangi: Latihan Ilmiah, Jabatan Antropologi dan Sosiologi, Universiti Kebangsaan Malaysia, 1979.

Salmon, Claudine. "La communaute chinoise de Surabaya". *Archipel* 53 (1997): 121–206.

Shamala G. "Fixing the Conversion Tangle". *The Sun*, 24 June 2001.

Shamsul Amri Baharuddin. "Identity Construction, Nation Formation, and Islamic Revivalism in Malaysia". In *Islam in an Era of Nation States: Politics and Religious Renewal in Muslim Southeast Asia*, edited by Robert W. Hefner and Patricia Horvatich. Honolulu: University of Hawaii Press, 1997.

————. "Identity Contestation in Malaysia: A Comparative Commentary on 'Malayness' and 'Chineseness'". *Academica* 55 (1999): 17–37.

Tan Chee-Beng. "People of Chinese Descent: Language, Nationality and Identity". In *The Chinese Diaspora Selected Essays*, Vol. I, edited by Wang Ling Chi and Wang Gungwu. Singapore: Eastern Universities Press, 2003.

Tan Yeok Seng. "Chinese Element in the Islamization of Southeast Asia". *Journal of the South Seas Society* 30 (1975): 19–27.

The Siauw Giap. "Islam and Chinese Assimilation in Indonesia and Malaysia". In *Chinese Beliefs and Practices in Southeast Asia*, edited by Cheu Hock Tong. Petaling Jaya: Pelanduk Publications, 1993.

3

QUO VADIS[1]: THE CHINESE IN MALAYSIA

Lee Kam Hing

A larger than expected swing against the ruling coalition Barisan Nasional (BN) in the March 2008 election altered the political landscape of Malaysia to an extent that few had thought possible. The opposition Pakatan Rakyat gained more than a third of the parliamentary seats, thus denying the ruling BN a two-third majority for the first time. Five large and important states fell to the opposition, and these include Penang, Selangor, Perak, and Kedah. In this election there had been a significant shift of Chinese votes against the ruling BN.[2] Most observers, including opposition leader Lim Kit Siang, acknowledged that the people mostly voted not for the opposition, but against the BN. Non-Malay voters were critical of non-Malay parties within the BN for not defending their interests and there was a strong underlying protest against what non-Malays saw as UMNO's display of overwhelming political power and arrogance. There was also the waving of an unsheathed keris by UMNO Youth in the last two UMNO General Assembly and this particularly dismayed the non-Malays.[3] Given the fact that March 2008 was a significant watershed in Malaysian politics, this chapter looks at how the political changes could affect the politics of the Chinese and the future of this community.

Since the country's Independence in 1957, Malaysian politics have incrementally been dominated by the BN. But it is UMNO that is dominant and this is reflected in the power relations of the various institutions in the country. Within the Executive, UMNO prevails over the other BN component parties and the Executive is seen as overriding the judiciary and the legislature, and a federal government exercising power over the states, including Sabah and Sarawak. It is UMNO that decides major national policies and key government positions in the country. The prime minister, deputy prime minister, and senior ministers come from UMNO and proceedings of the party's general assemblies are followed more closely by the public than parliamentary sittings.[4]

As the March 2008 election approached there were openly voiced criticisms about the government's ability to deal with the increasing social, economic, and political problems in the country. Allegations abounded of corruption on a scale unimaginable and complaints of New Economic Policy (NEP) abuse that benefited only a few while neglecting the majority, a judiciary lacking independence as highlighted by the Lingam tape, scandals of serious moral lapses of senior government figures, and reports of growing crime and social problems. There was also rising cost of living and high inflation, and these were felt by voters of all ethnic groups and social classes. The government might post impressive growth figures, but voters only felt the high cost of living. These were concerns that cut across ethnic lines. Through the alternative media and even mainstream press, these negative reports reached a wider number of Malaysians in towns and villages. This display of unchecked power and political arrogance was cited as an important factor in the swing against the ruling coalition. It was an election where the Internet and text messages have had major impact than previously. Today with more than half the population having Internet access and an estimated eighty-five out of a hundred Malaysians using a mobile phone, there is greater access to information than what could be obtained from the government-controlled media. And the influence of the alternative media and the Internet can be expected to open up Malaysian politics further in the future, with greater numbers of users who are also younger voters.[5]

This dominance in power relations in Malaysia has since the March 2008 election been tempered to an extent, at least for now. There is presently a slightly stronger opposition and, with that, a livelier parliament able to engage robustly with the Executive; state assertiveness, especially in the five Pakatan Rakyat-held states; and a restive Sabah and Sarawak over the federal government/East Malaysia relations. There is also the promise of a more independent judiciary. That the opposition has won the majority of the by-elections since the March 2008 election suggests that the sentiment against the BN is still strong. Arising from the present political fluidity is an evolving two-coalition system made up of alternative alignments of multi-ethnic or ethnic-based parties. This two-coalition system is threatening to sculpt out a new political landscape, but how successful and sustained this would be is difficult to say. The outcome could have major implications on interethnic relations and on nation building, within which the role of Chinese politics in this country rests.

A QUADRILATERAL MODEL OF MALAYSIAN POLITICS

Immediately after the elections and with the forming of a new Pakatan Rakyat coalition, there were Chinese Malaysians who hoped that politics in the country would now be more competitive and, through this, help address some of their concerns, such as the community's weakened political position, the lack of preferred higher education opportunities, NEP limitations to business opportunities, and desecularization of the state. The evidence of cross-ethnic voting in the elections, especially in Penang and in the Klang Valley, also encouraged many Chinese, especially the younger ones, to believe that there would be a less communal and more, *bangsa* Malaysia approach to politics in the coming years, and they hold this as the only option to an otherwise divisive course governed by narrow ethnic demands from all sides.

Yet, there are also those who have more modest expectations and argue that the 2008 election results follow a trend where voters, particularly the Chinese, swing their support alternately between the BN and the opposition. There was an expected swing against the BN in the 1999 election, but this did not happen when the Chinese supported the ruling coalition amidst the turbulence of the Asian Financial Crisis and the Reformasi movement, and again in 2004, when they voted BN to give Abdullah Badawi a mandate as the new prime minister.[6] In 2008, the delayed swing against the BN became therefore more pronounced. BN supporters are now hopeful that the pendulum will swing back to the BN's favour in the next election, and there will be a return to the pattern of Malaysian politics of pre-March 2008.

Although events are still unfolding in Malaysia and it is difficult to assess as yet whether the transformation in Malaysian politics, particularly with regard to the position of the Chinese, would consolidate, some tentative observations can nevertheless be made. For this I would like to draw attention to Wang Gungwu's article entitled, "Reflections on Malaysian Elites", first published in 1986, and to use a model he discussed there to try to understand what happened in 2008 and what possibly lies ahead in Malaysia's politics.[7] In the article Wang explained that there are four major centres of power in Malaysian politics: Malay rulers, Islam, *Bumiputra* nationalism, and non-*Bumiputra* society, and he likened these four centres to four legs of a table, or, in this case, the state. Wang argues that the influence of the four centres of power and their relations to one another have changed over time and his article traces developments from pre-colonial times to the present. He suggested that should these legs or four institutions become seriously out of proportion in relation to one another, then the stability of the table, or Malaysian politics, would be threatened. Wang, writing in 1986, was particularly interested in finding out whether then Prime Minister Mahathir Mohamad could, given the events then, subordinate the other power centres one at a time and thereby bring about a presidential style administration. It would, at the same time, ensure dominance of *Bumiputra* nationalism. The result would then be a pyramid-shape power structure with *Bumiputra* nationalism on top, and this model would replace the quadrilateral or four-legged diagram which currently represents Malaysian society. Wang's model of four centres is particularly relevant to helping us understand Malaysian politics and the Chinese today.[8]

Developing from Wang's quadrilateral model, it could be argued that since Independence, two of these centres, *Bumiputra* nationalism and Islam, have greatly expanded their influence and power. Increasingly there has been a drive by *Bumiputra* nationalism towards political hegemony and, supported by a largely Malay bureaucracy, strong advances being made in the strategic fields of higher education and the economy. At the same time, Islam has taken an expanded and influential presence as it is being pushed forward by the dynamics of the PAS-UMNO political competition.[9]

It is the other two legs that, by contrast with the first two, have had their influence circumscribed. The Malay rulers, as represented by the third leg, have had some of their powers reduced, particularly by the constitutional amendments of 1983 and 1993. These amendments have removed some of their legal immunity. Despite this the Malay rulers have largely retained their powers as defined by the 1957 Constitution and, in a situation where the ruling coalition and opposition are more evenly balanced, can play a critical role.

It is the fourth leg of non-*Bumiputra* society or plural society in Wang's model, within which are the Chinese and the Indians, that has weakened since Independence, and whose position, the community fear, could be further eroded in the coming years. The political position of the non-*Bumiputra* elite has been weakened due to several reasons. Among these was the acceptance by non-Malays at pre-Independence talks of constitutional compromises which conceded political pre-eminence to *Bumiputra* nationalism, a relative decline of the Chinese in the total population because of their lower birth rate, and consequently decreasing number of Chinese-majority seats in parliament. In 1957, the year of Independence, the Chinese formed an estimated

37.2 per cent of the population, but this has gradually declined to 34.31 per cent in 1970, and 32.1 per cent in 1980. There was a sharper decline in 1990 when the population of the Chinese fell to 27.6 per cent, and even further to 25.1 per cent in 2006. The decline is expected to continue so that by 2021 the Chinese are expected to form barely 21 per cent of the population and by 2050 about 16 per cent. By contrast the Malays, who made up less than 50 per cent of total population in 1957 and only became a majority in the early 1970s, now form more than 60 per cent.[10]

With this population decline, there are relatively fewer parliamentary constituencies that have a Chinese majority. The relative decline in Chinese-majority seats is accentuated by an electoral weightage favouring rural seats. Some largely Malay rural seats have less than half the number of voters than urban, mainly Chinese, seats. In the first election in 1959, there were twenty-nine Chinese parliamentarians or roughly a quarter of the members of parliament (MPs). This percentage of Chinese representatives in parliament is maintained even though percentage of Chinese-majority seats have fallen. It is because many Chinese MPs from the ruling BN were elected in Malay-majority areas. Ong Ka Chuan, then secretary general of the MCA, won in Tanjong Malim, Perak, which has 51 per cent Malays and only 31 per cent Chinese, and Ng Yen Yen, the Wanita MCA head, won in Raub, Pahang, where the Malays form 49.2 per cent, and the Chinese 43.1 per cent, of the voters. Several other MCA and Gerakan seats were won with substantial Malay support. These have implications because Chinese MPs dependent on Malay votes tend to be more circumspect in their public rhetoric on Chinese issues. With the Chinese weakened electorally, UMNO, or UMNO in alliance with PAS, could conceivably form a government without the support of non-Malay parties. And with less representation in parliament, Chinese BN parties have been unable to stake claims for larger number of cabinet positions, including strategic portfolios, which they once held, such as finance and trade.[11] This is reflected in the fact that no federal Chinese politician has enjoyed the same standing in relation to Malay leaders since the departure of Tan Siew Sin, former minister for Finance and president of the MCA.

The non-*Bumiputra* power centre is further weakened by deep divisions, firstly between those in opposition and in government; secondly within the ruling coalition, between Gerakan and the MCA, and thirdly, intraparty splits that occur at regular intervals, such as those in the MCA, and these sap the energy and resources of the largest Chinese-based party.[12] The Chinese have swung their support between the ruling coalition and the opposition, as well as engage in what some regard as strategic voting: supporting the opposition at the parliamentary level to articulate issues of larger concern and backing BN non-Malays at the state level to access basic amenities and licences. But this manner of voting has the effect of splitting the effectiveness and electoral strength of the non-Malay parties.

As non-Malays become less of a factor in the power balance, critical political engagement will increasingly be between the other two centres: *Bumiputra* nationalism and Islam. Wang referred to earlier *Bumiputra* nationalism as secular nationalism, one led by graduates of secular schools, colleges, and overseas institutions. Politically today, *Bumiputra* nationalism is equated with UMNO. Islam, meanwhile, is represented by those Muslim elite outside officialdom, whose role in religious and educational affairs gives them leadership status. Currently, the PAS could arguably be seen to represent this group, although not entirely. According to Clive Kessler, support for these two centres has intermittently been evenly divided. Intense competition has forced UMNO to adopt PAS positions incrementally in order "to match its ever expanding demands concerning the public, formal and legal standing of Islam" and win the Malay heartland.[13] UMNO finds it politically necessary to take the Islamic route against the PAS to reach a Malay electorate which is responding to a more religious appeal, partly the result of greater individual spirituality, and partly the effect of a worldwide Islamic resurgence.

In this contest with the PAS, UMNO does not have to worry too much about the non-*Bumiputra* power centre. Indeed in the 2004 general election UMNO won enough seats to come close to being able to govern the country all by itself. In 2004 while obtaining only 35.9 per cent of the popular vote, UMNO gained almost 50 per cent of the parliamentary seats and held 70 per cent of the ministerial positions. Given this political arithmetic, some UMNO leaders see the plural society leg as increasingly dispensable. It partly explains the behaviour of UMNO Youth in waving an unsheathed keris at the 2006 General Assembly as a form of political warning to non-Malay political demands. *Bumiputra* nationalism is deploying the symbol of the keris as well as its interpretation of history to advance the idea of *Ketuanan Melayu* or Malay Supremacy or Sovereignty.

The fourth centre of power, particularly the Chinese, watches with concern a *Bumiputra* nationalism that has not only expanded, but has increasingly taken on an Islamic thrust, and Islam, as represented by a PAS that is gaining electoral influence. As *Bumiputra* nationalism and Islam grow, the state is being reshaped and redefined, thereby further narrowing the political space for the Chinese. Early nationalist leaders such as Tunku Abdul Rahman, together with non-Malay leaders, decided in 1957 that while Islam was to be the religion of the state, the state itself would be secular. This was later re-emphasized under the Malaysia Agreement. However, beginning from the 1980s, there has been a gradual desecularization of the state so much so that in late September 2000 Mahathir Mohamed, and later in July 2007 Najib Razak, declared Malaysia to be an Islamic state.[14] While the Islamic state they declared might not conform to what classical Islamic theorists would want, the mere declaration endorses and encourages those pushing to replace the secular character of the state with an Islamic one. Incrementally, through changes in the legal system and an Islamization process in the bureaucracy and education, non-Malays find that the secular state, which they see as a safeguard for their religious and cultural interests, has been eroded. Where the Civil Court was once supreme, the *Syariah* Court has since gained parity in status and power. Increasingly disputes over religious conversion, properties, the custody of children, and burial rights are handed over to the *Syariah* rather than the Civil Courts. It is not just that it is increasingly difficult for non-Malays to get land for places of worship, and to use Bahasa Malaysia fully for their scriptures, but also that senior positions in bureaucracy, government, and universities are now reserved for Malays on both nationalist, as well as Islamic, imperatives. The fear is that Islam is being used to legitimize Malay dominance.[15]

Non-*Bumiputra* leadership's reaction to the expansion of Islam and a more Islamic *Bumiputra* nationalism has been mixed. For the main Chinese-based BN parties, religion has hardly been a core issue in party programmes. Where for Malays, it is Islam that is indisputably central, for the Chinese who are adherents of more than one religion, it is language and education that provide identity and cohesion to the community.

The MCA, through the Institute of Strategic Analysis and Policy Research (INSAP), its think tank, argues just before the March 2008 election that the Chinese had three key concerns, which it describes as the three pillars of the Chinese community, and that these define the identity and interests of the Chinese in Malaysia. According to INSAP these pillars are Chinese education, Chinese newspapers, and the guilds, associations, and non-government organizations.[16] These three pillars are interdependent and cannot exist without one another. If Chinese education were to cease, the Chinese dailies would close because of a lack of readers. There are six Chinese dailies in Peninsular Malaysia and eight in Sabah and Sarawak. The Chinese media, which is relatively free compared with the English and Malay papers, is the pulse of the community. And the community trusts the Chinese media more than its political leaders.

INSAP sees the MCA and the other Chinese-based parties as part of the 5,000 or so associations that form the third pillar. The MCA leaders thus believe that the party has to defend the three pillars including continued operation of the 1,291 Sekolah Kebangsaan Jenis Cina (SJKCs) and the sixty independent secondary schools, and to engage with the Chinese media and the 5,000 associations in order to maintain support within the community. The MCA sees its interest as being tied to these core concerns and therefore places priority in dealing with them.

Hence, when Mahathir declared that Malaysia is an Islamic state, the response from the BN parties was mostly muted because the Chinese-based parties did not then see it as a core concern. A firmer response was subsequently made to a similar declaration of Malaysia being an Islamic state by Najib Razak in July 2007. The MCA in this case issued a statement insisting that Malaysia is a secular state. The subsequent firmer stand of the Chinese-based parties was a response to the growing alarm of various religious groups within their community to growing Islamization. On 21 January 2006 non-Malay ministers submitted a memorandum to the prime minister on Islam and the legal system, but subsequently withdrew it when asked to do so. UMNO leaders regarded the memorandum as an ultimatum from non-Malay BN parties.

Many among the Chinese tend to fear the PAS more than UMNO, believing that the latter is willing to develop a moderate interpretation of an Islamic state, such as Islam Hadhari. Generally they have difficulties distinguishing between the Islamic programmes espoused by UMNO and the PAS. Both parties declared a commitment to an Islamic state, but in fact it is UMNO which has so far been more effective in pushing through Islamic programmes. When this happens Chinese-based parties within the coalition are attacked by the community and blamed for their ineffectiveness to stem the desecularization process.[17]

ISSUES OF EDUCATION AND THE ECONOMY IN *BUMIPUTRA* AND NON-*BUMIPUTRA* DYNAMICS

Other than the desecularization process of the nation, the March election showed that there are broader concerns troubling the Chinese community. Of these, opportunities in education and the economy continue to rank high. Chinese language education, especially maintaining national-type primary schools, remains a core concern of the Chinese community. But increasingly, the real unhappiness of the Chinese is the declining proportion of non-Malays admitted into the public universities and preferred courses.

In June 1979, following representation from Gerakan and the MCA, Hussein Onn, the then prime minister, fixed the ratio of university intake at 55 per cent *Bumiputra* and 45 per cent non-*Bumiputra*. The MCA also partially resolved the problem of limited educational opportunities by setting up the Tunku Abdul Rahman College which offers professional diploma courses.

Tension over admission to higher education eased further when in 1980s the government allowed the setting up of private colleges which, through twinning arrangements with U.K., Australian, and other overseas universities enabled thousands of Malaysians, mainly non-Malays, to obtain tertiary education. The move, which was consolidated under the 1996 Private Higher Educational Institutions Act, was timely, given that local public universities could not cope with demand, while fees for overseas universities were becoming unaffordable for many. In 1996 the government allowed several of the larger and more established colleges to be raised to university college status. The government itself has increased the number of public universities and today there are twenty of these public institutions.

There are now 365,800 students studying at private institutions of higher learning (IPTS) and 507,438 at public institutions of higher learning (IPTA). The 2007 intake saw 167,788 students enrolling at IPTSs and 190,265 at IPTAs. This indicates that enrolment in IPTSs is increasing and the gap between public and private institutions is closing. The growth is largely in about a dozen large private universities and colleges out of nearly 500 of such registered institutions.[18]

There are, however, implications in the continuing education trend which finds more Chinese students in private colleges and universities, and Malays in public universities. More significantly, the teaching and management staff of the public universities, to which research and government funding are allocated, are mostly Malays. The private universities and colleges are largely teaching rather than research-oriented although a few institutions have encouraged research. There will be relatively fewer non-Malay research scholars and public intellectuals in the years to come. There are therefore, three discernable segments in higher education — a largely public sector in higher education catering largely to lower-income Malaysians, a private sector for higher-income non-Malays, and an overseas sector for Malaysians who are relatively well off or government-sponsored. Few Malaysians graduating from overseas choose to teach in local universities and there is also a reluctance on the part of public universities to recruit them. This situation does not encourage an improvement in higher education, as reflected in the low world ranking of Malaysian universities.[19]

In their participation of the economy, the Chinese continue to view the implementation of government policies as seriously disadvantaging them. Two years ago, the Centre for Public Policy Research, then headed by Lim Teck Ghee, released a report showing that *Bumiputra* have more than achieved the target of 30 per cent corporate equity. And indeed there is a very strong *Bumiputra* presence in finance, telecommunications, and transport. Non-*Bumiputra* complain that they continue to face business restrictions, and at the same time, are required to give up 30 per cent of their companies' equity.[20]

The one sector where the Chinese continue to be important is in manufacturing, which in 2007 contributed to 80 per cent of export, 34.4 per cent of GDP, and 27 per cent of employment. There is Malaysian Chinese presence in a number of large manufacturing companies, but their contribution is mostly through small and medium enterprises (SMEs), of which they form the majority. The bulk of manufacturing is produced by multinational corporations, with Chinese SMEs being a significant part of the production and supply chain. Chinese SMEs also produce goods on behalf of overseas companies under an Original Equipment Manufacturer (OEM) arrangement.[21]

However, Chinese SMEs are encountering several challenges. Firstly, many SMEs are facing problems of succession. While there are examples of children of businessmen taking over SMEs and transforming them into modern enterprises, this is not the case for many others. Secondly, many SMEs have difficulties getting funding from government allocation to expand and innovate. And thirdly, many are not willing to expand because this would place them in a capitalization category where they would have to fulfil NEP requirements. Business opportunities in the coming years will be the concern of many Chinese. Their main anxiety is the economic downturn worldwide which would affect exports. They are also worried about competition for overseas markets from products coming out of China where costs are much lower than in Malaysia. Foreign investors are also moving to China and re-locating production plants there.[22]

So how are Malaysian Chinese businessmen responding and what options do they have? There are three possible options. Firstly, they have to be more competitive and advance into high-value areas, such as digital electronics, and thereby stay ahead of China's competition. Secondly, there is the option to relocate. Many are moving to China to take advantage of lower costs in labour and land there. Already, Pensonic, a Penang-based company, which is the largest electrical and electronics manufacturer in Malaysia, is thinking of shifting some of its production to China to take advantage of the lower costs there. But China is not necessarily the best option because Vietnam and Thailand offer similar advantages of costs and China may not be as attractive in the long run. Relocation also becomes necessary in order to remain in the supply chain of production when large manufacturers, such as MNCs, have moved. This migration of contract and OEM manufacturers would further reduce contract manufacturing opportunities for the smaller SMEs left behind. The relocation of Malaysian Chinese businesses particularly manufacturers, could lead not only to the shifting out of, or extending, production lines overseas, but would see an increase in the number of Malaysian Chinese working, for instance, in China. It is estimated that there are some 30,000 to 40,000 Malaysian Chinese working in China today. Many are in the financial services, in banks and accounting firms, but others are plant managers of factories. In a sense this is a reflection of the globalization process where Malaysians seek work not only in China, but also in other parts of the world.[23]

To move up the value chain or to relocate are not easy options. Only the larger ones are able to invest in research and development (R&D) to stay competitive, or relocate. According to the Malaysian Institute of Microelectronic Systems (MIMOS) Berhad, a government-funded technology company, expenditure on R&D in Malaysia is 0.4 per cent of GDP, compared with 0.8 per cent in China. For many middle-size and smaller SMEs, given the loss of markets, the choice is to close down. There is, for many small manufacturers, another option, and that is to turn from being manufacturers of textile and shoemaking, for instance, to being traders. It has been noted that it is more viable and profitable to buy products from China, which are cheaper than what they themselves could produce, and distribute or sell these in the region and in markets they have long been familiar with. However, this intermediary role remains until such time when entrepreneurs from China acquire the contacts themselves.

The third option is to search out *Bumiputra* business or political partners. Under such arrangements, Chinese businessmen offer entrepreneurial and technical skills, business networks, and possibly capital, while the *Bumiputra* partner secures capital and contracts, either as a principal or supporting partner. But this is increasingly harder as many *Bumiputra* businessmen are able to venture out on their own or with government backing.

The political dynamics between the non-*Bumiputra* leg and *Bumiputra* nationalism in Wang's quadrilateral model is thus most evident in the area of higher education and business. As *Bumiputra* nationalism makes impressive advances in education and business, some innovative and resilient approaches, as well as compromises with Malay nationalism, have to be developed to allow for a continuing and meaningful role for non-Malays. Non-*Bumiputra* continue to call for fair implementation of government policies so that affirmative action favouring *Bumiputra* would not disadvantage the Chinese in business, employment, and enrolment in universities, and that meritocracy should eventually be a criterion accepted by all.

THE FUTURE

In the 8 March 2008 election, the BN, a coalition of largely ethnic-based parties that has ruled the country since 1957, suffered losses on a scale not seen since 1969. Most notable was the strong swing of the Chinese and, to an extent, Malay and Indian votes, to the Opposition. There was also significant cross-ethnic voting for opposition parties, with non-Malays voting for the PAS and the Malays for the DAP. In the past, non-Malays voted for UMNO against the PAS, and Malays voted for non-Malay parties in UMNO against opposition parties such as the DAP.

The MCA, the largest Chinese-based party in the country, lost sixteen of the seats it held in the last parliament. It won only fifteen of the forty parliamentary seats contested. The Gerakan, another largely Chinese-based party in the BN, suffered an even greater electoral defeat. The party conceded all its state seats in Penang and, with this, the post of chief minister. It retained only two parliamentary and three state seats compared with ten parliamentary and thirty state seats it previously held. Of the fifty-two parliamentary constituencies where non-Malays formed the majority, BN won only thirteen.[24]

The opposition DAP, in the meantime, won as many Chinese-majority seats as the BN Chinese-based parties combined, even when the latter figure includes the Sabah and Sarawak seats. The DAP took twenty-eight seats, of which twenty one were won by its Chinese candidates. With the PKR, another opposition party, its seven new Chinese MPs, there are now more Chinese MPs in the Opposition than in the ruling coalition. Both the DAP and PKR are multiracial parties although the former is largely Chinese based, while the latter is Malay led.

The March 2008 election and emergence of two coalitions suggest that the hegemonic drive of *Bumiputra* nationalism, whether those pushing for *Ketuanan Melayu* or an Islamic state, has for the moment stalled, or been blunted. In losing five large and important states, an internal crisis and leadership struggle broke out immediately within UMNO. Whether the loss of momentum is only temporary is unclear, but it appears that a pyramid-shape structure of *Bumiputra* nationalism is unlikely to replace the power balance as depicted in a quadrilateral diagram at the moment. UMNO's weakened position and the emergence of a two-party system in the parliament has given the Malay rulers, and, to an extent, non-*Bumiputra*, a chance to return to a situation resembling the old quadrilateral model.

The rulers, as a separate power centre, demonstrated a more assertive position immediately after the elections when the rulers' choice for *menteri besar* in Perlis and Terengganu prevailed over that of the UMNO leader, Abdullah Badawi. And in the forming of the state governments in Perak and Selangor, the rulers ensured that both tradition and the provision of the Constitution were observed. That role has assumed greater political significance in early February 2009 when the sultan of Perak acceded to the BN's claim to the state, following the defection of three Pakatan assembly representatives. Their constitutional power has assumed significance and, as a result, it is to the rulers that the major political groups are beginning to turn to for support.

The non-*Bumiputra* leg, where the Chinese is the largest component group, is at a critical point after the elections. With the hegemonic drive of *Bumiputra* nationalism stalled and the Malay political constituency divided, non-*Bumiputra* have the space to reassess the kind of role and response they could take. Non-*Bumiputra* support had been critical in the past when there is a split within *Bumiputra* nationalism or UMNO. It was non-Malay support of UMNO in 1990 and 1999 that helped stave off Keadilan and the PAS's challenge. This time it was the sizeable non-Malay support that enabled the emergence of an alternative coalition, Pakatan Rakyat, consisting of non-*Bumiputra*, and Islam, and dissident *Bumiputra* nationalism proponents in the 2008 election.

Whether a non-*Bumiputra* leg can sustain itself as a viable power centre, either as part of the BN or Pakatan, in a four-legged model, depends on political developments presently taking place. Changes within the Chinese community will determine the future direction Chinese support would take. The type of divisions within Chinese society that operated in the past, such as between the China-oriented and local-oriented, and Chinese-educated and English-educated Chinese have, as Wang anticipated, become less clear and may not be relevant. Today most Malaysian Chinese are local-born. More than 60 per cent of the population are below the age of twenty-four. An entire generation born after Independence has gone through the national education system that is Malaysia-oriented and they are fluent in Malay as well as Chinese and, to an extent, English.[25] Those forty-five years of age and below would only have heard or read of the UMNO's struggle against the Malayan Union, Communist Emergency, the forging of UMNO-MCA-MIC ties to negotiate independence, and the early years of economic development.

The young would have less sentimental attachment or identification with those events, compared with the generation that participated in the political struggles. The present generation views UMNO and the MCA less for the historic role these parties played, and more on their present policies and performance. Young Chinese view the MCA, not for its part in the Independence movement alongside UMNO, but as a party that is a lesser partner in the ruling coalition. Thus these new and younger voters may not be natural supporters of the BN.

The MCA, still considered a major element within the non-*Bumiputra* centre of power, has weakened in relation to UMNO and in its standing within the community following poor electoral performances recently. This decline in its political ranking and effectiveness has led to a shortening of the non-*Bumiputra* leg in the quadrilateral model. In the past many Chinese saw the need for an expressly Chinese party to defend their core community concern. Indeed in 1953 when there was the choice before the MCA of either allying itself with the multiracial Independence of Malaya Party, or with UMNO, leaders such as H.S. Lee opted for UMNO because they feared that Chinese issues such as citizenship and education, might not get attention in a largely multiracial party.[26] And in 1969, after the MCA performed badly in the elections, there was a Chinese unity movement to revitalize the party, and this attracted a large number of young Chinese professionals such as Lim Keng Yaik, Alex Lee, and Paul Leong.[27] In the immediate aftermath of the 2008 election, there was no such campaign for reforms in the MCA or for Chinese unity. Rather the call was by older members to save the party.

Fewer of the younger Chinese are seeing the MCA as the party that could pursue the interests of the community effectively. The election results show that while Chinese education and language remain very important, the Chinese community has moved to broader concerns, such as equal economic and education opportunities, religious freedom, and an independent judiciary. A narrowly Chinese approach has little long-term prospects. Already younger leaders in the MCA see the need for a more assertive MCA to articulate issues within a multiracial framework, if the party is to regain Chinese support and have continuing political relevance. But before that, the MCA has to move out of what some of its own leaders criticize as a welfare-oriented framework, concerned with issues it started with back in the 1940s, such as New Village and Chinese education programmes.

Others suggest that the MCA should take the lead in becoming a multiracial party and that the BN be restructured eventually into a single, non-racial party. Critics see ethnic-based parties as hardening communal sentiments that are not helping national integration. Such a proposal, however, is not getting much support and runs against the mood within the party that wants the MCA to be more assertive on Chinese issues. Party leaders believe that the recent election losses were due to the BN Chinese-based parties being seen by the electorate as unable to stand up to the recent displays of political arrogance by sections of UMNO. Furthermore, becoming a multiracial party is unlikely to gain the MCA non-Chinese support or UMNO's approval.

It is even more challenging for Gerakan, the other major non-Malay party in the BN, which faces the prospect of becoming irrelevant. Some of its leaders see two options for the party. One is to rediscover its original ideals of being multiracial. It could become a voice of conscience or critic within the BN.[28] Or it could leave the BN altogether. Neither option offers much prospects. If it remains in the BN it is likely to become another People's Progressive Party, surviving to split Chinese representation within the BN, or be another Pekemas if it leaves to be an opposition group and having to compete with the DAP or PKR. Its chances of regaining Penang and the chief ministership in either capacity are bleak, unless the Pakatan performs disastrously or the coalition there breaks up. Even then Gerakan is unlikely to get back the chief ministership since UMNO has several senior assemblymen waiting to claim the post.[29]

In general, the leaders of the two parties are convinced that their future is with the BN coalition. The MCA still wields some influence within the community and it has institutions that were set up in the past that could sustain its continuing political programme. The party has a long history as well as close links with many local leaders and these could help in a future electoral recovery. The MCA and Gerakan are also keen to remain in the BN to ensure, as they contend, that there is Chinese representation in the government to speak up on non-Malay concerns. There must also be a government whose composition reflects the country's ethnic diversity to ensure stability and, in particular, the confidence of foreign investors in the country. Above all, at a time when UMNO itself suffered electoral losses and is undergoing a leadership struggle, to leave the BN now would be seen as abandoning a partner and, therefore, politically unwise.

The appeal by MCA for support to ensure Chinese representation in government resonates with many Chinese. A Chinese presence in the coalition, they believe, would help moderate ethnic politics and government policies. And there have been some Chinese who are prepared to rally behind the government such as during the Asian Financial Crisis.[30] The MCA-Gerakan team also faces a DAP which, in the past, had difficulties fielding a full team of strong candidates. Studies have shown that there remains significant non-Malay support for the BN.[31] In the absence of surveys rigorously and regularly conducted, it is possible to only suggest the reasons for there being some 30 per cent of committed MCA supporters, and Chinese swing votes going to Chinese-based parties in the BN in particular elections. In many communities, especially in rural and semi-rural areas, support for the MCA is built through local networks of personal and business relationships. Many Chinese also vote for the MCA because they regard the BN as standing for political stability. This was clearly the case in the 1999 election when, in the midst of the Reformasi movement, the Chinese in Malaysia were reminded of the violence in Indonesia the year before.[32]

Pakatan Rakyat and its performance in the coming years will determine the fourth leg, that is the non-*Bumiputra*. So far Pakatan has created new political excitement and a sense of empowerment within the non-Malay constituency. Many Chinese now feel that their votes can contribute to a more competitive political system and have dispelled the long-held fear and caution that voting for the opposition leads to less Chinese representation in the government and political instability. A more competitive system and a less dominant UMNO would allow the non-*Bumiputra* a voice that is commensurate with their size and role. Pakatan has attracted young Chinese to join its ranks. For those still concerned with Chinese issues, there is the DAP which is now, with political power in the states and a stronger position at the federal level, an attractive alternative. For those seeking a non-communal approach, there is Parti Keadilan Rakyat. Some have noticed a degree of parity status within the Pakatan Rakyat, and reasoned that this in itself might serve as pressure on the BN to accord similar standing to its partners if UMNO wants to fend off Pakatan Rakyat's challenge.

One may need to consider new groups when discussing the quadrilateral model, especially in the changing non-*Bumiputra* leg. These new groups include civil society organizations that are of growing influence. There are also the political parties of Sabah and Sarawak. Within the growing number of civil society groups are many young and capable Chinese fired with idealism. Drawn to voluntary, non-government organizations and social movements, these young Chinese share with Malaysians of other communities a concern for religious freedom, human rights, alleviating social conditions, corruption, an independent judiciary, and raising awareness on global concerns, such as the environment, nuclear non-proliferation, and human rights.[33]

While many of these non-governmental organizations represent ethnic and religious interests, others have transcended narrow ethnic preoccupations, and in expressing a more Malaysian approach, help promote integration. Through these multiracial civil society organizations, young Chinese are beginning to play an influential political role in encouraging non-racial politics. Although many of the civil society groups are single-issue movements, they often have wide impact. The role of civil society groups in politics is not new and organizations such as Suqiu were already active in the 1999 election. More recently, in November 2007, the Hindu Rights Action Force (Hindraf) was able to mobilize thousands into the streets. The boldness of the Hindraf was an important factor in the elections.

There are also religious groups such as Christians who are increasingly involved. Mostly middle-class and conservative, they tended in the past to support the establishment. However in recent years, because of allegations of corruption and detention without trial under the ISA, Christian groups are conscientizing their members into active political participation or, at least, to exercise their vote on election day. Compared with other non-Muslim religious groups, Christians are better organized through churches and parachurch institutions.

There has been a religious resurgence among the Chinese, particularly, among the Buddhists and Christians. Some 10 per cent of the Malaysian Chinese or 539,600 are Christians. Although they form only slightly more than 25 per cent of the Christian population, the Chinese provide leadership of Christian national organizations such as the Christian Federation of Malaysia and its three component member organizations: the National Evangelical Christian Fellowship, the Council of Churches of Malaysia, and the Catholics. Smaller parachurch organizations are also headed by Chinese.

This active participation of a growing number of young Chinese in civil society groups and Chinese-based organizations, including Christian groups, reflect a growing spirit of voluntarism among the Chinese that needs further studies. It indicates that many politically concerned Chinese are disenchanted with political parties as an effective instrument for change. They see the Chinese-based parties, particularly in the ruling coalition, as weak and subordinate to UMNO. Nevertheless, many of those active in the NGOs have also gravitated towards party involvement. Elizabeth Wong of SUARAM and P. Ramasamy, a former Universiti Kebangsaan Malaysia professor, who was active in the campaign against locating an incinerator in Broga, Selangor, joined the PKR and DAP respectively.

Finally the Chinese in Sabah and Sarawak could increasingly be important in the non-*Bumiputra* power centre. The Chinese there are largely involved with indigenous parties in the two states which are multiracial. These include the Sarawak United Peoples Party, the Sabah Progressive Party, and the Liberal Democratic Party. The Chinese in these parties have articulated state rights and interests. They work increasingly with non-Muslim *Bumiputra* within their parties and with other predominantly non-Muslim *Bumiputra* parties in the two states. The Chinese there therefore offer a slightly different approach to multiracial politics and could be instructive to those in Peninsular politics.[34]

The multiracial politics in Sabah and Sarawak raise questions about where to place non-Muslim *Bumiputra* in the quadrilateral model of the Malaysian state. As *Bumiputra* nationalism takes on an increasingly Islamic character, non-Muslim *Bumiputra* may begin to distinguish themselves and seek a stronger and separate voice. In opposing *Ketuanan Melayu* and an Islamic state, non-Muslim *Bumiputra* find political affinity with the non-*Bumiputra*. They may seek to work with non-*Bumiputra* and more liberal Malay nationalism. The PBS, under Pairin Kitingan, tried to do that in 1990 when it allied with Semangat 46 and the DAP. There were also efforts to bring the PBS and Gerakan together. Increasingly, non-Muslim *Bumiputra* share with non-*Bumiputra* a concern for a state that is religiously neutral. With fifty-four out of 222 parliamentary seats, Sabah and Sarawak politics would figure significantly in the quadrilateral state.

Recent developments suggest that a quadrilateral pattern deserves a re-look to understand politics in Malaysia. The emergence of two coalitions could help sustain the fourth leg of non-*Bumiputra* or plural society. It could push political parties to take a less ethnic approach and accommodate the expectations and aspirations of those concerned with justice, religious freedom, transparency of government, environmental concern, and an independent judiciary, so as to maintain a quadrilateral balance of power. Finally, the emerging two-party system could encourage a greater degree of mutual respect, debate, and accountability. Leaders of the opposition Pakatan Rakyat, such as Lim Guan Eng, Anwar Ibrahim, and PAS leaders presently engage one another with respect and on an equal basis similar to the Alliance Party in the 1952–53 period. Would this nudge the BN to move towards recovering the old parity which it once embraced? However the risk is also that recent developments, particularly the emergence of a two-coalition arrangement, could push *Bumiputra* nationalism into a renewed hegemonic drive to retain continued relevance and power, and there are signs of a hard-line Malay backlash.

Appendix 1
Parliamentary Elections, 1959–2008

Year	1959	1964	1969	1974	1978	1982	1986	1990	1995	1999	2004	2008
Alliance	74	89	74^a									
BN^b				135	130	132	148	127	162	148	199	140
MCA	19	27	13	19	17	24	17	18	30	29	31	15
Gerakan^d			8	5	4	5	5	5	7	6	10	2
PAS^c	13	9	12		5	5	1	7	7	27	6	23
Keadilan										5	1	31
DAP			13	9	16	9	24	20	9	10	12	28
Socialist Front	8	2										
PPP	4	2	4									
Parti Negara	1											
Malayan Party	1											
UDP		1			1							
PAP		1										
USNO			13									
SCA			3									
SNAP			9	9								
SUPP			5									
Pesaka			2									
Semangat 46								8	6			
Pekemas				1								
PBS^e								14	8	3		
Independents	3		1	2	2	8	4	4			1	
Total	104	104	144	154	154	154	177	180	192	193	219	222

Notes:

a – Figure includes seven seats won by the Sarawak Alliance

b – The BN replaced Alliance as an enlarged coalition

c – The PAS was in the BN in the 1974 general election

d – Gerakan joined the BN in the 1974 general election

e – PBS was in the BN in the 1986, 2004, and 2008 general elections

Sources: Compiled from *The Star* and *New Straits Times*

Appendix 2
Number and Percentage of Chinese Members of Parliament in Malaysia, 1959–2008

Year	1959	1964	1969	1974	1978	1982	1986	1990	1995	1999	2004	2008
Perlis	0	0	0	0	0	0	0	0	0	0	0	0
Kedah	2	2	2	2	2	2	2	2	2	2	2	1
Kelantan	0	0	0	0	0	0	0	0	0	0	0	0
Terengganu	0	0	0	0	0	0	0	0	0	0	0	0
Penang	4	4	3	5	4	5	5	4	5	7	7	6
Perak	8	8	9	9	8	9	9	10	10	10	9	9
Pahang	1	1	1	1	2	2	3	3	3	3	3	2
Selangor	5	6	7	5	4	4	4	4	6	6	8	6
Kuala Lumpur	—	—	—	3	3	4	5	5	7	7	8	7
Putrajaya	—	—	—	—	—	—	—	—	—	—	0	0
Negeri Sembilan	2	2	1	2	2	2	2	2	2	2	2	1
Malacca	2	2	2	2	2	2	2	2	2	2	2	2
Johor	5	5	5	5	5	4	5	5	6	6	9	9
Labuan	—	—	—	—	—	—	0	0	0	0	0	0
Sabah	—	—	3	3	3	3	3	3	4	4	4	4
Sarawak	—	—	6	6	6	6	6	7	8	7	7	7
Total number of Chinese MPs	29	30	39	43	41	43	46	47	55	56	61	54
Parliament Seats	104	104	104	144	154	154	177	180	192	193	219	222
Percentage	27.9	28.8	37.5	29.9	26.6	27.9	26.0	26.1	28.6	29.0	27.9	24.3

Sources: Compiled from *The Star* and *New Straits Times*

Notes

1   Latin, meaning, where are you going?

2   The 2008 Malaysian election results pull-out, *New Straits Times*, 9 March 2008.

3   Voon Phin Keong, "When 'petty' men ruled: The Malaysian general election of 2008", *Centre for Malaysian Studies Bulletin*, no. 3 (2008): 1–7.

4   Ong Kian Ming, "Making sense of the political tsunami", *Malaysiakini*, 11 March 2008; William Case, "Testing Malaysia's pseudo-democracy", in *The State of Malaysia: Ethnicity, Equity and Reform*, edited by Edmund Terence Gomez (London: RoutledgeCurzon), pp. 29–48.

5   Only 15 per cent of the population was using the Internet in the year 2000, but this increased to 59.0 per cent in 2008. From Internet World Statistics: "Malaysia Internet Usage Stats and Marketing Report", <http://www. interenetworldstats,com/asia/my.htm>; Oon Yeoh, "New media more than blogs", *The Star*, 18 September 2008.

6   Meredith Weiss, "The 1999 Malaysian General Elections", *Asian Survey* 40, no. 3 (2000): 413–35.

7   Wang Gungwu, "Reflections on Malaysian Elites", in *Only Connect: Sino-Malay Encounters* (Singapore: Eastern Universities Press, 2003), pp. 87–110.

8   Wang Gungwu, "Race in Malaysia: A Fine Balance", *Straits Times*, 26 November 2008.

9   Edmund Terence Gomez, *Politics in Malaysia and the Malay Dimension* (Abingdon, Oxon, England; New York: Routledge, 2007).

10 Tey Nai Peng, "Demographic Trends and Human Capital: The Case of Malaysian Chinese", in *Malaysian Chinese and Nation-building: Before Merdeka and Fifty Years After*, vol. 1, edited by Voon Phin Keong (Kuala Lumpur: Centre for Malaysian Chinese Studies, 2007), pp. 307–38.

11 Lim Hong Hai, "A Case for Fairer Representation", *The Sun*, 5 June 2008.

12 Ting Chew Peh, *Kris MCA: Ujian Prinsip Demokrasi* (Kuala Lumpur: Penerbit Abadi, 1984); Ho Kin Chai, *Malaysian Chinese Association: Leadership under Siege* (Kuala Lumpur: Ho Kin Chai, 1984); Ong Kian Ming, "Chinese-in-a-box? The Future of Chinese Parties in Peninsular Malaysia", in *Reflections: The Mahathir Years*, edited by Bridget Welsh (Washington: Southeast Asia Studies Program, John Hopkins University, 2004), pp. 189–98.

13 Clive Kessler, "Islam, the State and Desecularization in Malaysia: The Islamist Trajectory during the Badawi Years", in *Sharing the Nation: Faith, Difference, Power and the State 50 Years after Merdeka*, edited by Norani Othman et al. (Petaling Jaya: Strategic Information and Research Development Centre, 2008), pp. 59–80.

14 Aneel David Kannabhiran, "Fifty Years of Islamisation", *Catholic Asian News*, 7 August 2007.

[15]   "Final Report on the State of Religious Liberty in Malaysia for the Year 2007",
       presented by the Religious Liberty Commission, National Evangelical Christian
       Fellowship, Malaysia.

[16]   Rita Sim and Soong Fui K., "Three Pillars of the Chinese Community", *New
       Straits Times*, 9 September 2007.

[17]   Lee Kam Hing, "Mahathir's Administration and the Chinese", in *Reflections: The
       Mahathir Years*, edited by Bridget Welsh (Washington: Southeast Asia Studies
       Program, Johns Hopkins University, 2004).

[18]   Lee Hock Guan, "Affirmative Action in Malaysia", in *Southeast Asian Affairs
       2005*, edited by Chin Kin Wah and Daljit Singh (Singapore: Institute of
       Southeast Asian Studies, 2005); "Malaysia and the Knowledge Economy:
       Building a World Class Higher Education System", EPU-World Bank Report,
       2007.

[19]   B.A. Hamzah, "My Say: Are We Miles behind the World's Best", *The Edge*,
       Kuala Lumpur, 16 June 2008.

[20]   Beh Loo See, "Malaysian Chinese Capitalism: Mapping the Bargain of a
       Developmental State", in *Malaysian Chinese and Nation-building: Before Merdeka
       and Fifty Years After*, vol. 1, edited by Voon Phin Keong (Kuala Lumpur: Centre
       for Malaysian Chinese Studies, 2007), pp. 223–67; Chin Yee Whah, "Chinese
       Economic Activities in the Emerging Malaysian Nation-state: Changing with the
       Times", in *Malaysian Chinese and Nation-building: Before Merdeka and Fifty Years
       After*, vol. 1, edited by Voon Phin Keong (Kuala Lumpur: Centre for Malaysian
       Chinese Studies, 2007), pp. 269–306.

[21]   Bank Negara Malaysia, Annual Report 2006 (Kuala Lumpur: Bank Negara,
       2006); *Economic Report 2004/2005* (Kuala Lumpur: Ministry of Finance,
       2004).

[22]   Lee Poh Ping and Tham Siew Yean, "Malaysia Ten Years after the Asian Financial
       Crisis", *Asian Survey* 47, no. 6 (November–December 2007): 915–29.

[23]   Lee Poh Ping and Lee Kam Hing, "China's Economic Rise and Its Impact
       on Malaysian Chinese Business", in *Southeast Asia's Chinese Businesses in an
       Era of Globalisation: Coping with the Rise of China*, edited by Leo Suryadinata
       (Singapore: Institute of Southeast Asian Studies, 2006).

[24]   The 2008 election results pull-out, *The Star*, 9 March 2008.

[25]   Wang Gungwu, "Traditional Leadership in a New Nation: The Chinese in
       Malaya and Singapore", in *Community and Nations: Essays on Southeast Asia
       and the Chinese* (Singapore: Heinemann Educational Books (Asia) Ltd., 1981).
       Originally published in *Leadership and Authority: A Symposium*, edited by G.
       Wijeyewardene (Singapore: University Malaya Press, 1968); Heng Pek Koon,
       Chinese Politics in Malaysia (Singapore: Oxford University Press, 1988).

[26]   Letters from H.S. Lee to Tan Cheng Lock, 3 March 1952; and H.S. Lee
       to Tengku Abdul Rahman, 7 March 1952, both letters in the unpublished
       "Collection of H.S. Lee Private Papers", Kuala Lumpur.

27 Loh Kok Wah, *The Politics of Chinese Unity in Malaysia: Reform and Conflict in the Malaysian Chinese Association, 1971–1973* (Singapore: Maruzen Asia, 1982).

28 Parti Gerakan Rakyat Malaysia (PGRM), *A Selection of Speeches (1981–1992) by Dr Lim Keng Yaik, President, Parti Gerakan Rakyat Malaysia* (Kuala Lumpur: PGRM, 1984).

29 Chok Suat Ling, "It's Time for Gerakan to Go Back to its Roots", *New Straits Times*, 3 September 2008.

30 Lee Kam Hing, "Differing Perspectives on Integration and Nation-Building in Malaysia", in *Ethnic Relations and Nation-building in Southeast Asia*, edited by Leo Suryadinata (Singapore: Institute of Southeast Asian Studies, 2004), pp. 82–108.

31 James Chin, "The 1995 Malaysian General Elections: Mahathir's Last Triumph?" *Asian Survey* 36, no. 4 (April 1996): 392–409; Khoo Boo Teik, "The Malaysian General Elections of 29 November 1999", *Australian Journal of Political Science* 35 (July 2000): 305–11; Meredith L. Weiss, "The 1999 Malaysian General Elections", *Asian Survey* 40, no. 3 (May 2000): 413–35.

32 Khoo Boo Teik, *Beyond Mahathir: Malaysian Politics and its Discontents* (London, New York: Zed Books Ltd., 2003), pp. 134–66.

33 "Youth Vote: BN Losing Battle to Opposition", *Straits Times*, 20 January 2009.

34 Chin Ung-Ho, *Chinese Politics in Sarawak: A Study of the Sarawak United People's Party* (Kuala Lumpur: Oxford University Press, 1997).

References

"2008 election results pull-out". *The Star*, 9 March 2008.

"2008 Malaysian election results pull-out". *New Straits Times*, 9 March 2008.

Bank Negara Malaysia. *Annual Report 2006*. Kuala Lumpur: Bank Negara, 2006.

Beh Loo See. "Malaysian Chinese Capitalism: Mapping the Bargain of a Developmental State". In *Malaysian Chinese and Nation-building: Before Merdeka and Fifty Years After*, vol. 1, edited by Voon Phin Keong. Kuala Lumpur: Centre for Malaysian Chinese Studies, 2007.

Case, William. "Testing Malaysia's Pseudo-democracy". In *The State of Malaysia: Ethnicity, Equity and Reform*, edited by Edmund Terence Gomez. London: RoutledgeCurzon, 2004.

Chin James. "The 1995 Malaysian General Elections: Mahathir's Last Triumph?" *Asian Survey* 36, no. 4 (April 1996): 392–409.

Chin Ung-Ho. *Chinese Politics in Sarawak: A Study of the Sarawak United People's Party*. Kuala Lumpur: Oxford University Press, 1997.

Chin Yee Whah. "Chinese Economic Activities in the Emerging Malaysian Nation-state: Changing with the Times". In *Malaysian Chinese and Nation-building: Before Merdeka and Fifty Years After*, vol. 1, edited by Voon Phin Keong. Kuala Lumpur: Centre for Malaysian Chinese Studies, 2007.

Chok Suat Ling. "It's Time for Gerakan to Go Back to its Roots". *New Straits Times*, 3 September 2008.

EPU-World Bank. "Malaysia and the Knowledge Economy: Building a World Class Higher Education System". EPU-World Bank Report, 2007.

Gomez, Edmund Terence. *Politics in Malaysia and the Malay Dimension*. Abingdon, Oxon, England, New York: Routledge, 2007.

Hamzah, B.A. "My Say: Are We Miles Behind the World's Best". *The Edge*. Kuala Lumpur, 16 June 2008.

Heng Pek Koon. *Chinese Politics in Malaysia*. Singapore: Oxford University Press, 1988.

Ho Kin Chai. *Malaysian Chinese Association: Leadership under Siege*. Kuala Lumpur: Ho Kin Chai, 1984. <http://www.interenetworldstats,com/asia/my.htm>.

Kannabhiran, Aneel David. "Fifty Years of Islamisation". *Catholic Asian News*, 7 August 2007.

Kessler, Clive. "Islam, the State and Desecularization in Malaysia: The Islamist Trajectory during the Badawi Years". In *Sharing the Nation: Faith, Difference, Power and the State 50 Years after Merdeka*, by Norani Othman et al. Petaling Jaya: Strategic Information and Research Development Centre, 2008.

Khoo Boo Teik. "The Malaysian General Elections of 29 November 1999". *Australian Journal of Political Science* 35 (July 2000): 305–11.

————. *Beyond Mahathir: Malaysian Politics and Its Discontents*. London, New York: Zed Books Ltd., 2003.

Lee H.S. Letters to Tan Cheng Lock, 3 March 1952; and Tengku Abdul Rahman, 7 March 1952. Both letters in the unpublished "Collection of H.S. Lee Private Papers", Kuala Lumpur.

Lee Hock Guan. "Affirmative Action in Malaysia". In *Southeast Asian Affairs 2005*, edited by Chin Kin Wah and Daljit Singh. Singapore: Institute of Southeast Asian Studies, 2005.

Lee Kam Hing. "Differing Perspectives on Integration and Nation-Building in Malaysia". In *Ethnic Relations and Nation-building in Southeast Asia*, edited by Leo Suryadinata. Singapore: Institute of Southeast Asian Studies, 2004.

————. "Mahathir's Administration and the Chinese". In *Reflections: The Mahathir Years*, edited by Bridget Welsh. Washington: Southeast Asia Studies Program, Johns Hopkins University, 2004.

Lee Poh Ping and Lee Kam Hing. "China's Economic Rise and Its Impact on Malaysian Chinese Business". In *Southeast Asia's Chinese Businesses in an Era of Globalisation: Coping with the Rise of China*, edited by Leo Suryadinata. Singapore: Institute of Southeast Asian Studies, 2006.

Lee Poh Ping and Tham Siew Yean. "Malaysia Ten Years after the Asian Financial Crisis". *Asian Survey* 47, no. 6 (November–December 2007): 915–29.

Lim Hong Hai. "A Case for Fairer Representation". *The Sun*, 5 June 2008.

Loh Kok Wah. "The Politics of Chinese Unity in Malaysia: Reform and Conflict in the Malaysian Chinese Association, 1971–1973". Singapore: Maruzen Asia, 1982.

Ministry of Finance. Economic Report 2004/2005. Kuala Lumpur: Ministry of Finance, 2004.

Ong Kian Ming. "Chinese-in-a-box? The Future of Chinese Parties in Peninsular Malaysia". In Reflections: The Mahathir Years, edited by Bridget Welsh. Washington: Southeast Asia Studies Program, Johns Hopkins University, 2004.

————. "Making Sense of the Political Tsunami". Malaysiakini, 11 March 2008.

Oon, Yeoh. "New Media More than Blogs". The Star, 18 September 2008.

Parti Gerakan Rakyat Malaysia (PGRM). A Selection of Speeches (1981–1992) by Dr Lim Keng Yaik, president, Parti Gerakan Rakyat Malaysi. Kuala Lumpur: PGRM, 1984.

Religious Liberty Commission. "Final Report on the State of Religious Liberty in Malaysia for the Year 2007". National Evangelical Christian Fellowship, Malaysia, 2008.

Sim, Rita and Soong Fui K. "Three Pillars of the Chinese Community". New Straits Times, 9 September 2007.

Tey Nai Peng. "Demographic Trends and Human Capital: The Case of Malaysian Chinese". In Malaysian Chinese and Nation-building: Before Merdeka and Fifty Years After, vol. 1, edited by Voon Phin Keong. Kuala Lumpur: Centre for Malaysian Chinese Studies, 2007.

Ting Chew Peh. Kris MCA: Ujian Prinsip Demokrasi. Kuala Lumpur: Penerbit Abadi, 1984.

Voon Phin Keong. "When 'Petty' Men Ruled: The Malaysian General Election of 2008". Centre for Malaysian Studies Bulletin, no. 3 (2008): 1–7.

Wang Gungwu. "Traditional Leadership in a New Nation: The Chinese in Malaya and Singapore". In Community and Nations: Essays on Southeast Asia and the Chinese. Singapore: Heinemann Educational Books (Asia) Ltd., 1981. Originally published in Leadership and Authority: A Symposium, edited by G. Wijeyewardene. Singapore: University Malaya Press, 1968.

————. "Reflections on Malaysian Elites". In Only Connect: Sino-Malay Encounters, edited by Wang Gungwu. Singapore: Eastern Universities Press, 2003.

————. "Race in Malaysia: A Fine Balance". Straits Times, 26 November 2008.

Weiss, Meredith. "The 1999 Malaysian General Elections: Issues, Insults, and Irregularities". Asian Survey 40, no. 3 (2000): 413–35.

"Youth Vote: BN Losing Battle to Opposition". Straits Times, 20 January 2009.

4

AT A CROSSROADS: MALAYSIA'S COALITION POLITICS AND CHINESE-BASED POLITICAL PARTIES

Ho Khai Leong

The 8 March 2008 Malaysian general election stunned the incumbent Barisan Nasional (BN) coalition for it was bereft of the two-third parliamentary majority the coalition traditionally has held since the country obtained political independence in 1957. The electoral outcome was considered a tremendous shock to the BN and Prime Minister Abdullah Badawi. Not only did the BN see its share of the popular vote fall to 50.6 per cent, it now also lacked the necessary two-third majority to amend the Malaysian Constitution in Parliament. Indeed, compared with the 2004 general election when the newly appointed Prime Minister Badawi led the BN to its biggest electoral win, the results of the 2008 were shocking.

Do the results of the 2008 general election signify the transformation, albeit transitional, of Malaysia into a two-coalition party system — hence a more "democratic" — wherein the power of the people is truly exercised? Or do the election results simply indicate that things are out of balance? In the Malay dominated politics of Malaysia, what could have caused the sudden shift away from the BN to the opposition, which is composed of the ethnically Chinese-dominated DAP, the multi-ethnic Parti Keadilan Rakyat (PKR), and the religiously inspired PAS? What are the implications for the Malaysian Chinese, who voted overwhelmingly for the opposition? Can the Chinese-based parties, the MCA and the Gerakan, survive into the future?

ELECTION OUTCOME:
2004 VS. 2008

The 2008 election results were all the more startling when compared with the overwhelming and decisively strong BN electoral victory in 2004. A comparison of the breakdown of parliamentary and state seats in 2008 and 2004 (see Table 4.1) will clearly show that all the parties in the BN coalition, even UMNO, lost a sizeable number of parliamentary and state seats in the 2008 *vis-à-vis* their overwhelming electoral victory in 2004.

Table 4.1
Malaysian General Election 2008 and 2004 Results (Seats Won)

Political Parties				Parliament		State	
	2008	2004		2008	2004	2008	2004
BN			GERAKAN	2	10	3	30
Parliament	140	198					
State	307	453					
			LDP	1	—	2	3
			MCA	15	31	32	76
			MIC	3	9	7	19
			PBB	14	11	—	—
			PBDS	—	6	—	—
			PBRS	1	1	1	1
			PBS	3	4	12	13
			PRS	6	—	—	—
			SAPP	3	2	5	4
			SPDP	4	4	—	—
			SUPP	6	6	—	—
			UMNO	79	109	239	302
			UPKO	3	4	6	5
Independent			IND	—	1	2	11
Parliament	0	1					
State	2	1					
Opposition			DAP	28	12	73	15
Parliament	82	20					
State	196	51					
			PAS	23	7	83	36
			PKR	31	1	40	—

Sources: The Star Online, Malaysia General Elections 2008 outcome.[1] *The Star* Online, Malaysia General Elections 2004 outcome.[2]

Although analysts and the Internet political pundits have postulated that the BN would return to power, they were also unanimous in their predictions that the BN votes for the 2008 election would be severely reduced owing to its alienation of the Chinese and Indian voters.[3] This prediction is largely correct as demonstrated by comparing the 2004 and 2008 election results.

As the 2004 and 2008 election results show, the MCA, Gerakan and the MIC lost over half their seats at both the state and parliamentary levels. The electoral setback was so dramatic that an electoral post-mortem even revealed that MIC president Samy Vellu and Gerakan acting president Koh Tsu Koon were heavily defeated in the constituencies they contested.[4] It has been widely pointed out that most of the states in which the BN lost were traditional BN strongholds where the BN had taken pains to develop its support over the years.

HOW THE MCA, GERAKAN, THE DAP AND PKR FARED

Let us look at the performance of the MCA, GERAKAN, the DAP, and PKR in the 2008 election in greater detail.

The Malaysian Chinese Association (MCA)

The MCA has traditionally had a pro-Chinese agenda in politics and entered the BN coalition as a means to furthering that agenda for the benefit of the minority Chinese in Malaysia. However, owing to the perception that the MCA is not as corruption-free and not serving Chinese interests as it should, it lost half its parliamentary seats in the 2008 election, winning a paltry fifteen seats compared with the thirty-one it had secured in the 2004 election.

GERAKAN

Gerakan suffered a tremendous setback with its performance in this election as it was so trounced that the party retained only two seats, compared with the ten seats it had before the election. This, in turn, resulted in Gerakan losing the only cabinet post it held in the post-election cabinet shuffle. The party that had prided itself on its multi-ethnic appeal demonstrated that it was, for the first time since 1969, pretty much unable to retain its seats at the state or federal level.

The DAP

The DAP's landslide victory in Penang was an unexpected one. It came as a surprise to most observers when the DAP swept over two-thirds of the votes in Penang. In contrast, the BN only won two of the thirteen parliamentary seats, and eleven of the forty state seats, making its showing in Penang its worst performance thus far.

The DAP performed astonishingly well by winning twenty-eight seats in Parliament, which was a substantial gain when compared with the twelve seats it had won in the 2004 election. Collectively, the DAP, with the PAS and PKR, won a total of eighty-two parliament seats, while the BN won 140. DAP chairman Lim Kit Siang was pleasantly surprised with the outcome, especially since the party managed to sweep all the seats it contested in Penang and could form the Penang state government with the PKR and PAS, and with DAP's Lim Guan Eng as the state's chief minister.

Lim Guan Eng, in his first task as chief minister, waived all the summonses issued to hawkers, and parking offences by the Penang Municipal Council and Seberang Prai Municipal Council before March 2008. He also promised to look into removing the NEP constraints from doing business in Penang and from the state government's policies. In a hitherto unprecedented move, Lim embarked on the technological trail by answering online and through press conferences any questions on his proposed review of the NEP. This gave him the reputation of a chief minister who practises transparency, does things openly and consultatively. Indeed, the Penang state became the first in Malaysia to implement the CAT (competency, accountability, transparency) policy. Moreover, Lim's proposal to amend the NEP so as to focus on assisting poor Malaysians, regardless of ethnic background, was also shared by Anwar Ibrahim and his People's Front Coalition.

KEADILAN

When compared with its dismal showing in the 2004 election, where it won only 9 per cent of the popular vote and obtained only one parliamentary seat, the PKR did remarkably well in the 2008 election, where the party won thirty-one parliament seats. Together with its allies in the Pakatan Rakyat or People's Alliance (a coalition between the DAP, PAS, and PKR), the opposition came away with eighty-two out of the 222 seats in parliament, making this the best opposition performance in Malaysia's electoral history. Since the PKR clinched the most number of parliament seats won by the opposition parties, it advanced Wan Azizah (Anwar Ibrahim's wife) to assume the leadership of the opposition in parliament. In August 2008, when Anwar Ibrahim won the Permatang Pauh by-election held when Wan Azizah resigned, he became the opposition leader.

Subsequently, the PKR, DAP, and PAS came together to form the state governments in Kelantan, Kedah, Penang, Perak, and Selangor. After some hard bargaining the three parties agreed on Lim Guan Eng assuming the chief ministership of Penang, while Khalid Ibrahim was selected to be the *menteri besar* of Perak, and three PAS representatives to head the state governments of Kelantan, Kedah, and Perak.[5]

ISSUES SURROUNDING THE 2008 GENERAL ELECTION

2007 was a bumpy year, not just for Malaysia, but for the rest of the world as well. With the rising prices of foodstuff and other basic necessities, soaring oil prices, the rising cost of living, as well as the continuance of the BN's NEP, 2007 ended on a note of uncertainty. It is likely that these uncertainties continued unabated into 2008, which subsequently triggered thoughts among Malaysian citizens that the BN government was not doing all it could to alleviate their livelihoods and lives in general. These thoughts were probably the most rampant among Malaysians who had not benefited from the NEP. Since the Malays were perceived to benefit from the government subsidies and privileges extended to them — albeit only a disproportionately small number of them were the main beneficiaries — in view of the economic slowdown affecting all Malaysians, it caused an outcry amongst the non-Malays. The Indians and Chinese complained that they have become marginalized as they faced restrictions on jobs, education, freedom of religion, rights as well as loss of dignity.[6]

Indeed, when the independent polling agency, Merdeka Centre, conducted a pre-election public sentiment survey, it discovered that most Malaysians were worried about the BN's ability to successfully manage the issues of inflation, shortage of goods, fuel subsidies, rising crime, majority government, mismanagement, and corruption successfully.

Furthermore, owing to accusations of vote malapportionment and gerrymandering in the 2004 election, whereby opposition parties such as the PKR only obtained one parliamentary seat despite winning 9 per cent of the popular vote, several NGOs and opposition political parties formed the Coalition for Clean and Fair Elections (BERSIH) to demand "free and fair elections" in Malaysia. From 2007 until the 2008 election, several policies and issues also came under intense criticism by a growing number of Malaysians such as: the NEP which favours the Malay majority, the use of the Internal Security Act (ISA) to detain without trial Malaysians who are alleged a security threat, the suspected illegal intervention in the judicial appointment process of Malaysian judges in 2002,[7] and the inquiry into that affair, and the eligibility of former Deputy Prime Minister Anwar Ibrahim to run for elections.

All the above developments invariably culminated in the opposition parties' doubt over the fairness of the Malaysian electoral process. They claimed that the BN manipulated the process through the gerrymandering of electoral districts, granting uneven media access to the opposition parties, relying on an outdated electoral system, election fraud, and vote buying.[8] There were also rampant accusations from former Prime Minister Mahathir Mohamad that Prime Minister Badawi's politics were influenced by his son-in-law, Khairy Jamaluddin.[9]

Thus the 2008 general election contest became a highly polarized one where the factors of race, economics, and social reform coincided with the day-to-day politics of administration. The unfavourable developments for the ruling coalition preceding the elections may account for the astounding performances of the PKR and DAP, both parties campaigning on the platform of forming a Malaysia that was free from its current pro-Malay/pro-*Bumiputra* slant for the betterment of social and economic justice, as well as the elimination of political corruption.

Economics

One of the overriding issues surrounding the elections seemed to be economics. In part, because of the global economic slowdown triggered by the subprime crisis in the United States, inflationary pressures impacted many developing countries, especially in terms of rising prices leading to a rising cost of living. Malaysia was thus badly hit by the global economic downturn in the period before and after the elections. This led to an air of economic uncertainty over several government projects and initiatives. As soon as the DAP heard that it had won Penang, it immediately raised doubt about the feasibility of several large-scale BN projects. Indeed, the DAP's decision to question and review the construction of the BN-proposed Penang Global City Centre, a 7.8 billion-ringgit (MYR) real estate development project, was popular with many Penangnites. This is because many in Penang felt that the BN government had not obtained the permission of the local state council and had simply gone ahead with the official launching of the project.

Similarly questioned were the BN's previous proposals to develop economic corridors in the north, east, and south of the peninsula. Given the then existing economic climate of the global economic slowdown and the shortage of liquidity, it was not certain that the BN government would have the means to pay for all these projects.

Politics, Corruption, and Fraud

The Malaysian Election Commission (EC) has frequently been labelled as subservient to the BN as it was alleged that it closed a blind eye to gerrymandering and vote fraud. The BN has also been accused of manipulating the state-controlled media and of misusing government resources for vote buying. Moreover, international observers have also made the claim that the electoral roll was suspect because it listed some 9,000 people aged over 100 years. In light of this claim, it was suspected that the electoral list might be "contaminated" as it were with dead voters, thus leading to the very real possibility of electoral fraud.[10] Malaysians for Free and Fair Elections (MAFREL), an NGO, has also unearthed the registration of people with identical names and born the same year — but holding different identity cards and living in different localities — to vote in various places throughout the country.

It also came to light that some voters who had opted to vote by post were issued with two ballot sheets. BERSIH activists claim that since each ballot was attached to a letter identifying the voter, along with the voting slip serial number, it would be easy to trace who voted for the opposition. In seats where the winning margins were small and postal votes made up a significant percentage of the total votes, electoral reform activists and some observers claimed that the opposition could have won those seats if not for the postal votes which probably favoured the BN as voters casting postal votes did not have the freedom to choose the candidate they wanted.[11] Neither was the balloting process free from controversy. BERSIH claimed that in the 2008 election, 72,058 unreturned ballot papers (of which 41,564 were for parliamentary seats and 30,494 for state assembly seats) were originally cast for the opposition or spoilt and thence discarded.[12] Not surprisingly, Human Rights Watch has labelled the Malaysian electoral process "grossly unfair" and has made repeated calls to the BN government to address the various allegations of fraud.

The Anwar Factor

Anwar Ibrahim, former deputy prime minister of Malaysia, was released from prison in early 2004 after serving his term for corruption (that is, abuse of power), and his sodomy conviction was overturned by the High Court on appeal. However, because of his corruption conviction he was banned from politics until April 2008, thus disqualifying him from contesting in the March 2008 general election. Anwar is generally acknowledged as having both the charismatic personality as well as political clout amongst the people to make a comeback in politics. Indeed, he is often said to have changed the political landscape with his *Reformasi* movement in 1998 in the lead-up to his incarceration on allegations of sodomy and corruption.

Although he was unable to contest in the 2008 general election, he must have derived some satisfaction from seeing the BN coalition losing its two-third majority in parliament. For the 2008 general election, Anwar propounded his reformist political platform which criticized the NEP for privileging the Malays, and argued for the equality of all races in Malaysia. This platform appeared to have the support of Malaysians from all walks of life.

In touching on the concerns of all Malaysians, such as the rising cost of living and rising fuel prices, Anwar managed to win over not just the Indian and Chinese voters, but also the Malay voters, especially those who had not benefited from the NEP. Anwar also pledged to defend and promote a free-market economy and foreign investment and to continue the development process to benefit the poor of all races. Hence, Anwar's reformist agenda and criticisms of the excesses of UMNO and the Abdullah Badawi administration managed to appeal to the masses and he could stage his successful political comeback.

BREAKDOWN AND ANALYSIS OF THE PERFORMANCES OF THE MCA, GERAKAN, THE DAP AND KEADILAN

Owing to the above reasons, the MCA and Gerakan, which were allied to UMNO, lost heavily in the polls. This was due to their inability to distance themselves from accusations of corruption and electoral fraud, as well as their failure to come up with a definitive platform which addressed the ordinary Malaysians' concerns amid the climate of economic uncertainty at the time. However, this does not mean that there were no internal factors within the parties affecting their respective electoral performances. Indeed, in the cases of the MCA and Gerakan, it appears that former supporters were put off by both the parties' internal scandals, as well as the external allegations of electoral fraud, corruption, and the seeming inability of the BN to do anything about the depressing economic situation.

The MCA

On top of being associated with UMNO, which was accused of electoral fraud and economic mismanagement, the MCA was also beleaguered by its own internal problems, especially a scandal involving the top brass within the party.

In 2008, before the election, DVDs of then MCA vice-president Dr Chua Soi Lek "having sex" with a woman was widely circulated in Johor. Although he claimed neither involvement in the filming nor production of the DVD, Chua's credibility and public image suffered following this. Subsequently, he admitted being the man in the DVD and resigned from all his posts, including as member of parliament for Labis, vice-president of the MCA, and health minister at a press conference.

The MCA's reputation also took a further beating when one of its woman leaders, Chew Mei Fun, cautioned Chinese voters against electing fewer MCA representatives in the BN, claiming that less MCA involvement in the BN would result in reduced rights for the Chinese in Malaysia, and would culminate in a racial riot on the scale of the 13 May 1969 riots. This comment not only did not go down well with the Chinese community, but, instead, saw them take offence with this brazen MCA attempt to "punish" the Chinese for not demonstrating more support for the party.

Furthermore, the MCA had only been overtly concerned with appealing to the Chinese voters and forwarding the interests of the Chinese Malaysians. Doing so put the MCA at a disadvantage because it ended up alienating potential voters from other walks of life. It appears that its pro-Chinese agenda has now come under fire, for it could be interpreted as a Chinese version of the NEP. Also, it has become a matter of debate as to how much the MCA is able to protect and promote Chinese interests if it remains as one of the non-Malay component parties of a Malay-dominated BN. Accordingly, after the party's poor performance in the 2008 general election, Ong Ka Ting stated that the MCA must strive to look into the interests of all Malaysians and not just Malaysian Chinese interests.

GERAKAN

In the case of Gerakan, it lost its stronghold of Penang, which it had held since 1969, due to a culmination of the aforementioned economic crisis, as well as its complacency. While some analysts have hypothesized that Gerakan's enduring appeal for the mostly Chinese Penangnites was the party's predominantly Chinese membership, it appears that the party did not do enough to promote the interests of the Penangnites, and it had seemingly become complacent, assuring that the Penangnites would re-elect it on the grounds that the party was mostly made up of Chinese members. For instance, despite the widespread public opposition to the Penang Global City Centre (PGCC), Gerakan allowed the BN to go ahead with the project, even going so far as to bypass consultation with local state council. It is understandable that Gerakan had to allow the BN to develop the PGCC due to the fact that the party is a member of the BN coalition. But going over the head of the local state council by not consulting it about the PGCC sparked an outcry on the Gerakan's high-handedness and highlighted the party's inability to do anything for the people *vis-à-vis* the federal government. Gerakan's inability to address and quell this public sentiment successfully eventually led to their poorest electoral showing in its history.

The use of blogs and various cyberspace and communication technologies, such as SMS, YouTube, and online political commentaries, put the opposition successfully at the fore while also painting Gerakan as part of a group of old fogeys unable to keep up with the changing times. Generally then, the Internet and new telecommunication technologies enabled Malaysians to have better access to the opposition parties and thus insights into their workings as well as their platforms. The situation was starkly different for the BN coalition parties, such as Gerakan, whose carefully crafted political promises were publicized by Malaysian newspapers, television, and radio. Since nearly all Malaysian newspapers, television, and radio stations are controlled and owned by the large parties in the BN coalition, the opposition was given scant coverage in the mainstream media so blogs and other telecommunication technologies were particularly important.

The use of these encouraged online debates as to the efficacy of the BN in dealing with the socio-economic climate in Malaysia then and what the opposition hoped to do about things. Nowhere was this more apparent than in the case of Jeff Ooi, a blogger-turned-politician. Ooi, who became a candidate for the DAP, criticized the BN and highlighted the importance of pluralism in Malaysian politics, as well as his perceptions of the inadequacies and complacency of Gerakan, of which he was a former member. He was so successful and eloquent online that on his first venture into politics under the DAP banner, he won the Jelutong parliamentary seat in Penang.

Furthermore, the BN and its coalition partners came under fire for being both out of date, and out of touch with the people, when they collectively lambasted these online political debates and attempted to sue bloggers for libel for posting online articles which they deemed to have painted the BN government unflatteringly. The BN's claim that political debates online had no place in Malaysia as politics in the country was purely a matter of politicians addressing local issues, not debating these issues, only further alienated the Malaysian public.

The defeat of the Gerakan acting president, Dr Koh Tsu Koon, also demonstrated that Gerakan was out of touch with the people. Believing that his eighteen years of experience as Penang chief minister would stand him in good stead, he gave up his state seat and contested the Batu Kawan parliamentary seat, in a move some analysts have claimed was part of a larger ambition for a post in the post-election BN cabinet. However, this speculation about his ambition did not paint him or the Gerakan in a positive light. Instead Penangnites came away with the impression that Gerakan was more interested in promoting its political ambitions at the national level, rather than seeing to the needs of its constituents at the state level. The upshot to this perception of Koh and Gerakan was the widespread withdrawal of electoral support for the party's acting president in favour of DAP newcomer P. Ramasamy, who thus won the Batu Kawan seat with a sizeable majority.

The DAP

With the astounding rout of Gerakan, the DAP came into its own in Penang, effectively sweeping the popular vote in the state by a large majority. One of the means through which it did so was its platform of a Malaysian Malaysia, that is, a Malaysia that is really for all Malaysians, regardless of ethnicity. This was a particularly pertinent issue to the Chinese and Indians in the country who feel marginalized by the NEP's dispensing of privileges to the Malays. It did not help the BN cause that when the deputy prime minister derided the DAP platform for being a threat to the *Bumiputra*/Malay privileges granted under Article 153 of the country's Constitution. Such a comment from UMNO only provided fuel for DAP supporters who debated online the issue of Malay privileges versus that of equal treatment for all Malaysians.

One of those who did so was Jeff Ooi. Indeed Ooi's blog has been dubbed "Malaysia's Most Influential Blog" by the popular Malaysian online news publication, *Malaysiakini*. As one of the pioneers in the Malaysian blogosphere, Ooi's insightful comments and analyses on the issues touching ordinary Malaysians' lives brought him to the attention of Internet political commentators, as well as the DAP. Sufficiently impressed by him and his blog's popularity, the DAP wooed him to join their party. Perhaps because he had become disillusioned with Gerakan and its failure to consult the Penang state council on several major socio-economic decisions, Ooi decided to accept the DAP's offer to join the party and run for public office, formally rejecting the Gerakan of which he was a former member. After officially joining the DAP on 31 July 2007, he later contested the Jelutong parliamentary seat in Penang in the 2008 election and won by a huge majority margin of 16,246 votes.

The DAP, together with its coalition partner, PKR, successfully used the online medium for raising public awareness of Malaysian politics, and to solicit funds, as well as to involve members of the public in their campaigns by inviting them to help with the printing of campaign posters and the holding of public forums. By doing so the opposition parties made the public feel involved in the run-up to the electoral process, a thing undreamt of in the days before the Internet and technological revolutions. In the end, the Internet and new telecommunications and the ways the DAP has utilized them enabled the party to match the ruling coalition's massive spending power in the elections.

Parti Keadilan Rakyat (PKR)

After its disastrous performance in the 2004 general election where it only obtained one parliamentary seat, the PKR revamped itself with the reinsertion of Anwar Ibrahim into the party when he was released from prison after the 2004 election — earlier than expected because his sodomy conviction was overturned by the Federal Court. The timing of his release was opportune as it helped to energize the PKR to organize its second national congress in December 2005. At this congress, the New Economic Agenda (NEA) was announced, which became one of the defining platforms of the PKR. In essence, the NEA sought to replace the BN's NEP, which had hitherto dispensed privileges to the Malays. Under the PKR manifesto, its NEA would be a socio-economic policy benefiting all Malaysians, regardless of race. This platform proved to be immensely popular with the Chinese and Indians, and as well as the needier sectors of Malay society.

For the 2008 general election, the PKR adopted a more aggressive strategy of wooing supporters from within the BN and from external groups so as to improve its political clout. As part of this strategy, it won over several notable personalities in Malaysia to the PKR, such as Khalid Ibrahim, former chief executive officer of Permodalan Nasional Berhad and Guthrie (Malaysia), who was appointed treasurer of the party; and Jeffrey Kitingan, a Kadazan politician and brother of Joseph Kitingan, president of the BN-aligned Parti Bersatu Sabah.

In light of the global economic slowdown, the PKR and DAP platforms of conceptualizing a new socio-economic model that would alleviate and offset the impact of the rising cost of living and rising fuel prices proved immensely popular with the people. Also, the DAP and PKR proposal to review the NEP's issuance of privileges to the Malays proved to be popular as well. This is because the recent global economic slowdown has led many Malaysians to believe that the NEP policy has been flawed by UMNO and their supporters.

CAN THE BN COALITION SYSTEM HOLD TOGETHER IN THE FUTURE?

The 2008 general election was a blow to the BN and it indeed raises an important question: is the BN system capable of holding together in the future, given the overwhelming withdrawal of popular support? The BN was originally conceptualized as a confederation political parties representing the main ethnic groups in Malaysia, namely the Malays (UMNO), Chinese (MCA), and Indians (MIC). Under the BN umbrella, its member parties collectively espouse racial harmony while retaining their individual sectarian nature. What this means is that the BN is reflective of the unintegrated nature of Malaysian society. Although Malaysian society is a multiracial one, the country is still divided along racial lines. Indeed, the unintegratedness is so pervasive that the BN racial-based coalition mirrors how race-based organizations have been encouraged at even the school level. There is no inspiration within the Malaysian society towards real integration. It would appear that the existence of the BN serves to maintain and promulgate further the practice of racial politics in Malaysia.

This continuance of racial politics has in recent years come under fire in the run-up to, and aftermath of, the 2008 general election because the BN government has called for the institution of more privileges to the Malays on top of what they have already received as part of the NEP. UMNO has gone as far as to claim staunchly that *Bumiputra* (son of the soil or generally Malays) special rights are part and parcel of the BN's manifesto, enshrined in Article 153 of the Malaysian Constitution. This has further fanned the dissatisfaction and opposition of the non-*Bumiputra*, especially the Chinese and Indians. The latter's frustrations hit a new high when a report claimed that the Malays had already achieved the 30 per cent equity target as outlined in the NEP, and yet UMNO insisted that the Malays would continue to receive privileges by virtue of their race.

The release of this report led to some infighting within the BN as its Chinese and Indian component parties cried foul with the continuance of privileges to the Malays. The situation was especially grating to the Chinese and Indian component parties in light of the fact that the global economic slowdown has adversely hit *all* Malaysians. Given that the BN is still very separated along racial lines and its non-Malay member parties have realized that concentrating and promoting the existing agenda would further alienate non-Malay Malaysians, the BN system may be unable to sustain itself in the long run.

The 2008 general election has demonstrated that race is no longer as important an issue as it once was to Malaysians. The reason behind this lies in the growing reality that the issues of inflation, shortage of goods, fuel subsidies, rising crime, majority government, government mismanagement, and corruption, affect the quality of lives for all Malaysians of all races. Further compounding this is the fact that the people do not feel the trickle down effects of widespread government spending, which it claims is alleviating the impact of the economic slowdown. Even the Malays themselves are not exempt from the effects of the economic slowdown. This in turn has further exacerbated speculation of government mismanagement of the economy and corruption.

CONCLUSION

Another interesting question to ask, given the recent developments, is: what happens if Anwar's Pakatan Rakyat takes over the government? There are of course insurmountable obstacles for this to happen, or if it ever happens, problems such as the controversial notion of the Islamic State, national leadership, and (lack of) administrative experience might make the new coalition government untenable. However, if the three components of the PR are able to put aside their differences and get along, it is possible that Malaysia could reform its policies, institute the NEA, and work at chipping away the sectarian nature of Malaysian politics and gradually ameliorate the polarization of racial politics.

What should be obvious to even the most casual observer is that the future of the BN and its dominant party, UMNO, as well as its Chinese-based political parties, MCA and Gerakan, are inextricably intertwined. They may all well be approaching an historical "make or break" crossroad. The BN coalition government must rethink whether a political system based on ethnic interests is still viable in the long run. Malay upper-class dominance has not only alienated the non-Malays, it has also energized those Malays who have not benefited from the system, and certain educated class to rethink the viability of *Bumiputrism*. For the Chinese-based political parties within the BN, already there were revolts against their conservative leaders who are trying very hard to reinvent themselves. However, in a transforming system where any ethnic interests have become suspect, the MCA and Gerakan will find it difficult to get out of their quandary. For the Malaysian Chinese voters, they may rejoice at the electoral outcome in the short run, but their political future remains as unpredictable as the 2008 general election.

Notes

1   *The Star* Online, 10 March 2008, available at <http://thestar.com.my/election/results/results.html> (accessed 1 May 2008).
2   *The Star* Online, 5 April 2004, available at <http://thestar.com.my/election/results2004/results.html> (accessed 1 May 2008).
3   "Malaysia's General Elections Open", Agence France-Presse, 7 March 2008.
4   "Malaysia's BN coalition suffers worst electoral defeat", *Channel NewsAsia*, 9 March 2008, available at <http://www.channelnewsasia.com/stories/southeastasia/view/333807/1/.html> (accessed 1 May 2008). "Abdullah: BN to form govt with simple majority", *New Straits Times* Online, 9 March 2008, available at <http://www.nst.com.my/Sunday/National/2182245/Article/index_html> (accessed 1 May 2008).
5   Mohammad Nizar Jamaluddin, the PAS *menteri besar* of Perak, was, however, ousted by UMNO in early 2009, with the defection of three opposition state legislators over to the UMNO-led camp.
6   Vijay Johsi, "Ethnic Tensions in Malaysian Election", Associated Press, 7 March 2008.
7   "Cabinet Nod for Panel's Terms of Reference", *New Straits Times*, 29 November 2007.
8   Sanjeev Miglani, ed., "FACTBOX: Malaysian Elections: Are they fair?", Reuters, 25 February 2008, available at <http://www.reuters.com/article/worldNews/idUSKLR683920080307> (accessed 8 May 2008).
9   Abdul Halim Mohd Rashid, "Khairy bertannngungjaweb kekalahan BN — Dr M", available at <http://www.harakahdaily.net/index.php?option=com_content&task=view&id=13189&Itemid=28> (accessed 8 May 2008).
10   "Dead or Alive, Malaysia Voters Among World's Oldest", Reuters, 29 February 2008.

11   "46 Ismail Ibrahims born in '62 on EC's rolls", *Malaysiakini*, 6 March 2008, available at <http://www.malaysiakini.com/news/79253> (accessed 9 May 2008).
12   Azreen Madzlan, "Bersih: Opposition Could Have Won Govt", *Malaysiakini*, available at <http://malaysiakini.com/news/79977> (accessed 9 May 2008).

References

Abdul Halim Mohd Rashid. "Khairy bertannngungjaweb kekalahan BN – Dr M". <http://www.harakahdaily.net/index.php?option=com_content&task=view&id=13189&Itemid=28> (accessed 8 May 2008).

Agence France-Presse. "Malaysia's General Elections Open", 7 March 2008.

Azreen Madzlan. "Bersih: Opposition could have won govt". *Malaysiakini*, 17 March 2008. <http://malaysiakini.com/news/79977> (accessed 9 May 2008).

Channel NewsAsia. "Malaysia's BN Coalition Suffers Worst Electoral Defeat", 9 March 2008. <http://www.channelnewsasia.com/stories/southeastasia/view/333807/1/.html> (accessed 1 May 2008).

Johsi, Vijay. "Ethnic Tensions in Malaysian Election". Associated Press, 7 March 2008.

Malaysiakini. "46 Ismail Ibrahims born in '62 on EC's rolls", 6 March 2008. <http://www.malaysiakini.com/news/79253> (accessed 9 May 2008).

Miglani, Sanjeev, ed. "FACTBOX: Malaysian Elections: Are they fair?" Reuters, 25 February 2008. <http://www.reuters.com/article/worldNews/idUSKLR683920080307> (accessed 8 May 2008).

New Straits Times. "Cabinet Nod for Panel's Terms of Reference", 29 November 2007.

New Straits Times Online. "Abdullah: BN to Form Govt with Simple Majority", 9 March 2008. <http://www.nst.com.my/Sunday/National/2182245/Article/index_html> (accessed 1 May 2008).

Reuters. "Dead or Alive, Malaysia Voters among World's Oldest", 29 February 2008.

The Star Online, 10 March 2008. <http://thestar.com.my/election/results/results.html> (accessed 1 May 2008).

————., 5 April 2004. <http://thestar.com.my/election/results2004/results.html> (accessed 1 May 2008).

5

THE END OF CHINESE MALAYSIANS' POLITICAL DIVISION? THE MARCH 8 POLITICAL TSUNAMI AND CHINESE POLITICS IN PENANG, SELANGOR, AND PERAK

Wong Chin Huat

INTRODUCTION

For many Chinese Malaysians, a major concern in Chinese politics is the problem of "political division" in the community. Since 1959, Chinese electoral politics in West Malaysia has been characterized by fragmentation, with Chinese voters splitting their support between the ruling coalition, the Alliance, and later the National Front (Barisan Nasional, BN), and the opposition parties. To further complicate matters, even the two camps were severely fragmented; before 1969 the anti-establishment Chinese votes were divided by several leftist parties, and after 1969 the Malaysian Chinese Association (MCA) and the Chinese-dominant Parti Gerakan Malaysia (Gerakan) competed to represent the Chinese voters in the BN government. This political division has commonly been blamed for the erosion of the so-called "community interests" as the Chinese-based parties could not get their act together amidst the implementation of pro-Malay or pro-*Bumiputra* policies in economic, sociocultural, and political fields.

In sharp contrast, with the exception of the 1969 general election, the majority of ethnic Malay voters had always backed a single party, the United Malays National Organization (UMNO), as the driving force of national politics, not withstanding the significant presence of its long-term rival the Pan-Malaysia Islamic Party (PAS). In return for the community's support, UMNO has implemented many pro-Malay policies since winning the 1955 Home Rule election. From a communal perspective, the ethnic Malays' political unity in multi-ethnic Malaysia is extremely effective and rewarding, and many would attribute that to the group's political unity. In the paradigm of the ethnic zero-sum game, where monopartism is inevitably superior to multipartism for an ethnic group, the Chinese Malaysians have failed miserably, given their political division.

The March 8 election in 2008 have reversed the configuration of ethnic politics in Malaysia. It was "the day Malaysia woke up" (Kee 2008) because it was in a profound sense "eclipsing May 13" (Ooi, Saravanamuttu and Lee 2008). This chapter will focus on how the post-1969 Chinese politics in West Malaysia has been transformed. From the previous pattern of "United Malays v Divided Chinese", Malaysian ethnic politics has shifted towards a new "Divided Malays v United Chinese" format. While both the Malay and non-Malay voters in West Malaysia swung towards the opposition parties — the Islamist PAS, the centrist People's Justice Party (Parti Keadilan Rakyat, PKR) led by former Deputy Prime Minister Anwar Ibrahim, and the Chinese-based Democratic Action Party (DAP), the two groups swung in different magnitudes and intensities. For the Malay-Muslims, since the swing reduced the concentration of votes in UMNO, the end result was that the community shifted from unity to division. In contrast, the Chinese voters moved from division to unity by deserting the BN to back the opposition solidly.

The March 8 political tsunami has therefore brought greater consequences than just the end of the BN's customary two-third parliamentary majority — in itself a key symbol of UMNO's and Malay dominance because it is a prerequisite for Constitutional amendments — and the opposition's unprecedented victories in five states in the peninsula. If the voting trend continues, it could well mean the beginning of a new configuration of communal politics in Malaysia. But has the Chinese political division truly come to an end? First of all, what were the factors that drove the majority of the Chinese to vote for the opposition parties? Have these factors been reinforced or weakened in the aftermath of the political tsunami? Would this seemingly "Chinese political unity" with the People's Alliance (Pakatan Rakyat, PR) eventually become a given in Malaysian politics, like the so-called "Malay political unity" under UMNO once was?

This chapter will try to address the questions above by focusing on three states — Penang, Perak, and Selangor. These three states have significant percentages of non-Malay voters, ranging from Selangor's 49.26 per cent, Perak's 53.02 per cent, to Penang's 65.51 per cent (Wong and Yeoh 2008, p. 42). These three states were amongst Malaysia's most developed states in party politics. Incidentally, in the 1969 election, the last time when the ruling coalition's rule was threatened, the opposition parties too had particularly strong showings in these three states — they captured Penang and left Perak and Selangor with hung state assemblies. In 2008, these three states not only voted for regime change, but they also placed strong Chinese representation in the new state governments, hence allowing us a close analysis.

RATIONALITY OF THE CHINESE POLITICAL DIVISION

In any highly ethnicized political competition, "political unity" or monopartism — namely, concentrating the votes of the entire community in one party or bloc — is a natural choice. Division or fragmentation only obstructs the ethnic group from acting in unison and weakens its threatening and bargaining power. In extreme cases, every major ethnic group would be completely aligned to a particular party; for example, in Guyana, elections are effectively "ethnic census", with one party representing the African-Creole community and another party championing their East Indian rivals. Election campaigns in extreme cases are thus essentially about the competition in "calling the votes out" (Horowitz 2000, pp. 311–22).

In the ethnicized politics of Malaysia, it is perfectly rational for Malays in West Malaysia, feeling threatened by an economically powerful ethnic minority group, to back one single party. On the other hand, although it may seem counter-intuitive, the division of the Chinese prior to 2008 is also a "rational" response as the community's strategy entails balancing two competing political goals. If we treat ethnic communities as unitary actors, then political division could be regarded as the Chinese community's "best response", even though it might not yield good outcomes; this is because unity in supporting either the ruling coalition or the opposition could be a much worse response. Failing to understand the dilemma the ethnic Chinese faced would prevent us from appreciating the party realignment impact of the March 8 political tsunami.

Politics of Negotiation v Politics of Pressure

The ethnic Chinese's political dilemma is split between two contradictory goals; representation within, and ability to pressure, the government. In a functioning democracy, these two goals would usually be one since the stronger an ethnic group was represented in the coalition government, the greater the pressure it could apply on the government as the ethnic group could bring down the government by withdrawing its support. This option does not exist, however, for ethnic minorities in Malaysia as they need to be represented in the government. In particular, immediately after the 1969 election, when the ruling Alliance coalition suffered a disastrous electoral setback, the MCA's announcement to withdraw from the government worsened ethnic tensions and anxieties so much so that on the very same day the party made its announcement, ethnic riots broke out (Means 1976, p. 397).

Nevertheless, what the Chinese Malaysians have learnt over time, as have the Indian Malaysians after the 2007 Hindu Rights Action Force (HINDRAF) rally, is that their goals are better served by voting against the BN. In other words, weakening their communal representation in the government would, in fact, help to advance their interests. When the Chinese gave full support to the BN, the BN was so strong that UMNO could afford to lose ethnic minority votes. On the other hand, when the Chinese retracted their support for the BN, a weakened BN would have to take their grievances seriously. For example, in 1982 the Chinese education movement, Dong Jiao Zong, endorsed Gerakan hoping that the latter, through negotiations within the BN government, could bring about more favourable education policies. But when the BN government did not change the education policies, the movement switched to backing a "two-coalition system", hoping that the emergence of a second multi-ethnic coalition would pressure the BN government, and indeed replace the BN government if necessary (Gomez 1996, p. 36; Thock 1994, pp. 148–77). Following the UMNO split in 1987–88, the opposition parties were united under the leadership of former UMNO Finance Minister Tengku Razaleigh and supported by the majority of the Chinese voters (Khong 1991). Although the united opposition failed to deny the BN its two-third parliamentary majority, the ruling coalition was forced to address the grievances of the ethnic minority, resulting in Prime Minister Mahathir's inclusive nation building blueprint, "Vision 2020", and some liberalization policies in culture, education, and the economy (Loh 2000; Gomez 1996, pp. 35–36).

The Chinese support for the BN in the 1995 and 1999 elections, however, did not bring further concessions to the community. *Bumiputraism* was further institutionalized and the marginalization of the Chinese persisted. Yet, the community leaders were split over the issue of strategy, between "politics of negotiation" (voting *for* the BN to negotiate within it) and "politics of pressure" (voting *against* the BN to pressure it) (Ng 2003). In the 1999 election, deserted by half of the Malay electorate, the BN was arguably saved by stronger support from the non-Malays. Even the DAP's most prominent leaders, Lim Kit Siang and Karpal Singh, lost their parliament seats in 1999 (Weiss 2006, pp. 143–45). After the election, the Chinese community not only was not "rewarded" with more policy concessions, on the contrary, UMNO condemned the community for "extremism". Specifically, UMNO accused David Chua, a Chinese businessman, and the Chinese reformist lobby group, Suqiu, of challenging Malay special rights. UMNO employed this strategy hoping it would win back the Malay votes the party lost in the 1999 election. Again in 2001, the hope to win back the Malay votes led Mahathir to declare Malaysia an Islamic state in order to out-Islamize PAS (Lee 2004, pp. 185–86). Similarly, the Chinese support for the BN under new Prime Minister Abdullah Badawi in the 2004 election was unpleasantly reciprocated with UMNO's ultranationalist statements and gestures due to the party's efforts to wrench Malay-Muslim support from the PKR and PAS.

In the post-1969 era then, while "political unity" behind ruling coalition was not desirable, "political unity" behind the opposition parties did not materialize due to various factors such as fear of ethnic violence, fear of losing representation in the government, and fear of instability or uncertainty. The only exception to this happened in 1990 when an estimated 70 per cent of the Chinese voted for the opposition when they thought the Malays were split and there could thus be sufficient votes to elect a new government under Tengku Razaleigh.

The Fear of Ethnic Violence

The fear of ethnic violence factor is best illustrated by the constant invocation of the May 13 ethnic riots. It has long been interpreted that the May 13 riots occurred because the Chinese abandoned the power sharing arrangement with the Malays when they switched their support to the opposition. In reality, however, the vote share of the Chinese-based opposition parties in West Malaysia remained at 26 per cent in both the 1964 and 1969 elections. The opposition's electoral gain was largely due to their better coordination. The real threat to the Alliance government was that about 9 per cent of the West Malaysian Malay voters had abandoned the ruling coalition for the PAS, hence challenging the validity of UMNO's claim as the party championing the Malays (Wong 2007). The subtle message in the popular version of the "1969 lesson" is that voting for UMNO and the BN is the ethnic minority's price to pay for harmony and peace. This message was not only repeated by the UMNO-controlled campaign machinery when the BN's two-third majority was threatened (Lim 1991, p. 5), but also echoed by some Chinese BN leaders such as MCA parliamentarian Chew Mei Fun.[1]

The Fear of Losing Representation in Government

Another factor for the Chinese is the fear of losing representation in the government. Without Chinese leaders in the cabinet to object or mitigate exclusivist policies, it is claimed that the community would be on the receiving end of Malay ultranationalism. This fear of losing representation is in fact used to justify the "politics of negotiation" (Ng 2003). To drive home this point, UMNO has constantly refused to negotiate with the DAP or other opposition parties for policy concessions. Thus as long as UMNO is in power, voting for its preferred Chinese partners is a must for many Chinese voters. This factor may also be perceived as an extension of the fear of ethnic violence factor since the community's participation in the government would help to prevent or check excesses, including ethnic violence, of state or non-state actors.

The Fear of Instability or Uncertainty

Chinese voters are also deterred from fully backing the opposition because of their fear that regime change may bring about instability or uncertainty. While the fear of losing representation in the government could be eased, many Chinese would still fear that the opposition parties would not run the country well due to inexperience and ideological differences. The differences between the Islamist PAS and the secularist DAP is often cited as a case in point; in fact, DAP had twice — in 1995 and 2001 — pulled out of opposition coalitions over the PAS's Islamization policy. This fear factor may also be seen as an extension of the fear of ethnic violence face, since instability and uncertainty after regime change are feared, not least, because of the possibility of their leading to ethnic riots.

THE CAUSES OF THE MARCH 8 POLITICAL TSUNAMI

From a communal perspective, the March 8 political tsunami brings up two interesting questions: what caused the Malay-Muslims to shift from "unity" to "division", and non-Malays and non-Muslims from "division" to "unity"? This section tries to answer the latter question by examining the three fear factors experienced by the Chinese.

The Fear of Ethnic Violence

Did the ethnic Chinese overcome the fear of ethnic violence? The answer may be both yes and no. Three mass rallies were held by civil society groups and supported by opposition parties in less than six months before the 2008 election campaign. No ethnic riots took place even though one of the rallies — organized by the Hindu Rights Action Force (HINDRAF) — was mono-ethnic in both rhetoric and participation. The post-rally peace was a blow to the May 13 discourse that mass demonstrations would lead to chaos and riots. In other words, the success of these three rallies helped legitimize political actions and emboldened many voters to consider the critical issues affecting Malaysian public life.

The first rally was the Walk for Justice on 26 September 2007, organized by the Malaysian Bar Association. Two thousand demonstrators — mostly lawyers, with some bloggers and activists — marched past the Palace of Justice in Putrajaya to demand that a Royal Commission of Inquiry investigate the Lingam Tape scandal which implicated that judicial appointments were allegedly fixed by a well connected lawyer. The Bar Council president, Ambiga Sreenevasan, explained aptly the novelty of this protest: "Lawyers don't walk everyday. Not even every month. But when they walk, then something must be very wrong." (Malaysian Bar 2007). Less than two months later, the Coalition for Clean and Fair Elections (BERSIH) — a coalition of opposition parties and civil society groups — mobilized some 40,000–60,000 people to march in downtown Kuala Lumpur to call for electoral reform. Instructed and marshalled by PAS volunteers, the demonstrators — mostly ethnic Malays, but with a small number of middle-class non-Malays — overcame the police blockade and marched orderly and assembled peacefully in front of the National Palace (Saravanamuttu 2008, pp. 45–46; Mohammad Khairie 2008).

Finally, on 25 November 2007, again in central Kuala Lumpur the Hindraf rally occurred where about 30,000 Indian protestors defied police tear gas and water cannons. They shouted "*Makkal Sakthi*" (People's Power) in protest against the marginalization of their community — from the demolition of

Hindu temples to police violence to urban poverty. "There was genuine fear as well that with the protesters all being Indian (and a sprinkling of sympathizers of other races) and the police being almost wholly Malay, a racial clash might erupt and blood spilled on the streets." (Saravanamuttu 2008, pp. 46–48; Ang 2008, p. 92). Not only did no May 13 occur, but instead the Hindraf struggle for their communal rights received the support of the PAS besides the DAP and PKR. The intercommunal solidarity between various anti-BN forces hence lowered the credibility of the ethnic violence threat.

It would, however, be wrong to conclude that Malaysia in 2008 was free from the threat of violence. The UMNO Youth chief and education minister, Hishamuddin Hussein Onn, for three consecutive years from 2005–2007 waved a *keris* (Malay dagger) during the youth wing's annual assembly. While then party president Abdullah Badawi tried to rationalize the *keris*-waving antics as "reaffirming its struggle within the boundaries of the Federal Constitution", the non-Malays generally read the gesture as UMNO Youth's thinly veiled threat of ethnic violence if the powerful youth wing did not get its way on ethno-religious issues, such as the continue pursuance of *Bumiputraism*. In the 2006 Assembly, Malacca delegate Hasnoor Sidang Hussein bluntly said that "Umno is willing to risk lives and bathe in blood in defence of race and religion", a sentiment echoed by seasoned Executive Council member Azimi Daim who said "when tension rises, the blood of Malay warriors will run in our veins". Perlis delegate Hashim Suboh took this further by asking Hishamuddin, "Datuk Hisham has unsheathed his keris, waved his keris, kissed his keris. We want to ask Datuk Hisham when he is going to use it." (Lim 2007, Khoo 2006).

Hence, while the threat of ethnic violence was still felt by the Chinese and other non-Malays in 2008, they could clearly see that such a threat came only from the UMNO Malays, but not from the PKR and PAS Malays who were attacked by UMNO for reaching out and embracing the non-Malays. This was a world of difference from the 1969 scenario where there was little link and cooperation between the West coast and urban anti-establishment Chinese voters and the East coast and inland anti-establishment Malay voters.

The Fear of Losing Representation in Government

This fear factor was certainly overcome in the March 8 political tsunami. One of the MCA March 8 election advertisements shows two vacant arm chairs, one labelled Parliament, and the other, Cabinet. The message to the Chinese voters was straightforward: they may regret later for not having representatives in the government should they abandon the incumbents. The rejection from the Chinese voters could not be clearer: MCA won only fifteen out of forty seats it contested, a sharp drop from its forty seats in 2004. MCA candidates were completely wiped out in Chinese-majority Penang while only one parliamentary seat and two state seats were won in Selangor and Kuala Lumpur, another region with a high percentage of Chinese population.

The party president, Ong Ka Ting, who advocated a "low-profile but pragmatic" style of politics through closed-door negotiations with UMNO, was blamed for "running away from politics" and turning the MCA into a charity organization that focused on education and community projects rather than formulating national policies. Ong was eventually forced to assume responsibility for the party's electoral defeat and resign as party president.

The anger of the Chinese community was not hard to comprehend. After the 1999 election, the community felt insulted when their strong support for the BN, when Malay support for BN was at its lowest point, was met by Prime Minister Mahathir's vicious attack on Suqiu and the Chinese education lobby, Dong Jiao Zong. In the 2004 election, won over by the fatherly and friendly style of Prime Minister Abdullah Badawi, the Chinese continued to give strong support to the BN. Together with other voters, they gave the Abdullah-led BN a 64 per cent landslide victory in popular votes and a 91 per cent majority in parliament. However, after the election Abdullah failed to fight the corruption problem and exclusivist politics he had promised to do. In fact, Malaysia's Corruption Perception Index (CPI) deteriorated from the 37th most corrupt country in 2003, to the 39th in 2004 and 2005, the 44th in 2006, and only improved slightly to 43rd in 2007 (Ooi 2008, p. 95). Abdullah was simply too weak to push through reforms in tainted key institutions such as the judiciary and the police force.

What infuriated the non-Malay voters even more was the deterioration of their rights as citizens as UMNO's ethno-religious agenda became increasingly unassailable. For a start, UMNO politicians such as the *keris* waving Hishamuddin Hussein Onn reacted intolerantly to critics of *Bumiputraism* in order to silence public debate. While Abdullah propagated his version of moderate Islam, called Islam Hadhari (Civilizational Islam), the long march towards desecularization continued (Kessler 2008). The religious conflicts that deeply alienated the non-Muslims include tussles over the bodies of allegedly new converts to Islam when they die, conversion cases involving marriage and family, the demolition of Hindu temples, and restrictions on non-Muslims' religious practices.

In December 2005, the Federal Territory Department of Religious Affairs (JAWI), claiming that the deceased M. Moorthy, the first Malaysian to climb

Mt. Everest, had converted to Islam, snatched his body away from his Hindu wife and family for a Muslim burial. His wife's application to claim his body back was rejected by the High Court which ruled that the Civil Court had no jurisdiction to review the decision of the Kuala Lumpur *Syariah* Court, which had ruled that the deceased died a Muslim, as stipulated in Article 121 (1A) of the Federal Constitution (Suaram 2006, pp. 102–03). Earlier, in April 2004, citing the same constitutional provision, the Kuala Lumpur High Court rejected Shamala Sathyaseelan's application to nullify the conversion of her two children to Islam unilaterally by her estranged husband, who had converted to Islam after their marriage fell apart (Suaram 2005, p. 109).

Besides the contentious decisions on conversion cases made by judges, there were also other controversies triggered by state bureaucrats. The construction of places of worship for non-Muslims has always been obstructed by restrictive town planning guidelines. To add insult to injury, in recent years local councils have been more than eager to demolish non-Muslim places of worship. The demolition of temples was seen by Hindraf leaders as "nothing but provocative acts designed to humiliate, frustrate and belittle the faith and belief of the non-Muslims" (Ang 2008). In 2007, when the Shah Alam City Council demolished a Hindu temple just several days prior to the Hindu religious festival of Deepavali, it provoked Hindraf to organize a huge rally in November 2007. Another recurrent irritation is the Christian community's confrontation with the state, especially the Home Ministry, over the confiscation of Malay-language bibles and the banning of non-Muslims from using the word *Allah* ("the God" in Arabic) (Suaram 2009, pp. 118–19).

The strong support of non-Malays and non-Muslims for Abdullah in the 2004 election did not help to mitigate the exclusivist developments. The BN non-Malay politicians did nothing to put an end to UMNO Youth's *keris*-waving antics. If a reason for a community to have representatives in the government is to protect the community's interests, the failure of the BN non-Malay parties to do that seriously raised the question of whether the community should continue to support them. In January 2006, BN's non-Muslim ministers submitted a memorandum to Prime Minister Abdullah calling for a review of the above-mentioned Article 121(1A). When the prime minister rejected the demand, all but one of the ministers quickly retracted their initiative. The MCA even announced that the matter was settled and they would abide by the premier's wish (Ooi 2008, pp. 103–04). If the non-Malay/non-Muslim ministers cannot protect the minority's interest, then it would cost the minority groups nothing if they were to lose their ministerial positions.

The Fear of Instability or Uncertainty

Did the Chinese voters also overcome their fear of post-transition instability or uncertainty in the political tsunami? It will be difficult to answer this question since the three main opposition parties in general did not sell themselves as the next government. Presenting their individual manifestos, the parties did not form a formal coalition even almost a month after the poll. The central message targeting the Chinese voters was really about denying the BN a two-third majority and checking its excesses. In fact, the opposition leaders openly admitted that they were surprised by the election outcomes. They did not even position the right candidates to form a state government, especially in Perak.

The outcome of the Chinese-majority constituencies in the March 8 election can therefore be interpreted as the collective choice of ethnic Chinese voters who had largely overcome their fear of ethnic violence and of losing representation in the government. They did not fear ethnic violence much because they saw and found anti-UMNO Malays in large numbers by their side. As most of them did not expect a regime change, the decision to abandon the BN Chinese leaders can only be indicative of their disillusion with the BN's power-sharing myth. It is against this background that another phenomenon in Chinese politics — split ticket voting — might also have come to an end.

The End of Split Voting?

Over the years, Chinese voters have adopted a split voting strategy as a means to pressure the BN and maintain representation in the government. Thus Chinese split-voters would vote for opposition candidates in the parliamentary contests and BN candidates at the state level. In splitting their votes this way, the Chinese calculate that their protest votes would be more effectively felt through the federal Parliament, while representation in the state government would ensure development funding. This strategy was particularly common in those states where the BN Chinese-based parties were still perceived to have some power in the state government. For example, Sarawakian Chinese voters would not want to weaken the Sarawak United People's Party (SUPP) at the state level because the party's ability to promote and defend the community's interests depended on its ability to win the pivotal Chinese-majority constituencies. At the federal level, the SUPP would have minimal impact since the party would contest in only eight parliamentary seats, which are far too few for the party to have any bargaining power. As such, it would make more sense for the Sarawakian

Chinese to elect opposition parliamentarians to draw the BN's attention to their grievances (Chin 1996).

The stake for the Chinese voters is even bigger in Penang because this is the only state where the state government is still led by a Chinese. Indeed, since 1990 the Penang Chinese have consistently used the split voting strategy to advance their interests. In 1990, hoping for the birth of a two-party system, the Penang Chinese vigorously backed the DAP in its campaign to grab the state's chief ministership. But the effort fell short of three seats to win the state as the DAP won only fourteen out of thirty-three seats and its allies won no seat at all. For the next three elections, 1995, 1999, and 2004, the DAP could win only a seat in the Penang state legislature as Chinese voters decided to back Gerakan and the MCA at the state level to check UMNO's ambition for the top post. They were however more generous to the DAP at the federal level, electing three to four DAP parliamentarians in those trying years.

Ceteris paribus, if the Chinese have overcome their fear so as to attain political unity under the opposition parties, we should see the disappearance of split voting. However there was neither an exit poll nor polling-district-level data for estimation techniques such as Gary King's "ecological inference"[2] for us to conjecture the voting pattern of the Chinese or any other ethnic group. Even parliamentary vote breakdowns at the state seat level are not readily available for all constituencies. A way to estimate the extent of split voting in Penang, Perak, and Selangor is to compare the BN vote shares in parliamentary and state contests at the parliamentary constituency level. Since constituencies are redelineated for every two elections, only the 2004 and 2008 elections can be analysed to assess the possible trends.

In Penang, split voting was still found in all six parliamentary seats involving two-third or more Chinese voters. For example, in Tanjung and Bukit Mertajam, the BN won 10 per cent more votes at the state level, but lost both parliament seats to the DAP. In part, because both the DAP parliamentary candidates in these constituencies are hugely popular, they won about 69 per cent to 74 per cent of the valid votes whereas the opposition state candidates bagged only 62 per cent to 70 per cent of the votes in total. Nevertheless, in the 2004 election the split voting in favour of the BN state candidates in three of these constituencies ranged from 12 per cent to 21 per cent. The diminished presence of split voting in the 2008 election would suggest that the Penang Chinese voters have abandoned their habit of voting for the BN at the state level, and for the opposition at the federal level. As the DAP and other opposition parties did not campaign on regime change in 2008, one could interpret that the majority of Penang Chinese voters did not mind being in the opposition camp at both federal and state levels (see Table 5.1).

Table 5.1
Estimated Split Voting in Penang, 2004 and 2008

Code	Constituency	Chinese, 2008	Total Electorate (TE), 2008	Winning Party (P)	2008			Winning Parties	2004			Change in Extra Support for BN (S), 2004–08
					BN/Total Valid Votes (P)	BN/Total Valid Votes (S)	BN/Total Valid Votes (S-P)		BN/Total Valid Votes (P)	BN/Total Valid Votes (S)	BN/Total Valid Votes (S-P)	
P49	Tanjong	86.10%	53,188	DAP	25.68%	36.24%	10.56%	DAP	44.59%	60.47%	15.88%	-5.31%
P48	Bukit Bendera	75.20%	64,545	DAP	32.63%	38.30%	5.68%	BN-Gerakan	61.69%	68.45%	6.76%	-1.08%
P51	Bukit Gelugor	74.50%	65,614	DAP	28.67%	33.81%	5.13%	DAP	48.56%	60.42%	11.86%	-6.73%
P45	Bukit Mertajam	74.00%	64,080	DAP	26.18%	37.00%	10.82%	DAP	40.24%	61.49%	21.25%	-10.43%
P43	Bagan	70.60%	59,385	DAP	25.71%	30.00%	4.29%	DAP	45.75%	54.61%	8.87%	-4.58%
P50	Jelutong	67.96%	61,181	DAP	31.23%	37.14%	5.91%	BN-Gerakan	58.79%	60.41%	1.62%	4.29%
P46	Batu Kawan	55.57%	47,244	DAP	37.06%	32.91%	-4.15%	BN-Gerakan	53.85%	57.14%	3.29%	-7.44%
P52	Bayan Baru	48.50%	60,713	PKR	37.53%	44.30%	6.77%	BN-MCA	73.56%	74.15%	0.59%	6.18%
P47	Nibong Tebal	37.60%	47,540	PKR	45.87%	42.49%	-3.37%	BN-UMNO	59.49%	64.59%	5.10%	-8.47%
P53	Balik Pulau	35.30%	39,765	PKR	48.85%	51.88%	3.03%	BN-UMNO	72.23%	71.64%	-0.59%	3.62%
P44	Permatang Pauh	24.50%	58,449	Keadilan	35.84%	42.48%	6.63%	Keadilan	49.31%	55.19%	5.87%	0.76%
P41	Kepala Batas	20.50%	43,018	BN-UMNO	65.78%	60.02%	-5.76%	BN-UMNO	77.72%	71.08%	-6.64%	0.88%
P42	Tasek Gelugor	14.70%	44,466	BN-UMNO	56.25%	55.48%	-0.77%	BN-UMNO	65.05%	65.42%	0.38%	-1.15%

Source: The Sun.

In Perak, split voting was mild for the six constituencies with 50 per cent or more Chinese voters in both the 2004 and 2008 polls. In Kampar, the only constituency won by the MCA, the BN state candidates lost 19 per cent of the votes in total whereas the coalition parliamentary vote share dropped only by 9 per cent. While this may be due to the opposition having more popular candidates at the state level, it nevertheless still means that more Chinese were willing to forego their representation in the state government. This trend seems to be confirmed by another phenomenon: in the top three Chinese-majority parliamentary constituencies, more than 60 per cent of the voters were happy to be represented by opposition members in contrast to only around 50 per cent willing in 2004. This is interesting because a DAP-dominated state government was simply unimaginable before and during the 2008 poll (see Table 5.2).

Finally, Selangor — where the constituencies were much more ethnically mixed — presents a different picture with some anomalies. Out of six parliamentary constituencies with 40 per cent or more Chinese voters, only Puchong demonstrated considerable extra support in favour of the BN state candidates. On the other hand, two parliamentary constituencies showed greater support for the BN parliamentary, perhaps largely due to the personality factor; for example, in Pandan, the MCA incumbent and deputy minister, Ong Tee Keat, was known as an outspoken maverick in the ruling coalition. A look at the 2004 election results helps put things into perspective. Selangor was a heavily BN state in 2004 with the BN state candidates winning more than 65 per cent of the total popular vote. By 2008, these figures had dropped considerably from 21 per cent to 44 per cent. Unlike in Penang and Perak, regime change was not completely kept out of the opposition campaigning in Selangor, but judging from the post-election response, most voters did not expect that to happen. Hence, the increased willingness amongst the Chinese voters to elect a candidate who is expected to be in the opposition and denied government funding is significant (see Table 5.3).

While the preliminary analysis of the voting data shows that the political tsunami did not sweep away split voting amongst the ethnic Chinese voters, the traditional rationale for split voting has lost its appeal. Even where split voting happened, it did so more likely because of the personality factor and not because the Chinese voters wanted to keep the BN representatives in the state government to fight for their interests from within.

Table 5.2
Estimated Split Voting in Perak, 2004 and 2008

Code	Constituency	Chinese, 2008	Total Electorate (TE), 2008	Winning Party (P)	2008			Winning Parties	2004			Change in Extra Support for BN (S), 2004–2008
					BN/Total Valid Votes (P)	BN/Total Valid Votes (S)	BN/Total Valid Votes (S-P)		BN/Total Valid Votes (P)	BN/Total Valid Votes (S)	BN/Total Valid Votes (S-P)	
P64	Ipoh Timor	81.50%	76,647	DAP	29.22%	36.24%	7.03%	DAP	39.80%	50.04%	10.23%	-3.21%
P66	Batu Gajah	78.10%	77,313	DAP	27.70%	34.51%	6.81%	DAP	41.91%	47.96%	6.05%	0.76%
P65	Ipoh Barat	65.05%	69,773	DAP	34.35%	38.09%	3.74%	DAP	49.34%	55.99%	6.65%	-2.91%
P70	Kampar	63.10%	59,784	BN-MCA	53.59%	44.42%	-9.17%	BN-MCA	62.91%	63.66%	0.75%	-9.92%
P68	Beruas	54.80%	43,273	DAP	46.94%	41.57%	-5.36%	BN-Gerakan	58.40%	49.77%	-8.63%	3.26%
P60	Taiping	50.30%	65,889	DAP	37.42%	46.58%	9.16%	BN-PPP	47.41%	62.27%	14.86%	-5.70%
P71	Gopeng	47.34%	74,344	PKR	42.92%	47.19%	4.28%	BN-MCA	66.12%	58.83%	-7.30%	11.57%
P76	Telok Intan	44.60%	52,354	DAP	47.93%	37.73%	-10.20%	BN-Gerakan	55.78%	50.32%	-5.46%	-4.74%
P62	Sungai Siput	40.20%	47,424	PKR	45.80%	43.64%	-2.16%	BN-MIC	62.19%	61.99%	-0.20%	-1.96%
P74	Lumut	38.50%	72,763	BN-MCA	50.29%	43.03%	-7.26%	BN-MIC	63.44%	52.39%	-11.04%	3.78%
P72	Tapah	32.40%	38,236	BN-MIC	56.00%	63.02%	7.02%	BN-MIC	69.72%	76.78%	7.06%	-0.04%
P77	Tanjong Malim	31.00%	53,481	BN-MCA	57.41%	51.43%	-5.98%	BN-MCA	71.69%	65.55%	-6.14%	0.16%
P57	Parit Buntar	28.30%	45,219	PAS	39.18%	47.68%	8.50%	BN-UMNO	56.91%	57.72%	0.81%	7.69%
P59	Bukit Gantang	27.10%	55,471	PAS	46.90%	49.04%	2.14%	BN-Gerakan	61.79%	60.65%	-1.13%	3.28%
P67	Kuala Kangsar	26.00%	28,325	BN-UMNO	53.64%	56.10%	2.45%	BN-UMNO	65.73%	66.92%	1.19%	1.26%
P63	Tambun	24.00%	65,966	BN-UMNO	55.33%	55.17%	-0.16%	BN-UMNO	68.75%	67.45%	-1.30%	1.13%
P75	Bagan Datok	19.50%	34,670	BN-UMNO	55.72%	47.29%	-8.43%	BN-UMNO	79.08%	63.98%	-15.10%	6.68%
P61	Padang Rengas	18.70%	24,397	BN-UMNO	54.88%	52.70%	-2.19%	BN-UMNO	65.74%	64.54%	-1.20%	-0.98%
P54	Gerik	18.20%	26,229	BN-Gerakan	64.31%	73.83%	9.53%	BN-UMNO	74.92%	76.82%	1.89%	7.63%
P55	Lenggong	16.80%	23,223	BN-UMNO	64.41%	65.04%	0.63%	BN-UMNO	67.37%	67.02%	-0.35%	0.98%
P58	Bagan Serai	15.80%	47,111	PKR	45.05%	46.36%	1.31%	BN-UMNO	58.25%	58.31%	0.05%	1.26%
P73	Pasir Salak	14.60%	42,732	BN-UMNO	54.31%	54.45%	0.14%	BN-UMNO	64.11%	64.20%	0.10%	0.04%
P56	Larut	5.60%	39,697	BN-UMNO	53.20%	54.78%	1.58%	BN-UMNO	62.46%	62.57%	0.10%	1.48%
P69	Parit	3.30%	28,859	BN-UMNO	56.55%	59.83%	3.28%	BN-UMNO	61.22%	61.59%	0.36%	2.91%

Source: The Sun.

Table 5.3
Estimated Split Voting in Selangor, 2004 and 2008

Code	Constituency	Chinese, 2008	Total Electorate (TE), 2008	Winning Party (P)	2008 BN/Total Valid Votes (P)	2008 BN/Total Valid Votes (S)	2008 BN/Total Valid Votes (S-P)	Winning Parties	2004 BN/Total Valid Votes (P)	2004 BN/Total Valid Votes (S)	2004 BN/Total Valid Votes (S-P)	Change in Extra Support for BN (S), 2004–2008
P106	PJ Utara	76.70%	76,618	DAP	32.08%	29.05%	-3.03%	BN-MCA	62.59%	60.07%	-2.52%	-0.51%
P102	Serdang	52.10%	94,877	DAP	35.77%	37.62%	1.85%	BN-MCA	59.77%	63.29%	3.52%	-1.67%
P110	Klang*	47.10%	77,816	DAP	34.81%	35.08%	0.27%	BN-MCA	63.02%	60.20%	-2.82%	3.09%
P100	Pandan	45.04%	64,497	BN-MCA	53.12%	40.29%	-12.82%	BN-MCA	67.94%	60.70%	-7.24%	-5.58%
P105	PJ Selatan	44.50%	73,192	PKR	44.46%	37.22%	-7.24%	BN-MCA	71.99%	64.01%	-7.98%	0.75%
P103	Puchong	40.78%	75,625	DAP	39.06%	45.10%	6.03%	BN-Gerakan	53.38%	68.39%	15.01%	-8.98%
P104	Kelana Jaya	38.70%	79,648	PKR	43.97%	35.56%	-8.41%	BN-MCA	71.52%	74.56%	3.04%	-11.45%
P97	Selayang	38.24%	79,557	PKR	45.86%	46.84%	0.98%	BN-MCA	73.48%	69.98%	-3.50%	4.48%
P101	Hulu Langat	36.20%	90,319	PAS	48.76%	49.88%	1.12%	BN-UMNO	69.27%	66.58%	-2.70%	3.82%
P107	Subang	35.90%	84,414	PKR	44.70%	45.64%	0.94%	BN-MIC	65.33%	70.11%	4.78%	-3.84%
P109	Kapar	35.40%	112,224	PKR	42.69%	38.79%	-3.90%	BN-MIC	59.93%	59.59%	-0.35%	-3.55%
P99	Ampang	34.20%	69,132	PKR	46.35%	46.41%	0.06%	BN-UMNO	71.13%	68.35%	-2.78%	2.84%
P93	Sungai Besar	30.30%	34,073	BN-UMNO	59.23%	60.38%	1.15%	BN-UMNO	65.75%	60.93%	-4.82%	5.97%
P94	Hulu Selangor	26.70%	63,593	PKR	49.79%	56.66%	6.88%	BN-MIC	67.61%	77.51%	9.91%	-3.03%
P112	Kuala Langat	26.09%	66,515	PKR	49.06%	47.62%	-1.43%	BN-UMNO	72.99%	66.26%	-6.73%	5.30%
P113	Sepang	23.30%	62,044	BN-UMNO	55.06%	56.78%	1.72%	BN-UMNO	72.07%	70.67%	-1.40%	3.13%
P111	Kota Raja	23.20%	71,887	PAS	31.64%	35.62%	3.98%	BN-MIC	55.25%	62.18%	6.93%	-2.95%
P95	Tanjong Karang	16.70%	36,391	BN-UMNO	56.74%	55.85%	-0.90%	BN-UMNO	67.00%	66.60%	-0.40%	-0.50%
P96	Kuala Selangor	15.60%	47,203	PAS	48.83%	48.99%	0.16%	BN-UMNO	72.51%	67.69%	-4.82%	4.99%
P108	Shah Alam	15.50%	75,334	PAS	41.89%	44.98%	3.09%	BN-UMNO	63.04%	65.15%	2.11%	0.98%
P92	Sabak Bernam	13.61%	31,381	BN-UMNO	52.93%	50.51%	-2.42%	BN-UMNO	61.99%	59.82%	-2.17%	-0.24%
P98	Gombak	13.45%	99,153	PKR	45.35%	43.91%	-1.44%	BN-UMNO	59.93%	58.43%	-1.50%	0.05%

Source: The Sun.

THE AFTERMATH OF THE POLITICAL TSUNAMI

If the developments before March 8 had contributed to the political unification of the Chinese voters, what about the post-tsunami developments? Will they help to put to rest for good those fears that previously stopped them from backing the opposition in full force? Or will they help revive those fears?

The Fear of Ethnic Violence

The first casualty of the political tsunami is really the spectre of May 13. For generations, the ethnic minorities had been taught that ethnic riots would happen if they abandoned the ruling coalition. On the night of March 8, opposition supporters were asked to stay at home and not celebrate publicly, to avoid a replay of the riots thirty-eight years ago. Partly thanks to Prime Minister Abdullah Badawi and, in Penang, Chief Minister Koh Tsu Koon, who gracefully accepted the election outcome, nothing untoward happened. While there were initial hiccups in the formation of the state governments in Perak and Selangor, the problems were swiftly solved with important interventions from the respective state sultan.

Nearly two years later in 2009, the threat of ethnic violence was on the cards again. First, in late August, just a few days before National Day, a group of Shah Alam residents, including UMNO division leaders, marched to the Selangor State Government building with a severed cow head to protest against a decision to relocate a Hindu Temple. The severed cow head was not only meant to humiliate the Hindus who treat the cow as a holy animal, but also to signal bloodshed if the state government did not back down (Shazwan 2009).

In January 2010, a few churches were torched, followed by the desecration of mosques and a Sikh Temple. This was allegedly a response by angry Muslims to the High Court decision to allow the Christians to use the Arabic word, *Allah* (The God) in their Malay-language publications. The government and several Muslim groups claimed that this would confuse the Muslims to the extent that they may convert out of Islam (Parry 2010).

While this was a national issue, the first cases of church attacks happened in Selangor and neighbouring Kuala Lumpur, leading some conspiracy theorists to speculate that this was a plot to destabilize the Pakatan Selangor government.

In Penang and Perak, the DAP politicians were accused of marginalizing the Malays and insulting Islam. In February 2010, an effigy of Penang Chief Minister Lim Guan Eng was burned by some Malay non-governmental organizations in protest against his alleged discrimination against the Malays in the demolition of illegal hawker stalls (*The Star* 2010). Earlier in December 2009, similar Malay non-governmental organizations protested against a DAP parliamentarian in Perak for questioning the "Malay special rights". They demanded that his citizenship be stripped and threatened to take "whatever action necessary to protect Malay supremacy" (Chooi 2009).

The protests and attacks in the name of defending Islam and the Malay rights in Selangor, Penang, and Perak were clearly to signal that the Malays might run amok to protect their political power. However, so far no sign shows that such protests have terrified Malaysians into bowing to violence and modifying their political preferences. Instead, violence has been roundly condemned and delegitimized by civil society, including mainstream Islamic groups, for the cow-head protest and church arson incident.

In fact, the inter-ethnic solidarity of the BERSIH 2.0 rally participants to defy police crackdown and threats of ethnic violence is perceived as the official burial of the May 13 "bogeyman" (Chooi 2011).

The Fear of Losing Representation in Government

If representation in the government was the traditional justification used by the MCA to ask ethnic Chinese voters to vote for Chinese, this argument has now become a deadly weapon that is diminishing the BN Chinese-based parties day by day.

Chinese and Indian politicians are way better represented in all three Pakatan Rakyat state governments: Penang, Perak (up to the constitutional coup in February 2009) and Selangor. In Penang, with the DAP directly controlling nineteen out of Pakatan Rakyat's twenty-nine seats, the lawmaker, DAP's Lim Guan Eng, is a powerful chief minister, in sharp contrast to his predecessor, Koh Tsu Koon, who is seen by many as UMNO's puppet. Lim's cabinet consists of seven Chinese, two Malays (including the first deputy chief minister), and one Indian (the second deputy chief minister). In both Selangor and Perak, an ethnic Chinese DAP lawmaker was appointed as senior executive councillor, much like the deputy chief minister in Penang, except without the title. The non-Malays dominated the Perak state cabinet as in Penang and constituted nearly half of the Selangor one (see Table 5.4). (In sharp contrast, the post-coup BN state cabinet in Perak has only a Chinese member while the rest are from UMNO.) Both Perak and Selangor also appointed a non-Malay as the legislative speaker and both have turned out to be powerful players in state politics.

Table 5.4
Party and Ethnic Breakdown of State Executive Councillors in
Penang, Perak, and Selangor

	PKR- Malay	PKR- Chinese	PKR- Indian	DAP- Chinese	DAP- Indian	PAS- Malay	Total (including MB/CM)
Penang	2	1	—	7	1	0	11
Perak (2008–9)	2	1	—	5	1	2	11
Selangor	3	1	1	3	—	3	11

Source: Various news reports.

The communal power sharing in Pakatan Rakyat is, therefore, completely unmatched by the UMNO-dominated executive council before March 8 where the non-Malay members had no real power. Not only is its communal representation more balanced, but the Pakatan Rakyat state governments also implement several colour-blind or minority-friendly policies. The affluent Selangor gives the first 20 cubic meters of water for domestic use free and provides subsidies for newborns, and the funerals of senior citizens. Likewise, the Penang state government hands out money first to hardcore poverty households and then senior citizens. In pre-coup Perak, the financially constrained state government announced the conversion of leasehold titles to freehold for villagers, a move particularly welcomed by Chinese voters living in new villages.

The Fear of Instability or Uncertainty?

Unlike the fear of ethnic violence or that of losing governmental representation, the fear of instability or uncertainty with regime change does not go away easily. Despite the fact that the PKR, DAP, and PAS quickly formalized their coalition by 1 April 2009, the Pakatan Rakyat state governments in Penang, Perak, and Selangor have become plagued by three problems: infighting, defections, and regime change.

Infighting has taken place at both the intraparty and interparty levels. In Penang, the most stable of the three Pakatan Rakyat states, the conflict was largely between the dominant DAP and a PKR faction led by former UMNO leader, Zahrain Hashim, a parliamentarian. The conflict ended with the resignation of Zahrain and another two PKR parliamentarians from the PKR, but the state government remains intact.

The scenario in Selangor is much more complicated as the PAS — which is the second largest party by popular vote, but the third largest party by seats — has been continuously courted by UMNO to form a Muslim-dominated coalition government. The PAS Selangor chief Hassan Ali, who was offered the *menteri besar* position by UMNO, took a hard line position on religious matters such as alcohol and moral policing (Lau and Spykerman 2009). This landed him in conflict not only with the DAP, but also with his more open-minded colleagues in the PAS. For many, this confirmed their fear of the ideological incompatibility between the PAS and DAP, but the conflict somehow died down after a while, with Hassan Ali pledging his support for Pakatan Rakyat. While the PKR later lost a state assemblyperson, the defection was not related to the PAS-DAP conflict.

The greatest challenge for Pakatan Rakyat remains in Perak. In February 2009, two PKR executive councillors and the DAP deputy legislative speaker declared themselves BN-friendly independents. This reversed the tiny 31:28 lead the Pakatan Rakyat enjoyed in the fifty-nine-seat legislature. When the sultan of Perak turned down Menteri Besar Mohamad Nizar Jamaluddin's request to dissolve the legislature and sacked him instead, the state fell into an intractable political stand-off with two chief ministers and two legislative speakers challenging each other's legality. While Nizar enjoys greater support from the public, especially the non-Malay voters, he eventually lost his case in the Federal Court.

THE FUTURE TREND?

I have argued in this chapter that the March 8 political tsunami may have fundamentally transformed Chinese politics in West Malaysia. Ethnic Chinese voters have apparently overcome their fear of ethnic violence and of losing representation in government in order to attain political unity under the opposition's banner. The most interesting finding is perhaps that the majority of voters in Chinese-majority constituencies in Penang, Perak, and Selangor did not hesitate to vote for opposition parties at the state level, even though regime change was not expected. While split voting was still found, the phenomenon was a different animal from what was previously encountered.

The post-March 8 developments, however, have not diminished, but in fact, may have strengthened the last fear factor: the fear of instability. The continuing Perak crisis may induce some risk-adverse voters, both within and outside Perak, to return to the BN's fold and help secure its victory in the next elections. If this is the case, the Chinese political division is likely to continue, but with an even smaller representation in the BN government.

However, if the fear of instability is largely overcome, the ethnic Chinese voters would be politically united under Pakatan Rakyat, while the Malay voters are likely to remain split between the BN and the opposition coalition. This would have great impact on the emerging two-party politics in Malaysia. Even if the BN wins the next elections, it will be surviving mainly on Malay support with the MCA and Gerakan becoming a spent force. This will, in turn, constrain the BN's ability to move to the centre and appeal to the non-Malays. And without sufficient division within both the Malays and the Chinese, it is difficult to imagine that the current two-party competition can be sustained.

Note

1   See *China Press*, 21 January 2008, p. A11.

References

Ang, Helen. "The Force of 'Makkal Sakthi'". In *March 8: The Day Malaysia Woke Up*, edited by Kee Thuan Chyepp. Subang: Marshall Cavendish, 2008.

Chin, James. "The Sarawak Chinese Voters and their Support for the Democratic Action Party (DAP)". *Southeast Asian Studies* 34, no. 2 (September 1996): 387–401.

Chooi, Clara. "DAP veep lodges report on Malay supremacy attacks". *The Malaysian Insider,* 11 December 2009, available at <http://www.themalaysianinsider.com/index.php/malaysia/46193-dap-veep-lodges-report-on-malay-supremacy-attacks> (assessed 31 March 2010).

———. "Bersih rally shows May 13 'ogeyman' officially buried, says Bar Council". *The Malaysia Insider*, 12 July 2011. <http://blog.drdzul.com/2011/07/12/bersih-rally-shows-may-13-%E2%80%98bogeyman%E2%80%99-buried-says-bar-council/> (accessed 19 August 2011).

Gomez, Edmund Terence. *The 1995 Malaysian General Elections: A Report and Commentary.* Singapore: Institute of Southeast Asian Studies, 1996a.

Horowitz, Donald. *Ethnic Groups in Conflict.* 2nd ed. Berkeley, Los Angeles and London: University of California Press, 2000.

Kee Thuan Chye, ed. *March 8: The Day Malaysia Woke Up.* Subang: Marshall Cavendish, 2008.

Kessler, Clive S. "Islam, the State and Desecularisation in Malaysia: The Islamist Trajectory during the Badawi Years". In *Sharing the Nation: Faith, Difference, Power and the State 50 years after Merdeka*, by Norani Othman, Mavis C. Puthucheary and Clive S. Kessler. Petaling Jaya: Society for Inner Resources Development, 2008.

Khong Kim Hoong. *Malaysia's General Election 1990: Continuity, Change and Ethnic Politics.* Singapore: Institute of Southeast Asian Studies, 1991.

Khoo Kay Peng. "Apologize not justify". *Straight talk,* 21 November 2006, available at <http://khookaypeng.blogspot.com/2006/11/apologize-not-justify.html> (assessed 29 March 2010).

Lau, Leslie and Neville Spykerman. "Hassan Ali's Religious Police to Nab Errant Muslims". *The Malaysian Insider,* 24 August 2009, available at <http://www.themalaysianinsider.com/index.php/malaysia/35927-hassan-alis-religious-police-to-nab-errant-muslims> (assessed 31 March 2010).

Lee Kam Hing. "Mahathir's Administration and the Chinese". In *Reflections: The Mahathir years,* edited by Bridget Welsh. Washington, D.C.: Johns Hopkins University, 2004.

Lim Kit Siang. *The Dirtiest General Elections in the History.* Petaling Jaya: Oriengroup, 1991.

————. "Hishammuddin's Keris Desensitization and the Boiling-Frog Syndrome". Parliamentary speech on 6 November 2007. "Lim Kit Siang for Malaysia", available at <http://blog.limkitsiang.com/2007/11/06/hishammuddin%E2%80%99s-keris-desensitization-and-the-boiling-frog-syndrome/> (assessed 29 March 2010).

Loh, Francis, Kok Wah. "Developmentalism and the Limits of Democratic Discourse". In *Democracy in Malaysia: Discourses and Practices,* edited by Francis Loh Kok Wah and Khoo Boo Teik. Singapore: Institute of Southeast Asian Studies, 2000.

Malaysian Bar. "Walk for Justice: 'When Lawyers Walk, Something Must Be Very Wrong'", 26 September 2007, available at <http://www.malaysianbar.org.my/bar_news/berita_badan_peguam/walk_for_justice_when_lawyers_walk_something_must_be_very_wrong_.html> (assessed 28 March 2010).

Means, Gordon P. *Malaysian Politics.* 2nd ed. London: Hodder and Stoughton, 1976.

Mohammad Khairie. "We Walked United in Hope". In *March 8: The Day Malaysia Woke Up,* edited by Kee Thuan Chye. Subang: Marshall Cavendish, 2008.

Ng Tien Eng. "The Contest for Chinese Votes: Politics of Negotiation or Politics of Pressure?" In *New Politics in Malaysia,* edited by Francis Loh Kok Wah and Johan Saravanamuttu. Singapore: Institute of Southeast Asian Studies, 2003.

Ooi Kee Beng. *Lost in Transition: Malaysia under Abdullah.* Singapore: Institute of Southeast Asian Studies, and Petaling Jaya: SIRD, 2008.

Ooi Kee Beng, Johan Saravanamuttu, and Lee Hock Guan. *March 8: Eclipsing May 13.* Singapore: Institute of Southeast Asian Studies, 2005.

Parry, Richard Lloyd. "Attacks after Malaysian Court Rules Christians Can Worship Allah". *The Times,* 9 January 2010, available at <http://www.timesonline.co.uk/tol/news/world/asia/article6980360.ece> (assessed 31 March 2010).

Saravanamuttu, Johan. "A Tectonic Shift in Malaysian Politics". In *March 8: Eclipsing May 13*, edited by Ooi Kee Beng, Johan Saravanamuttu, and Lee Hock Guan. Singapore: Institute of Southeast Asian Studies, 2008.

Shazwan Mustafa Kamal. "Protesters Threaten Bloodshed over Hindu Temple". *The Malaysian Insider*, 28 August 2009, available at <http://www.themalaysianinsider. com/index.php/malaysia/36272-protesters-threaten-bloodshed-over-hindu-temple> (assessed 31 March 2010).

Suaram. *Malaysia Human Rights Report 2008: Civil and Political Rights*. Petaling Jaya: Suaram Komunikasi, 2009.

———. *Malaysia Human Rights Report 2005: Civil and Political Rights*. Petaling Jaya: Suaram Komunikasi, 2006.

———. *Malaysia Human Rights Report 2004: Civil and Political Rights*. Petaling Jaya: Suaram Komunikasi, 2005.

The Star. "Malay NGOs Hold Protest, Burn Effigy of Guan Eng". *The Star*, 5 February 2010, available at <http://thestar.com.my/news/story.asp?file=/2010/2/5/nation/20100205155351&sec=nation> (assessed 31 March 2010).

Thock Kiah Wah. *Deconstruction of Political Myth: The Study of Two-coalition Politics in Malaysia* (1985–1992) [in Chinese]. Kuala Lumpur: Huazi Resource and Research Centre, 1994.

Weiss, Meredith. *Protest and Possibilities: Civil Society and Coalitions for Political Change in Malaysia* Stanford: Stanford University Press, 2006.

Wong Chin Huat. "Watershed Elections of 1969". *The Sun*, 26 July 2007, available at <http://www.malaysianbar.org.my/echoes_of_the_past/watershed_elections_of_1969.html> (assessed 28 March 2010).

Wong Chin Huat and Oon Yeoh. "A Tale of Two Malaysias". In *March 8: The Day Malaysia Woke Up*, edited by Kee Thuan Chye. Subang: Marshall Cavendish, 2008.

6

FORCED TO THE PERIPHERY: RECENT CHINESE POLITICS IN EAST MALAYSIA

James Chin

This chapter will chart the development of Chinese politics in the East Malaysian states of Sarawak and Sabah in the past decade. In general, Chinese politics in both states has taken the same trajectory as Chinese politics in the peninsula, that is, the political marginalization of the community, especially in electoral politics. The only key difference between Chinese politics in the peninsula and East Malaysia is the continued pre-eminence of local-based Chinese parties in both states.

CONTEMPORARY SARAWAK CHINESE POLITICS

The most significant change in Chinese politics in Sarawak in recent years was the defeat of the Sarawak United People's Party (SUPP) in the 2006 state election. Hitherto, the Chinese community had largely supported the SUPP against the Sarawak Democratic Action Party (DAP). SUPP was Sarawak's first political party, established by the Chinese community in 1959 with significant Dayak support. Although it started out as a left-wing party, from 1970 onward it emerged as a right wing, conservative, Chinese-based party. Since then it has lost much of its Dayak support although it still retains some Dayak majority seats due to the Sarawak BN seat allocation formula.[1]

While the SUPP is the only Chinese-based party in the Sarawak BN, the main Chinese opposition is the DAP. The DAP was formed in the late 1970s by a renegade group of SUPP members who teamed up with anti-establishment Chinese who wanted a credible Chinese-based opposition party in Sarawak. The then Sarawak chief minister, Rahman Yakub, also encouraged the setting up of the DAP in order to weaken the SUPP. [2]

Sarawak politics revolves around three major political groupings; the Chinese, the Malay/Melanau Muslims (MMM), and the Dayak[3] (Non-Muslim Bumiputra [NMB]) community. Parti Pesaka Bumiputera Bersatu (PBB) serves as the main political party for the MMM, while the NMB spread their support among several Dayak-based parties such as the Pesaka wing of the PBB, SUPP, Parti Keadilan Rakyat (PKR), the Sarawak Progressive Democratic Party (SPDP), and the Parti Rakyat Sarawak (PRS). Although numerically the Dayaks constitute the largest segment of the community (about 40 per cent), they have never been united politically and are prone to political manipulation by the MMM and the Chinese elite.

THE 2006 SARAWAK STATE ELECTIONS

For years the SUPP has been taking the line that the Sarawak Chinese community was "different" compared with the Peninsular Chinese, as the SUPP had "real power". The SUPP points to the fact that SUPP ministers were traditionally in charge of two key state ministries: Finance and Infrastructure Development. These two ministries allowed the SUPP to channel enough government projects to Sarawak Chinese businessmen and mitigate some of the more blatant discriminatory *Bumiputra* policies pursued by the UMNO-led federal government.

The different timing of the federal and state elections[4] also allowed the SUPP to differentiate the issues. Although the SUPP did not say it openly, their operatives gave the impression that federal elections were "less important" than state elections, given that most of the decisions affecting the lives of Sarawak Chinese were made in Kuching rather than Kuala Lumpur.

This has meant that voters were told that if they were unhappy with the *Bumiputra* policy, they should "protest" by voting for the opposition at the federal level since these policies were "federal policies", but they should support the SUPP during state elections given that the SUPP "has real power" at the state level. Many Chinese voters bought this argument that they could have it "both ways", that is, they could vote for the opposition at federal elections to voice their unhappiness over the New Economic Policy (NEP), while voting for the SUPP at the state level in order to ensure that Chinese interests were taken care of at this level.[5]

In the 2006 state elections, there was a sea change among the Chinese voters. They voted in six DAP candidates in Chinese-majority constituencies at the expense of the SUPP, which lost a total of eight seats. The SUPP, in essence, lost its claim to be the voice of the Sarawak Chinese. What caused the sea change?

In a nutshell, the Chinese voters were no longer convinced that the SUPP held "power" at the state level. Several issues demonstrated that the SUPP was increasingly becoming politically impotent, and that all powers lay in the hands of Taib Mahmud, the Melanau chief minister, and the PBB. The first issue involved land, always a sensitive issue in Sarawak. Many of the land owned by the Chinese are leased from the state for a period of between sixty and ninety-nine years. Many of these leases are located in major urban housing suburbs and a large number of the leases are due to expire by the year 2015. Despite repeated public calls by the SUPP for the state government to renew the leases, there was no clear announcement from the chief minister that it would be done. For many Chinese families, their house was the only piece of family heirloom they could pass to the next generation and the inability of SUPP to get the state government to renew the lease became the number one campaign issue. The DAP kept repeating the simple message that if the SUPP could not even get the state government to renew something as simple as a land lease, then the SUPP was powerless.

The second issue was the relationship between the SUPP and PBB. SUPP's president, George Chan, a medical doctor, was seen as unusually close to Taib. His daughter was married to Taib's son, Sulaiman,[6] and many questioned if he was truly able to stand up to Taib if the need should arise. The answer appeared to be no. In July 2004, Taib removed Chan as state Finance and Public Utilities minister, and instead appointed him state Industrial Development minister and Agriculture Modernisation minister. These ministries were widely seen as less powerful than the Finance and Public Utilities Ministry. To add insult to injury, Taib appointed himself minister for Finance in addition to being the minister for Resource Planning, which controls timber licences.[7]

The SUPP was further marginalized politically when a year later, in 2005, it was allocated only two out of nine newly created state seats. The PBB, on the other hand, was allocated five. What was really politically damaging was that only one of the nine new seats, Pujut, was carved out of George Chan's own state seat of Miri. No new seats were created either in Chinese-majority Sibu or Kuching. Thus the Chinese community only gained one new Chinese-majority seat in the delineation exercise. Many blamed the SUPP and its president Chan, claiming that he did not fight hard enough for more Chinese-majority seats.[8]

A related issue was the long reign of Taib, leading to allegations of extensive corruption and dynastic politics. Taib became chief minister in 1981 (the same year Mahathir became prime minister) and is still in power after more than a quarter of a century. Mahathir's voluntary retirement in 2004 made Taib look bad politically. There were serious allegations of corruption as the family-controlled conglomerate Cahaya Mata Sarawak (CMS)[9] was seen to be given an unusually large portion of the state government's contracts.[10] Taib's brother was an elected assemblyman and rumours were that he was preparing his son to succeed him.[11]

Taken as a whole, the marginalization of the SUPP, corruption allegations against the long-serving Taib Mahmud, and the land lease issue, the Chinese community saw no reason to support the SUPP. The opposition DAP, on the other hand, was able to capitalize on the issues above and told the receptive Chinese voters that it was better to be represented by the DAP rather than a powerless SUPP. The DAP was also able to capitalize on the fact that most of its new candidates were young, "good looking", and professional.[12] In contrast, many of the SUPP candidates were incumbents who had already served several terms.

Thus, it was clear to the ordinary voter that the SUPP's powerbase among the Chinese community was severely clipped by the PBB through constituency delineation and seat distribution within the Sarawak BN. Table 6.1 clearly shows that although the number of Chinese seats has gone

Table 6.1
Sarawak: State Constituencies by Main Voting Groups

	1969	1987	1991	2008
Dayaks/NMB	28	25	24	29
MMM	12	15	18	27
Chinese	8	8	11	12
Mixed	—	—	3	3
Total	48	48	56	71

Notes: NMB: Non Muslim *Bumiputra*
MMM: Malay/Melanau/Muslims
Mixed: Where no single ethnic group constitutes more than 50 per cent of the voters
Source: Author's own calculations, using data from newspaper reports and political parties.

Table 6.2
Sarawak: Changes in Voting Groups

	1969	%	2008	%	change
Dayaks/NMB	28	58.3	29	40.8	−18%
MMM	12	25.0	27	38.0	+13%
Chinese	8	16.7	12	16.9	0%
Mixed	—	—	3	4.2	+4%
Total	48		71		

Source: Author's own calculations.

up since 1969, the number of Malay/Melanau/Muslim seats has increased dramatically. In percentage terms, the Chinese seats still constitute around 17 per cent despite several delineation exercises. The clear loser is the Dayak community while the clear winner is the MMM community (see Table 6.2). Even if all the Chinese seats were won by a single party, the Chinese would not be in a position to form the state government.

THE SUPP SPLITS

The DAP victory in the 2006 election caused ruptures in the SUPP. For the first time, it could no longer legitimately claim to be the "voice" of the Sarawak Chinese since most of the Chinese urban constituencies were now in the hands of the DAP. The internal revolt against party president George Chan Hong Ham was led by two Foochow leaders from the Rejang basin, Law Hieng Dieng and Wong Soon Koh. Law had been unhappy with Chan ever since he was dumped by Chan as a federal minister after the 2004 parliamentary polls. Law claimed that Chan had promised him that he could continue for one more term as federal minister before retiring. Instead Chan nominated his close ally, Peter Chin Fah Kui, for the cabinet position.[13]

Wong, on the other hand, was unhappy that Chan was undermining his leadership of the Sibu SUPP. It was known that Dr Soon Choon Teck, an assemblyman from Sibu, had the support of Chan in his quest to form a new SUPP branch in Dudong, which is a suburb of Sibu town. Hitherto, the Sibu branch controlled all the sub-branches located in the Sibu region, including the Dudong sub-branch. If Dudong was allowed to be an independent branch, this would effectively cut Wong's influence since he could not control the central delegates from an independent Dudong branch.

Matters came to a head when Dr Soon announced that he had obtained the permission of the Registrar of Societies (ROS) to establish the Dudong branch. The application to ROS was signed by party president George Chan back in August 2007. Wong Soon Koh refused to recognize the branch and refused to transfer membership of Dudong sub-branch to the newly created Dudong branch. Without the transfer of membership, the new branch could not be established.

Both Law and Wong then publicly asked Chan to resign and take responsibility for the SUPP's 2006 losses. Law also accused Chan of playing anti-Foochow politics.[14] Since its founding, the SUPP has roughly been divided into three regions — south, central, and north. South refers to the SUPP branches around Kuching, central refers to the branches in the Foochow triangle (Bintagor-Sarikei-Sibu), and north refers to the Bintulu, Kapit and Miri branches. Wong and Law accused Chan and the Kuching SUPP leaders such as Sim Kheng Hui of playing "anti-Foochow" sentiments in order to stop Wong from taking over as party leader.

Generally speaking, there is a strong anti-Foochow sentiment among the Hakka, Hokkien, Teochew and Cantonese communities in Sarawak. This sentiment is mostly due to economic envy: the Sarawak Foochow form the richest segment of the Sarawak Chinese community and commercially the most successful. Their economic dominance has spread outside the Foochow Triangle and they own about half of the businesses in Kuching, while dominating the business community in all other areas of Sarawak. Almost all timber barons in Sarawak come from the Foochow community. In the post-war period up to the early 1970s, it was the Hokkien community that dominated businesses in Kuching, and the Cantonese were the majority in Miri.

To stop Law and Wong, Chan suddenly announced that he would retire at the next party congress to be held in late 2007. However, this did not happen as the party congress was postponed due to the March 2008 parliamentary election. Unlike in 2006, the SUPP was able to hold on to its parliamentary seats and the party lost only one seat, the Bandar Kuching constituency, to the DAP. However, this was tolerable given that Bandar Kuching was already held by the DAP since the 2004 election.

In late 2008, Wong suddenly broke with Law and announced that he would support Chan as president. Chan was duly re-elected party president for another three-year term in the party's congress in December 2008. In turn, Chan announced that he would not support Dr Soon and the establishment of an independent Dudong Branch, prompting Dr Soon to resign from his position as assistant publicity chief.[15] One possible reason Wong decided not to proceed to challenge Chan may be his inability to get support from Taib and the majority of the Central delegates. Taib, as mentioned, is related to Chan (Taib's son is married to Chan's daughter) and is known to be close to Chan.

The re-election of George Chan as party president and the re-election of many other senior party holders has meant that the SUPP is now widely seen as an old and tired party incapable of rejuvenating. This is in stark contrast to the Sarawak DAP led mostly by young professionals. The SUPP's inability to bring new leadership was not lost on its long-serving deputy president and Chan critic, Law Hieng Dieng, who said:

> Once, the leader of a party asked his most trusted adviser to draw up a rebranding plan for the party. The young adviser did not hesitate to give his boss this immediate reply, "Sir, how can you expect me to rebrand anything in the party when all of you, old and senile leaders, still refuse to step down and want to continue in your party positions"?[16]

With George Chan and Wong Soon Koh on the same side, Dr Soon felt betrayed and tried to organize a Special Delegates Conference (SDC) to force the party to recognize the establishment of the Dudong branch in late 2009. However, using the excuse that the ROS would not recognize the SDC, George Chan cancelled the SDC, thus prolonging the crisis. One of the key promoters of the Dudong branch, Wong Chin Yong, resigned from the SUPP in protest.

In a political environment where the opposition made historic gains in 2006 and where a black U.S. president elected, the catchphrase, "Change", does not appear to apply to the SUPP. It is almost certain that the DAP had made major gains at the expense of the SUPP in the next state elections due to the popular perception that SUPP is led by long-serving leaders who refused to step down. The split over the Dudong issue will help push voters to the opposition as well.

CONTEMPORARY SABAH CHINESE POLITICS

Chinese politics in Sabah in the past decade has been mostly about which Chinese party represented the community.[17] Unlike Sarawak, where essentially one party represented the community in government (SUPP) or in the opposition (Sarawak DAP), there are several parties all claiming to represent the Chinese. This situation came about for two reasons. First, when the Parti Bersatu Sabah (PBS) pulled out of the BN in 1990, the main Chinese

BN parties in the peninsula (MCA and Gerakan) made an entry into Sabah together with UMNO.[18] The defection of the PBS also caused some Chinese elements in the PBS to break away, the prime example being Yong Teck Lee's Sabah Progressive Party (SAPP). Yong broke away from the PBS just days prior to the 1994 Sabah state elections.

Second, the Sabah Chinese have always spread their support among various parties and regularly switch their support. For example, there was significant Chinese support for Berjaya during its administration from 1976 to 1985. When the PBS came into power in 1985, it was able to attract significant Chinese support as well as from many of Berjaya's Chinese supporters.[19] During the PBS's reign, several Sabah Chinese parties, such as Liberal Democratic Party (LDP), were established in addition to the opposition Sabah Democratic Action Party (DAP).

Hence in recent years, the Chinese had a wide choice of parties — the PBS, MCA, Gerakan, SAPP, LDP, DAP, and, more recently, the PKR — to support. However, it is generally acknowledged that the parties with significant Chinese support after the 2008 parliamentary elections were the PBS, SAPP, and LDP.

One important point that needs to be made is that Chinese politics in Sabah is not as ethnically delineated as that found in the peninsula or Sarawak. There is a sizeable number of Sino-Kadazans in Sabah and they enjoy full *Bumiputra* status. Thus it is not uncommon for candidates from the PBS to be Sino-Kadazans and be yet regarded as more or less "full" Chinese by the Chinese community.

Because of the large number of BN parties purportedly representing them, Chinese-majority seats are divided among them, making a dominant Chinese BN party impossible. For example, in the 2008 state elections, of the six Chinese-majority seats, SAPP was allocated four seats, LDP three, and MCA one. In Sarawak, the SUPP would have been allocated all the Chinese constituencies seats.

Like the Sarawak Chinese, the Chinese in Sabah have seen their political weight decline because of delineation in successive elections. In Sabah, this problem was compounded by a deliberate policy of "importing" Muslim voters from Indonesia and the Southern Philippines. Since the 1960s, the percentage of the Chinese population in Sabah has fallen, from about a quarter in 1960 to about 12 per cent now. This does not mean that the community is getting smaller. Rather, the fall is due mainly to the rapid rise, in the last three decades, of the Muslim *Bumiputra* community in Sabah through immigration from the Southern Philippines and Indonesia.

The proof that there is manipulation of Sabah's population is almost irrefutable. The discrepancies in the population increase between 1970 and 2000 in Sabah, Sarawak, and Malaysia are stark: 10,439,430 to 22,202,614 or up by 113 per cent in Malaysia; 976,269 to 2,012,616 or up by 106 per cent in Sarawak; and 636,431 to 2,449,389 or up by 285 per cent in Sabah. It is impossible for this growth to take place naturally. [20]

Since the retirement of Mahathir in 2003, more information has come to the public domain of the policy to increase the number of Muslim voters. The plan was apparently adopted during the Mahathir years (the project was called "Project M" or "Project IC") when Mahathir realized that the only way to control Sabah was to make it a Muslim-majority state.[21] One must remember that during Mahathir's early years as prime minister in the mid-1980s, he was confronted by the PBS and its strong Sabah nationalism. In 1990, the PBS withdrew from the BN during the midst of a general election and threw its support behind his archrival, Tengku Razaleigh. Although Mahathir won the election, he was politically shaken by the Sabah betrayal. Mahathir was widely quoted to have said that he was "stabbed in the back" by the PBS. To ensure that the PBS and the NMB could no longer threaten the BN, it was logical to make Sabah a Muslim-majority state. Many illegal Indonesian and Filipinos were issued Malaysian identity cards,[22] allowing them to vote. Information compiled by the PBS and some NGOs suggests that close to half a million identity cards were issued, giving the Muslim-*Bumiputra* (MB) community an absolute majority among the voting population.[23] Despite clear evidence that illegal migrants were issued identity cards, the federal government has consistently refused to establish a royal commission to look into this key issue.[24]

The net effect of these "instant" Malaysians has been a dramatic shift in electoral power among the three political groupings (see Table 6.3). In 1975, before "Project M", the Muslim-*Bumiputra* accounted for eighteen of forty-eight seats (37.5 per cent). In 2008, this community accounted for thirty-six seats or 60 per cent of state seats. This also means that if all the Muslim-*Bumiputra* in Sabah supported one party, that party could win outright. In three decades, the Muslims have managed to become an absolute majority in terms of electoral politics.

The Chinese, on the other hand, have seen their share of seats drop by about 7 per cent to only 10 per cent now. The non-Muslim *Bumiputra* group suffered the most as they saw their representation plunge from 45.8 per cent of states to a mere 21.6 per cent now. It is clear that "Project M" or "IC" was an unqualified success.

Table 6.3
Sabah: State Constituencies by Main Voting Groups

	1976	%	2008	%	Change
NMB	22	45.8	13	21.6	−24.2
MB	18	37.5	36	60	+22.5
Chinese	8	16.6	6	10	−6.6
Mixed	—		5	0.83	+0.83
Total	48	100	60	100	

Notes: NMB: Non Muslim *Bumiputra*
MB: Muslim *Bumiputra*
Mixed: Where no single ethnic group constitutes more than 50 per cent of the voters
Source: Author's own calculations using data from newspaper reports and political parties.

Two recent events in Sabah that will shape Sabah Chinese politics for some years to come are SAPP's self withdrawal from the BN, and the Mazu affair.

SAPP'S SABAH NATIONALISM

SAPP was established by Yong Teck Lee, a lawyer and founding member of the PBS. In 1994, when the PBS state government was in the opposition, he led his Chinese supporters out of the PBS after he fell out with PBS president Joseph Pairin Kitingan, and secured Mahathir's help in registering a new multiracial, but Chinese-based party, the Sabah Progressive Party (SAPP). When the PBS state government fell and the BN took over, he became a major beneficiary. He was selected by Mahathir to be Sabah's chief minister under the "rotation chief minister" system.[25] He was Sabah's chief minister from 1996 to 1998.

Under Yong, SAPP has cleverly positioned itself as a Sabah nationalist party. The party projects itself as fighting for the rights of Sabahans, especially the non-Muslim community. This ideology is not surprising given that the founding of the PBS, of which Yong was a founding member, was based on Sabah nationalism as well. At the simplest level, Sabah nationalism means Sabah for Sabahans. Sabah nationalists often refer to the "Twenty Points". Prior to the formation of the Malaysian Federation in 1963, Sabah (and Sarawak) extracted constitutional safeguards for the Borneo states. The main features of the safeguards, known the "Twenty Points", were:[26]

(a) Islam's status as a national religion was not applicable to Sarawak and Sabah;

(b) Immigration control was vested in the state governments of Sabah and Sarawak;

(c) Borneanization of the civil service and English could be used as the official language of both states;

(d) No amendments or modification of any specific safeguards granted under the Twenty Points can be made by the federal government without the agreement of the Sabah and Sarawak state governments;

(e) There would be no right to secede from the Federation.

Since then, parties espousing Sabah nationalism accused the federal government of not respecting these guarantees and have argued that the federal government has breached these guarantees by taking away much of the political autonomy. The PBS's rise in the mid-1980s was largely due to these sentiments.[27]

When the PBS rejoined the BN in 2004, the SAPP's position in the Sabah BN was severely affected. Previously SAPP and LDP were the local-based Chinese parties in the Sabah BN. With the PBS rejoining the coalition, it was clear that the PBS could upset the fine equation since it had significant Chinese support as well. Matters came to a head when seats were allocated for the 2008 general election. With the PBS in the Sabah BN, the SAPP suddenly found it was "boxed to a 2 by 4", that is, only allocated two state and four parliamentary seats with no possibility of getting additional seats.

Yong wanted additional seats, in part because he wished to make a comeback to active politics after he was disqualified.[28] He wanted to stand in the Kota Kinabalu or the Sandakan parliamentary constituencies, but was rebuffed by the BN leadership. Badawi offered him a senatorship instead of an appointed post.[29]

At first Yong kept quiet, but after UMNO and the BN's historic loss in the 2008 parliamentary elections, he saw his chance to break out of the "2 by 4" formula. Sensing that the Sabah BN would lose big in the next election, he convinced the party to support him when the SAPP demanded that UMNO give back political autonomy to Sabah in September 2008.[30] At first, there was widespread speculation that Yong and SAPP would quit the BN and defect to Anwar Ibrahim's Pakatan Rakyat. Anwar had earlier predicted that he would take over the federal government by September 2008 using BN defectors. However, this did not happen when Anwar was not able to get the BN MPs to defect in large enough numbers. SAPP instead decided to go "independent" although it was understood that it would support Anwar's takeover of the federal government.

By taking the SAPP independent, Yong is cleverly positioning the party for the next election. He will no longer be constrained by the BN seat allocation formula, and by remaining friendly with Anwar, he will be able to contest most of the Chinese and mixed seats. His only real competitor on the opposition side will be the Sabah DAP. However, the Sabah DAP has been weak since the late 1990s due to its inability to attract leaders of calibre and infighting.

MAZU AND DIVINE INTERVENTION

On 13 April 2007, Sabahans woke up to some unusual news. The state minister for Tourism, Culture and Environment, Chong Kah Kiat, had suddenly resigned from the state cabinet. This was no ordinary event. Malaysian ministers almost never resign from their posts. In this case, it was even more significant as Chong was a former chief minister (under the rotation system just like Yong was from 2001–03) and leader of the Liberal Democratic Party (LDP). What was even more unusual was that his resignation was quickly accepted by the chief minister, Musa Aman, who is also the Sabah UMNO chief.

Within a few days, rumours circulated that Chong resigned over the "Mazu" project. Mazu or goddess of the sea, is a major deity among the Malaysian Chinese community. In early 2005, Chong received "divine" instruction that he would lead the Kudat Moral Uplifting Society and the Kudat Thean Hou Charitable Foundation (KTHCF) in building a 88-foot high statue of the Mazu "for the good and prosperity of the people in Kudat".[31] Despite obtaining the necessary planning permission from the Kudat Town Board, the project was halted on the orders of Musa in 2007. When Chong confronted Musa, the latter allegedly accused Chong of sabotaging a major tourism project. He also said the statue could not be built as it was too close to a mosque and that there was a *fatwa* against the statue. Chong then approached the prime minister, Badawi, and his deputy, Najib. Musa, however, refused to reconsider his opposition and Chong decided to resign so that he could sue the state government.

Musa tried to defuse the situation by allocating another piece of land to the Hainan Federation of Sabah and Labuan for the construction of the sea goddess statue. However his actions merely confirmed that his initial opposition to the project was personal — if the initial project had not been initiated by Chong, he may not have objected to it.

Chong's actions will have major political repercussions. Many Sabah Chinese saw the refusal of the government to approve the Mazu statue as a sign of increasing religious intolerance and UMNO's arrogance towards the Chinese community. In addition, the federal government's (read UMNO's) opposition to the use of the word, *Allah*, by the Christian NMB communities in East Malaysia had added fuel to the feeling among the non-Muslim community in Sabah that there is growing Islamization and intolerance towards the non-Muslims in East Malaysia. For generations, the NMB and Chinese communities in Sabah (and Sarawak) have been using the word, *Allah*, in their religious service. However in the past decade, the federal government has tried to restrict the word to only the Muslim community, causing the indigenous Sidang Injil Borneo (SIB) church to sue the federal government for the confiscation of Bahasa Indonesia bibles which used the word, *Allah*. There is a significant number of Chinese adherents in the SIB.

Chong's actions will benefit the opposition in the next election as they can use this widely reported case and the *Allah* controversy to win support from the Chinese and non-Muslim community.

CONCLUSION

In general, the trend towards electorally marginalizing the Chinese community in Sarawak and Sabah appears to be unstoppable. In both states, the Chinese community lost their kingmaker roles, and the percentage of Chinese-majority seats has declined significantly in the past two decades in Sabah. There is enough anecdotal evidence to suggest that this is deliberately done in order to ensure that the Chinese community can never play the role of kingmaker, or play a significant role in the formation of any state government. It is also clear that the biggest beneficiary from the changes to the electoral boundaries is the Muslim community. In both states, it would be politically unpalatable not to include them in any government. The Muslims made the biggest gain in Sabah, followed by Sarawak.

In the coming years, the trend of an increasing number of Muslim constituencies will continue and the biggest losers in this political game will be the Chinese and the non-Muslim *Bumiputra* communities.

The key difference between recent Chinese politics in Sabah and Sarawak is that in Sarawak, the Chinese voter is presented with a relatively easy choice; support the SUPP if they are government supporters, and the Sarawak DAP if they support the opposition.

In Sabah, the situation is more fluid. Sabah Chinese can choose SAPP and LDP, in addition to the MCA and Gerakan, and we can expect the formation of new Chinese-based parties if Chinese voters reject these parties. The Chinese voters here are much more volatile than Sarawak Chinese voters.

In the coming decade, when UMNO makes its entry into Sarawak, it is almost certain the MCA and Gerakan will follow. It is likely then that Sarawak Chinese politics will change and may go the way of Chinese politics in Sabah, where the Chinese community is faced with multiple parties all seeking to represent them.

Notes

1   Under the Sarawak BN's seat allocation formula, seats won by the SUPP cannot be taken away. Thus, Dayak seats won by the SUPP in the 1960s and 1970s remain with the party despite the party losing Dayak support.

2   For the early history of the SUPP and DAP, see Chin Ung Ho, *Chinese Politics in Sarawak: A Study of the Sarawak United People's Party (SUPP)* (Kuala Lumpur: Oxford University Press, 1997).

3   Dayak is normally used to refer to all non-Muslim indigenous groups in Sarawak, such as the Ibans, Bidayuh, and the Orang Ulu.

4   Sarawak is the only state in Malaysia where the federal and state elections are held at different times. All other states hold both simultaneously.

5   James Chin, "The Sarawak Chinese Voters and Their Support for the Democratic Action Party (DAP)", *Southeast Asian Studies* 34, no. 2 (1996): 387–401.

6   Sulaiman is currently an MP.

7   "Political Maestro Taib Gets His Way with Biggest Cabinet", *Malaysiakini*, 3 July 2004.

8   "Taib Bolsters His Party, Chinese Ally Discontented", *Malaysiakini*, 14 February 2005.

9   Referred to by his critics as "Chief Minister of Sarawak".

10   The growth of CMS and Taib's business empire was the subject of a doctoral dissertation. See Andrew Aeria, "Politics, Business, the State and Development in Sarawak, 1970–2000", unpublished Ph.D. dissertation, LSE, 2002.

11   The rumours proved to be partly right when his son, Sulaiman, was elected in the 2008 parliamentary elections and he was immediately appointed federal deputy minister for Tourism. Many saw this as a prelude for his son to gain some federal experience before returning to state politics. However, in December 2009, he abruptly resigned as the deputy minister.

12   Personal communication by a Sarawak SAP leader. He also said that the national DAP adopted the same strategy with great success in the 2008 general election in urban areas in the peninsula and it was one of key reasons the DAP did well.

13   Personal letter from Law to Chan. A copy is with the author.

14   Law hits out at Chan again, *Borneo Post*, 6 March 2007.

15   Assistant minister quits party post, *Malaysiakini*, 24 January 2009.

16   "Law: Time for Supp oldies to ship out", *Malaysiakini*, 13 December 2008.

17 For surveys on Sabah Chinese politics in the immediate post-Independence period, see Edwin Lee, *The Towkays of Sabah: Chinese Leadership and Indigenous Challenge in the Last Phase of British Rule* (Singapore: Singapore University Press, 1976).

18 James Chin, "Going East: UMNO's Entry into Sabah Politics", *Asian Journal of Political Science* 7, no. 1 (June 1999): 20–40.

19 Since its founding, the PBS has always reserved one of its vice-president slots for its Chinese wing, signifying the importance of its Chinese supporters.

20 "Loopholes' behind IC scam", *Malaysiakini*, 6 October 2008.

21 "Illegals problem in Sabah like 'cancer'", *Malaysiakini*, 3 August 2006.

22 In Malaysia, holding an identity card signifies citizenship.

23 See "PBS to ACA: Here's the proof", *Daily Express*, 6 February 2008; Kamal Sadiq, "When States prefer Non-Citizens over Citizens: Conflict over Illegal Immigration into Malaysia", *International Studies Quarterly* 49 (2005): 101–22.

24 "Royal Commission of Inquiry on Illegal Immigrants does not Guarantee Solution, says Musa", *Bernama*, 28 May 2008.

25 A promise made by Mahathir when the BN was trying to win Sabah was that the Sabah chief minister's post will be given on a two-year rotation among the three major political groupings: the MB, NMB, and the Chinese. The system was abandoned in the early 2000s when it was clear that Sabah UMNO was capable of winning almost half the state's seats.

26 Government of Malaya, "Malaysia Report of the Inter-governmental Committee", 1962 (Kuala Lumpur: Government Printer, 1963).

27 Francis Loh Kok Wah, "Modernisation, Cultural Revival and Counter-hegemony: The Kadazans of Sabah in the 1980s", in *Fragmented Vision: Culture and Politics in Contemporary Malaysia*, edited by Joel Kahn and Francis Loh Kok Wah (Sydney: Asian Studies Association of Australia in association with Allen & Unwin, 1992), pp. 225–53, and Audrey Kahin, "Crisis on the Periphery: The Rift Between Kuala Lumpur and Sabah", *Pacific Affairs* 65, no. 1 (Spring 1992): 41.

28 "Cracks in the BN Unity Widening in Sabah, Sarawak", *Daily Express*, 13 May 2008.

29 In Malaysia, senior politicians are regularly appointed to the Senate as a consolation when they are defeated electorally, or forced to retire.

30 See SAPP full statement, "The BN Has Lost is BN Spirit", issued on 16 September 2008.

31 Chong on why he quit the Sabah cabinet, *Malaysiakini*, 15 January 2009.

References

Aeria, Andrew. "Politics, Business, the State and Development in Sarawak, 1970–2000". Unpublished Ph.D. dissertation. London School of Economics, 2002.

Bernama. "Royal Commission of Inquiry on Illegal Immigrants does not Guarantee Solution, says Musa". *Bernama*, 28 May 2008.

Borneo Post. "Law hits out at Chan Again". *Borneo Post*, 6 March 2007.

Chin, James. "The Sarawak Chinese Voters and Their support for the Democratic Action Party" (DAP). *Southeast Asian Studies* 34, no. 2 (1996): 387–401.

———. "Going East: UMNO's Entry into Sabah Politics". *Asian Journal of Political Science* 7, no. 1 (June 1999): 20–40.

Chin Ung Ho. *Chinese Politics in Sarawak: A Study of the Sarawak United People's Party.* Kuala Lumpur: Oxford University Press, 1997.

Daily Express. "PBS to ACA: Here's the Proof". *Daily Express*, 6 February 2008.

———. "Cracks in BN unity widening in Sabah, Sarawak". *Daily Express*, 13 May 2008.

Government of Malaya. *Malaysia Report of the Inter-governmental Committee, 1962.* Kuala Lumpur: Government Printer, 1963.

Kahin, Audrey. "Crisis on the Periphery: The Rift Between Kuala Lumpur and Sabah". *Pacific Affairs* 65, no. 1 (Spring 1992): 41.

Lee, Edwin. *The Towkays of Sabah: Chinese Leadership and Indigenous Challenge in the Last Phase of British Rule.* Singapore: Singapore University Press, 1976.

Loh Kok Wah. "Modernisation, Cultural Revival and Counter-hegemony: The Kadazans of Sabah in the 1980s". In *Fragmented Vision: Culture and Politics in Contemporary Malaysia*, edited by Joel Kahn and Loh Kok Wah. Sydney: Asian Studies Association of Australia in association with Allen & Unwin, 1992.

Malaysiakini. "Political Maestro Taib Gets His Way with Biggest Cabinet". *Malaysiakini*, 3 July 2004.

———. "Taib Bolsters His Party, Chinese Ally Discontented". *Malaysiakini*, 14 February 2005.

———. "Illegals Problem in Sabah like 'Cancer'". *Malaysiakini*, 3 August 2006.

———. "Loopholes' Behind IC Scam". *Malaysiakini*, 6 October 2008.

———. "Law: Time for Supp Oldies to Ship Out". *Malaysiakini*, 13 December 2008.

———. "Chong on Why He Quit the Sabah Cabinet". *Malaysiakini*, 15 January 2009.

———. "Assistant Minister Quits Party Post". *Malaysiakini*, 24 January 2009.

SAAP. "The BN Has Lost its BN Spirit". 16 September 2008.

Sadiq, Kamal. "When States prefer Non-Citizens over Citizens: Conflict over Illegal Immigration into Malaysia". *International Studies Quarterly* 49 (2005): 101–22.

7

THE NEW MALAYSIAN ECONOMIC AGENDA: SOME PRELIMINARY OBSERVATIONS

Toh Kin Woon

INTRODUCTION

This chapter attempts to compare and contrast the much vaunted New Economic Policy (NEP) and its later variants, *viz.* the National Development Policy (NDP) and the National Vision Policy (NVP) with the New Economic Agenda (NEA) propounded by Anwar Ibrahim, the former deputy prime minister of Malaysia and *de facto* leader of Parti Keadilan Rakyat (PKR) (Peoples' Justice Party in English). This is, however, not an easy task. While much research and writing have been done on the NEP, the same cannot be said about the NEA, which is still very much at an early stage of conceptualization. Its detailed contents await further strengthening and fine-tuning. Be that as it may, the broad objectives and the underlying spirit and underpinnings of these two policies can be compared and contrasted. No one is sure as to whether the NEA will see the light of day, and if so, when. Should it be implemented sometime in the future, it will be done in a specific social formation that has its contradictions, competing interests, values, and institutions. Some of these may pose severe constraints and challenges to the successful realization of Anwar's, and by extension, PKR's new economic agenda.

STRUCTURE OF THE CHAPTER

In line with the above stated objectives, the structure of this chapter will be as follows:

(i) First, we will describe briefly the rationale behind the NEP; its tools of implementation; and the social contradictions that this policy has engendered.[1]

(ii) This provides the context for the contestation against the NEP via the articulation of the NEA. The differences between these two policies will be looked at.

(iii) The constraints inhibiting the successful implementation of the NEA and the social contradictions that it may potentially engender will then be discussed.

THE NEW ECONOMIC POLICY — ITS OBJECTIVES AND TOOLS OF IMPLEMENTATION

The NEP has been implemented for close to four decades now. It was first launched in 1971, with the overriding objective of bringing unity to a nation that was badly shaken by a major racial conflict that occurred two years before its launch. This was to be achieved through:

(i) reducing and eventually eradicating poverty among all Malaysians, irrespective of race; and

(ii) accelerating the process of restructuring Malaysian society to correct economic imbalances so as to reduce and eventually eliminate the identification of economic function with race.[2]

POVERTY ERADICATION

The first objective entails eradicating absolute poverty through the provision of income generating assets and enhancing the returns of these assets to identified poor groups. These assets include land, capital equipment, skills, and knowledge. The distribution of these assets to poor groups has been done through land resettlement schemes; the subsidized provision of productive means of production; the expansion of education opportunities at all levels, and skills training and retraining. In part, because of the ideological orientation of the state elite that promulgated the NEP, the focus of poverty eradication has always been on the raising of the productivity and income levels of the poor, without stressing the closing of the gap between the rich and poor. Distributive justice among the classes has not been given the attention due. However, there is a fair amount of attention paid to reducing the income disparity between the different races. This perhaps is in line with the race-based approach of the dominant UMNO elite in the governing stratum.

THE RESTRUCTURING OF MALAYSIAN SOCIETY

The second prong is by far the more controversial of the two prongs of the NEP. It aims to restructure society with a view towards removing a colonial legacy in which economic functions were identified with race. Besides restructuring employment, or, more specifically, enhancing greater *Bumiputra* participation in the employment structure of the more modern and productive sectors of the economy, this prong entails nurturing a Bumiputra Commercial and Industrial Community (BCIC). The measures adopted centre on a greater role for the state, a departure from the earlier, relatively more *laissez faire* stance of the state.[3] Legislation, such as the Petroleum Development Act (1974) and the Industrial Coordination Act (1975), the proliferation of state enterprises for the purpose of acquiring assets and wealth on behalf of the *Bumiputra*, and the use of quotas for admission to and employment in universities, were some of the measures used to achieve the restructuring objective. This enhanced role for the state was later complemented by large-scale privatization during the tenure of Prime Minister Dr Mahathir Mohamad. During this phase, largely from the 1980s to now, several state-owned enterprises were sold to a select group of cronies. Contracts for many mega infrastructural projects were given to them. This group comprises mainly, but not exclusively, *Bumiputra*.

SOCIAL CONSEQUENCES OF THE NEP

From the above brief description, we can conclude that the NEP is largely a race-based framework that has guided development in Malaysia over the past almost forty years. Its impact on the social fabric of the country has been immense, engendering in the process much class, ethnic and regional contradictions.

ACHIEVEMENTS

There have also been several positive outcomes of this massive social engineering project though. Absolute poverty has been brought down considerably over the period the NEP was implemented. The incidence of poverty has declined from 49.3 per cent in 1970 to 5.7 per cent in 2004.[4] Relative poverty, as measured by the Gini coefficient has, however, increased. Income inequality, especially intra-Malay inequality, has become worse, leading to a more socially unjust society, although the inter-ethnic income gap has closed somewhat. This growing inequality has been partly due to the system and partly policy induced. There have been many changes to the social structure of society as well. To be sure, a huge middle class across all ethnic groups has been nurtured. Specifically for the *Bumiputra*, there was a significant increase in the class of professionals across almost all high-income earning fields. The NEP's contribution towards enhancing the life chances of many *Bumiputra* through affirmative action in education cannot be denied.

CRONYISM

At the same time, a small class of rentiers, sometimes referred to as cronies, has been nurtured through state sponsorship under the guise of the NEP. Closed tenders in the award of contracts for mega infrastructural projects, alongside preferential treatment in government procurements, have been used to help nurture this small class of largely, but not exclusively, *Bumiputra* cronies. This stance of the state has no doubt sent the wrong signals to the market, leading to distorting effects such as an inefficient allocation of resources, waste, and declining competitiveness.

A CLASS-BIASED NEP

Since the launch of the NEP, the practice has been to apportion at least 30 per cent of corporate equity to the *Bumiputra* through both preferential allotment to individuals and state owned enterprises. The objective is to bring the share of equity ownership in public listed companies owned by the *Bumiputra* to at least 30 per cent. Whether this target has been achieved by now has always been a subject of contention. Independent analysts claim that the share owned by the *Bumiputra* has more than exceeded the official target, while official statistics claim the contrary.[5] Interestingly, when the official claim was challenged, the debate that ensued for a while became very heated. This shows the class orientation of the debate being skewed towards the interests of the upper strata of society.[6]

A CONFIDENT MIDDLE CLASS AND
THE LAUNCH OF *REFORMASI*

Meanwhile, the burgeoning middle class of *Bumiputra*, many of whom are well educated professionals living in the urban areas, has become increasingly confident and independent in terms of their political affiliation and support for the largely Malay-based parties. Although many still support UMNO, a significant number of them are now backing Parti Islam, which is more popularly known by its acronym, PAS, and the Peoples' Justice Party or PKR. Politically, the Malay society, like the Chinese society since a long time ago, has now become more fragmented. This split in the electoral support of the Malays became more pronounced after the sacking of Anwar Ibrahim, the then deputy prime minister, from the government and UMNO, and the subsequent launch of a massive *Reformasi* movement in 1998, a year after the Asian financial crisis hit the country. Following the Indonesian experience, this movement was inspired by the desire to combat corruption, cronyism, and nepotism. By the time of the economic and political crisis in 1997–98, these ills have engulfed the nation to a very serious degree, leading to considerable wastage and incompetence. As a result, support for UMNO generally, and even among the Malay polity, especially its middle and urban working classes, had been considerably eroded by the time of the last general election.

INCREASING ARROGANCE OF THE
BARISAN NASIONAL

Meanwhile, the ruling elite's continued hold on to political power, uninterrupted since the country's achievement of Independence by the ruling National Front (Barisan Nasional or BN in short) has made them increasingly arrogant and insensitive to the needs of the lower strata of society and minority groups, both in the peninsula and the two eastern states of Sabah and Sarawak. UMNO's dominance and hegemony within the BN was also reflected in the perceived lack of parity in power relations between UMNO and the other component parties such as the MCA, MIC, and Gerakan. The failure of the leaders of the latter to stand up against this political hegemony of the former has further exacerbated this negative image of the ruling BN coalition.

REVOLT AGAINST STATE ELITE

Frustrated by this insensitivity, and angry over the increasingly arrogant attitude of the ruling elite, marginalized groups, human rights' organizations and the lower strata of Malaysian society took to peaceful demonstrations and pickets to press the state to fulfil their basic demands for greater social justice, more equality in the distribution of wealth and economic opportunities, a cleaner and more just electoral system, and fairer treatment of the different religious faiths. Among these groups were the trade unions, which have become increasingly more vocal in their demand for a minimum wage. Another group is Bersih, a broad coalition of social activists from political parties and NGOs, which gathered tens of thousands of people to demand for a cleaner, more open, and just electoral system. Yet another group is Hindraf or the Hindu Rights Action Front, which successfully mobilized tens of thousands of followers in a peaceful march in Kuala Lumpur in November 2007, in an effort to impress upon the state the plight of the minority Indian community and the urgent need to redress this community's economic, educational, housing, and religious problems. Instead of looking into their plight, the state responded by detaining five Hindraf leaders under the notorious Internal Security Act (ISA).

REGIONAL CONTRADICTIONS

Besides class and ethnic contradictions, relations between the ruling elite at the federal level and the two East Malaysian states of Sabah and Sarawak have become increasingly strained, especially in the former. This enhanced contradiction became more obvious after the recently concluded general elections. Using the strong support for the BN from the electorate of Sabah as a basis, some leaders of component parties within the state BN expressed their disappointment over the failure of the federal government to give Sabah its due of the share of political appointments, revenue from the extraction of natural resources such as oil, and to address the illegal immigrant problem. The strain in relations was raised a notch recently when one of the component parties of the BN, the Sabah Progressive Party (SAPP) made a decision to either move or support a motion of no confidence against the prime minister in the Lower House of Parliament in its June/July sitting. This move, and the threat to cross over to the opposition — posed by some MPs from the BN in Sabah under the legitimate claim of wanting a higher share of revenue from oil extraction, a resolution to the illegal immigrant issue, and greater attention to the socio-economic development of poor

Sabahans — have raised anxiety among the ruling elite in the federal government in Kuala Lumpur.

THE LAUNCH OF THE
NEW ECONOMIC AGENDA (NEA)

After nearly four decades of implementing the NEP and its later variants, the NDP and NVP, the country seems mired in a whole host of tensions between the state and various groups of stakeholders. Governance of the country is also increasingly seen to be lacking in transparency and accountability. Although the NEP cannot be entirely blamed for this, its continued existence has been called into question. This is because the nurturing of cronies has often been done in the name of the restructuring prong of the NEP. People generally have also grown tired of its race-based policy framework. At the risk of gross oversimplification, the Chinese and Indians have generally felt unhappy over the race-based affirmative action of this policy. While the Malays have been perceived to be the main beneficiaries, the distribution of such benefits within this community is very uneven, and has been skewed largely in favour of the upper stratum, which has greater access to the key resource of political influence. For a long time, the NEP has directly or indirectly been used by UMNO to garner political support through taking an ethnic appeal. The party often calls on the Malays to unite under its banner to protect, consolidate, and further strengthen Malay Supremacy, best summed up by its Malay slogan, *Ketuanan Melayu*. For all its positive contributions, such as the reduction in the incidence of absolute poverty and the expansion of a Malay middle class, the NEP has also come to be identified with abuses, leading to the emergence of cronyism and nepotism. Increasingly, it is seen to be an instrument of the state to protect and expand the interests of a small class of rentiers and cronies allied closely with the holders of political power. It was in this context that Pakatan Rakyat (PR), in particular, its *de facto* leader, Anwar Ibrahim, put forward the New Economic Agenda.

NEA TENETS

It is difficult at the present juncture to describe the contents of the NEA, as it is still, I believe, at the stage of conceptualization. Its detailed policy proposals will, I am sure, be drawn up in due course. However, some glimpses into what will be in store for Malaysians may be made from some statements made by Anwar himself, the general election manifesto of the Parti Keadilan Rakyat (Peoples' Justice Party), and some policy pronouncements made and actions taken by the Pakatan Rakyat government in some of the states under their control in the first 100 days of their coming to power. So what are the major principles of the NEA?

Free Enterprise System

(i) For a start, Anwar has stressed that the country under the PR government will continue to adopt the free enterprise system.[7] Resource allocation will be based on the free operation of market forces. Market distortions caused by abuses, corruption, lack of transparency and accountability will be removed by opening tenders and granting awards based on efficiency and competence. The efficient operation of the market will be augmented through the practice of good governance. This will at once reduce transaction costs while enhancing improvements in service delivery.

Needs-Based Affirmative Action

(ii) Where there are market failures, as there are bound to be, the state will intervene to correct them. But such intervention will be largely needs-based, and not race-based. In a move towards achieving greater social justice, greater attention will be paid towards improving the economic livelihood of the disadvantaged groups, from all races and the Orang Asli.[8] Anwar also hinted at continuing with state support and subsidies for the provision of merit goods for the poor, such as fuel, health care, education, housing, and public transportation. Affirmative action will still be continued in order to level the playing field of competition. However, a radical departure from the current practice is that it will not be race-based, but needs-based.

Attracting FDIs – An Independent Judiciary System

(iii) Measures will be taken to ensure an expansion of productive capacity through inducing a greater inflow of foreign direct investments (FDIs) as well as promoting more domestic investments, especially by small and medium enterprises. To regain its status as one of the choice destinations for FDIs, the rule of law and a transparent regulatory framework will be stressed. This calls for an independent judiciary — one of the top priorities of the NEA — which will be further reinforced by the creation of a pro-business environment. It is hoped that there will be fair and impartial hearings in the enforcement of contracts, deemed so essential in attracting FDIs.

Sound Conservation and Good Labour Practices

(iv) The regulatory framework that will be put in place will promote sustainable development that encompasses sound conservation and good labour practices. Discussions will be carried out with both the international and local business communities to seek their inputs for drawing up this framework.

THE NEW ECONOMIC AGENDA VERSUS THE NEP
Similarities

From the brief presentation of the broad principles of the New Economic Agenda as articulated by Anwar, it does not seem that this new agenda is very much different in ideological terms from the NEP. Both use the free enterprise system as its underlying economic structure. Both have great faith in the efficient operation of markets. They likewise recognize that markets do fail and that the state does need to intervene in order to correct these failures. Indeed, the promulgation and subsequent implementation of the NEP was precisely premised on the belief that, unless the state intervenes through affirmative action, the *laissez faire* system that was practised in the first twelve years or so after the country's Independence would, if continued, systematically alienate the poor, the bulk of whom were Malays. An educational system that is based on merit would also work against the disadvantaged, again referring largely to the Malays, who would then be denied educational opportunities deemed so crucial for enhancing their life chances. Likewise, business opportunities will also be grabbed mainly by the more established Chinese businessmen as the playing field is not level, but tilted against the financially weak, in a free market system. While the basic ideological belief are the same, there are, however, several points of departure.

Differences

(i) Ketuanan Rakyat and not Ketuanan Melayu

The first is in the groups targeted for help under affirmative action. Although yet to be seen, the New Economic Agenda aims to help the poor, disadvantaged, and marginalized, irrespective of race. It will be needs-based and not race-based. It gives recognition to the fact that the poor, marginalized, and disadvantaged may comprise largely, but not exclusively, the *Bumiputra*, including those from Sabah and Sarawak. Hence, affirmative action must be inclusive and not exclusive. This way, there will be no feelings of alienation and deprivation, the way some minority groups are now feeling. This helps to promote national unity. *Ketuanan Melayu* (Malay Supremacy) will be replaced by *Ketuanan Rakyat* (People's Supremacy).

(ii) No to Cronyism

At the same time, the agenda will not allow the hijacking of state power by large corporate interests and the politically well connected for the promotion and enlargement of their businesses and commercial interests through getting lucrative contracts for mega infrastructural projects and government procurement. Cronyism and nepotism, which very much characterized the implementation of the last two decades of the NEP, will, in other words, be eschewed. This will help close the gap between the upper and lower strata of society, in particular, the *Bumiputra* community.

(iii) Greater Transparency

Another difference is that the state under the New Economic Agenda has promised to combat corruption and promote a more open and transparent government through a system of open tenders and awards. Transaction costs will be reduced while efficiency enhanced and waste educed at the same time. This will improve the country's competitiveness, which is important in an increasingly competitive global environment.

(iv) Developing Human Capital

There is also the likelihood that the New Economic Agenda, in line with its stress on efficiency, competence, and merit, will make serious attempts at producing high quality human capital. This will mean that the standard of the country's educational system will have to be raised. University standards, in particular, must be elevated to at least regional, if not, world standards. For this, the race-based quota system of admission and staff recruitment, as well as promotion, will have to be reviewed. In its place, a system that places more emphasis on meritocracy may be put in place, although a quota system of admission, based on socio-economic status, may be considered. This will ensure that the poor and marginalized will not be denied opportunities for higher education and hence be trapped in the vicious circle of poverty.

RESPONSE TO THE NEW ECONOMIC AGENDA
Abdullah's Failed Promises

The New Economic Agenda poses a challenge to the NEP, seen increasingly as having departed from its original spirit of lifting the socio-economic status of the *Bumiputra*, especially the poor among them. While there have been some positive achievements, the NEP has now come to be identified more with state elite using state power to nurture cronies. This has brought about much abuse, waste, and loss of efficiency. As a result, it is increasingly being questioned and challenged. The campaign against the abuses actually started in 1997–98, with the launch of the *Reformasi* movement. This was, however, stalled by the promise made by the former prime minister, Abdullah Ahmad Badawi, to execute many of these reforms, shortly after coming to office in November 2003. Hopes of genuine reforms were raised. Five years down the road, however, not only was the record of Abdullah Ahmad Badawi in 2008 one of broken promises, but also of the continuation of the excesses.[9]

Anwar's Consistent Campaign

It now waits to be seen how the charismatic Anwar will lead the charge with his New Economic Agenda. Initially, there was the understandable fear that while the new agenda will be welcomed by the non-*Bumiputra*, the *Bumiputra* may feel threatened and react negatively to it. Unperturbed, Anwar went into the campaign against the abuses of the NEP with passion and gusto. He not only spoke to the non-*Bumiputra*, but to the *Bumiputra* as well. This was an impressive display of political consistency that at once showed his disgust with the excesses of the present policy regime, and his commitment to the new agenda. In the event, Anwar's political and economic pronouncements won him considerable support among the non-*Bumiputra*.

Reaction of the *Bumiputra*

Although it is too early to tell, the *Bumiputra*, at the same time, did not seem to feel insecure and threatened by the proposed abolishment of the NEP and its replacement by the New Economic Agenda. There is preliminary evidence of this in the results of the 2008 general election. I have to add quickly, however, that this is not definitive as electoral outcomes are influenced by a whole host of factors and linking the generally much improved performance of the Pakatan Rakyat to the promise of abolishing the NEP may be premature. Be that as it may, I would still assert that it did not cause the PR any electoral harm either. In the 2008 general election, Pakatan Rakyat gained considerable support in what is called the "middle ground" or mixed constituencies, long regarded as the traditional strongholds of the ruling BN. At the same time, it retained support in the Malay heartland state of Kelantan and even won power for the first time in Kedah, another Malay heartland state. The assertion by Anwar that the new agenda will protect and promote the interests of the poor and even the middle classes, which would include a significant number of *Bumiputra*, seems to have gone down well with people from across ethnic boundaries. Perhaps Anwar's charisma and his high credibility as a true Malay nationalist may have helped lend credence to his campaign for change.

HOW FEASIBLE IS THE NEW ECONOMIC AGENDA?

The promise of change in the New Economic Agenda is all very well. But how politically and administratively feasible is it? Some quarters argue that it may not be that easy for Anwar and his PR, upon coming to power, to abolish the NEP.[10]

(i) Deeply Entrenched Malay Identity

The Malay identity, expressed through the slogan of *Ketuanan Melayu* or Malay Supremacy, is deeply embedded in the psyche of a large majority of Malays. To them, therefore, special Malay rights and privileges, as articulated in Article 153 of the Federal Constitution, and subsequently promulgated in the policy framework of the NEP, are their entitlements to be granted in perpetuity. Moreover, there is this so-called social contract agreed upon by leaders representing the different ethnic groups at the time of Independence, whereby the Malays agreed to the granting of citizenship rights to the non-Malays in return for recognition of their special status as *Bumiputra* or sons of the soil. Because of this deep rooted Malay identity, a lot of effort will have to go into convincing them that the NEP is not, and should not, be seen as a permanent instrument for granting them special status in the economy, education, housing, scholarships, etc, but merely an affirmative action programme meant to uplift their socio-economic status. Once this has been achieved, it will have to be done away with, and in its place, a needs-

and merit-based policy framework, such as the New Economic Agenda, will have to be put in place.

(ii) Resistance from the Ultra Malay Nationalists

But such a switch in mindset will clearly not be easy and will take time, especially when there will still be considerable resistance from the old forces bent on continuously harping on the racial agenda. Moreover, it is still unclear whether the Malays are merely against the corruption and abuse of power, which may not necessarily be inherent in the NEP, and not against the NEP per se. To call for the direct abolition of the NEP may therefore be going against the wishes of a significant proportion of the Malay community. The Malays certainly support efforts to wipe out corruption, cronyism, and nepotism, but they may still want poverty eradication, especially the eradication of relative poverty, and even the restructuring of society.

(iii) Institutionalization of the NEP

Moreover, the removal of the NEP will require the revamping of many of the institutions, such as the civil service, the procurement processes, amending the Securities Commission's requirements pertaining to the listing requirements of public listed companies, the Central Bank's requirements on housing loans, and the doing away with other requisite supporting legislation.[11] This clearly is not an easy task.

(iv) Lack of Implementation Capacity

The New Economic Agenda will have to be implemented by bureaucrats. A huge pool of highly skilled and top quality knowledge workers and professionals will be needed to move the economy forward and up the value chain. These key human resources are, however, not likely to be available. Instead, what will be in place will be a mediocre public sector filled with personnel largely from local universities that have dropped precipitously in academic standards. The civil service is not likely to have the implementation capacity that Anwar and his PR government so badly need to realize the goals of the new agenda. The other institutions of the state, such as the universities, the police, and the judiciary are equally unlikely to have the kind of quality that he and his new government would badly need, should he be successful in coming to power one day. Mediocrity, a negative product of many years of the NEP that neglects meritocracy, has permeated almost all levels of public sector institutions.

FAVOURABLE FACTORS
Support for Reforms

Against these problems and constraints, there are a few factors that favour reforms contained in the NEA. There is immense support from the people for the *Reformasi* movement. People from across all ethnic groups want cronyism, nepotism, and corruption totally stamped out. They want a clean, transparent, and accountable government that is committed to social justice. Such popular support for Anwar's socio-economic and political programmes will act as a deterrent against the old conservative forces bent on frustrating the new agenda.

UMNO's Influence Weakening

Even the change in the Malay mindset that we referred to earlier is not impossible, although initially difficult. Here, let me give you an anecdote. Shortly after coming into office as the new chief minister, Lim Guan Eng, announced that the new state government in Penang will implement an open tender system to award contracts and will not be following the guidelines of the NEP. Soon afterwards, UMNO attempted to mobilize a large crowd to protest against this move, which was seen as threatening the status of the Malays in Penang. The prime minister called on the chief minister to stop playing with racial politics. The response to UMNO's call was, however, poor. The non-Malays went about their business unperturbed. A few days later, a large group of Malay-based NGOs called on the new chief minister to pledge their support for his efforts to set up a clean, accountable, transparent, and efficient government. Banners pledging support for the new chief minister were put up in some areas in George Town that have a heavy concentration of Malay residents. This anecdote tells us that the hegemonic hold of UMNO over the Malays is now loosening. The Malay society is now fragmented and the race card, though not completely without a following, is slowly losing its appeal. This is in contrast to the situation many years ago when a similar call to protest this perceived encroachment on Malay rights would have been answered with huge turnouts at numerous protest meetings. Malay confidence, especially among the middle class, has increased. With UMNO being increasingly discredited for the excesses and abuse of power under the veil of the NEP, its appeal has been eroded.

THE NEW ECONOMIC AGENDA IN PRACTICE – THE FIRST 100 DAYS OF PR RULE IN THE STATES OF SELANGOR, PENANG, AND PERAK

Some glimpses into what the New Economic Agenda may have in store for Malaysians may be obtained by looking at a few of the measures that some of the PR-controlled states implemented in their first 100 days in office.[12] It is true that one should not read too much into this as 100 days are rather too short for any meaningful evaluation. However, these measures, even if limited, do provide some indications of the things to come. Here are some of them.

Promise of Good Governance

All have pledged to practise good governance through practising the open tender system of giving awards. Under the counter payments for licences and contracts will be strictly prohibited. Representatives of several NGOs have been appointed to be members of local councils, with a view to encouraging greater public participation in the decision-making processes at the third tier of government.

Relief for the Poor

Several pro-poor measures have also been announced. These include giving a once off grant of 100 ringgit to the poor in Penang to tide them over their difficulties, following from the fuel price increase. In Selangor, the state government has announced that revenue from natural resources extraction will be put into a fund to help the poor and elderly. This is in addition to providing twenty cubic metres of free water to all residents living in the state. Appeals for discounts of land premiums will be entertained only from the poor, but not the rich. A special fund for the children of plantation workers would be set up to provide them with scholarships and the building and maintenance of dormitories.

Cutting Down on Wasteful Expenditures

Almost all the PR state governments have announced measures to cut down on unnecessary expenditures. These include cancelling the order for a new fleet of vehicles for the new chief ministers and state executive councillors, and holding official functions in government-owned buildings rather than hotels. Mega projects that are of doubtful benefit to the people, especially the poor, and possibly environmentally destructive, will be reviewed. A major case in point is the Penang Global City Centre project in Penang.

No Racial Discrimination

All the PR state governments have pledged that there will be no discrimination in policy formulation and implementation on the basis of race, creed, or religion. This was made particularly clear by the *menteri besar* of Perak, who is from the PAS. He said, "I want to tell the public that Pakatan Rakyat does not tolerate any discrimination based on race, creed and religion."[13]

CONCLUSION

The above analysis shows that after nearly four decades of implementing the NEP, race as a defining social category, which has its roots in the colonial economic structure, has been further reinforced. The overriding objective of the NEP was to attain national unity and build social cohesion by redressing the economic imbalance between the *Bumiputra* — largely the Malays — and the non-*Bumiputra*. Removing class disparity has, however, never been its objective. At its very crux is the contest between those who see the NEP as merely an affirmative action programme to help lift the socio-economic status of the *Bumiputra* — especially the poor — through state support, and those who see it as an ongoing enforcement of the unwritten social contract agreed upon among the various communities at the time of Independence. The first group sees the NEP as only a transient measure, to be ended on the attainment of its objectives, while the latter group interprets it as a right by virtue of its status. Herein lies the underlying challenge to the much desired social cohesion, which has always been frail. A mentality of "us (the in-group) versus them (out-group)" has been entrenched. Racism has been institutionalized. Beginning from the 1980s, the state elite began deviating from the original spirit of the NEP by nurturing on a large scale a small group of cronies, using state power at its command. Corruption, waste, and abuses have become increasingly rampant at the same time as society becomes increasingly unequal. While the non-*Bumiputra* have long felt left out, even the poor *Bumiputra* feel increasingly excluded from the benefits of the NEP. It was in this social context that the New Economic Agenda was introduced and the NEP challenged. The New Economic Agenda is still at its early stage of conceptualization; hence it is difficult to compare the two. But suffice to say that the race-based underpinnings of the NEP are now being increasingly challenged by the New Economic Agenda. Many from among the poor and middle classes in the *Bumiputra* community and the non-*Bumiputra* are disenchanted, frustrated, and disappointed with the use of race to serve the interests of the elite from all ethnic categories. They are equally disaffected by the lack of transparency and accountability in governance. The promise to practise good governance and to recognize talent has given fresh hope to the people at large. It remains to be seen whether Anwar and his PR government, should they come to power, will be able to deliver on this promise. To be sure, there will be constraints restricting the space within which they can operate. Resistance against the abolition of the NEP will still be there. One comes from the deep-seated entrenchment of the spirit of *Ketuanan Melayu* that will lead to some Malays vigilantly safeguarding their special status against any encroachment by the perceived economically superior non-Malays. The abolition of the NEP is a very complex process that entails the dismantling of a whole host of institutions, processes, and legislation. This may not be easy, given the institutionalization of the practices of the NEP. Even if the New Economic Agenda can be introduced, its realization may not be easy, given the mediocrity of the institutions of the state, such as the civil service and the universities. But if the first 100 days of the PR-ruled states are anything to go by, there are early indications of some commitment to the ideals of the agenda. It is safe to say that many Malaysians are desirous of changes away from racism that does not bode well for social cohesion and nation building. Many are cheering the opposition coalition on in the hope that the current democratic space will be widened and deepened, social justice built, merit and talent recognized and promoted, and a more open, transparent, accountable, and responsible government put in place. The New Economic Agenda presents some hope for these ideals. Whether or not they will be achieved remains to be seen, but its articulation has minimally empowered the public to engage in greater discourse on a policy framework that has, until recently, come to be regarded as almost sacrosanct.

Notes

[1] The NEP in this chapter refers to the NEP, as it was when first formulated and implemented over the period 1971–90 and its subsequent variants, the National Development Policy 1991–2000, and the National Vision Policy 2001–10. Despite their different names, the latter two policies have continued to follow the design and spirit of the original NEP.

2   Malaysia, Second Malaysia Plan 1971–1975 (Kuala Lumpur: Government Press, 1971), p. 1.
3   See Toh Kin Woon, "The State in Economic Development: A Case Study of Malaysia's New Economic Policy", Ph.D. thesis submitted to the University of Malaya, Kuala Lumpur, 1982.
4   Malaysia, Ninth Malaysia Plan 2006–2010 (Malay version) (Putrajaya: Economic Planning Unit, 2006), p. 349.
5   An independent estimation by Lim Teck Ghee showed that the share of equity ownership by the *Bumiputra* has well exceeded the official target of 30 per cent. The political implication is that the continued resort to the use of the NEP to favour share accumulation by the *Bumiputra* lacks credibility. This challenge posed by Lim against official claims on this issue won him considerable support from among leaders of several influential Chinese-based NGOs, some of which even put up advertisements in one or two Chinese dailies to lend him support.
6   In an article published in the *Aliran*, Khoo Kay Jin showed that share ownership, even in the more advanced industrial economies, is concentrated in the hands of only a very small percentage of society. A large proportion of shares are invariably owned by a very small group of rich elite and institutions. See Khoo Kay Jin, "Gimme! Gimme! Gimme! Greed was the Agenda of the Day", in *Aliran Monthly* 25, no. 7 (2005).
7   Anwar Ibrahim, "Malaysia's Defining Moment and the New Economic Agenda", Keynote Address at the CLSA Corporate Access Forum, Singapore, 20 May 2008.
8   Syed Husin Ali, "Looking at the Malay Problem", Speech delivered at the launch of his book, *The Malays: Their Problems and Future*, held on 14 June 2008 in Petaling Jaya. Syed Husin Ali is the deputy president of the PKR.
9   For an account of this, see Ooi Kee Beng, "Lost in Transition: Malaysia under Abdullah", Strategic Information and Research Development Centre, Petaling Jaya, and Institute of Southeast Asian Studies, Singapore, 2008.
10   Tricia Yeoh, "Can Anwar Replace the NEP?", *The Edge*, 3 April 2008.
11   Yeoh, ibid.
12   For an account of the achievements in the first 100 days of office of the PR-controlled state governments in Kedah, Penang, Perak, and Selangor, see *Malaysiakini*, 17 and 18 June 2008.
13   Interview with *Malaysiakini*, 18 June 2008.

References

Anwar Ibrahim. "Malaysia's Defining Moment and the New Economic Agenda". Keynote Address at the CLSA Corporate Access Forum, Singapore, 20 May 2008.

Government of Malaysia. Second Malaysia Plan 1971–1975. Kuala Lumpur: Government Press, 1971.

———. Ninth Malaysia Plan 2006–2010. Putrajaya: Economic Planning Unit, 2006.

Khoo Kay Jin. "Gimme! Gimme! Gimme! Greed was the Agenda of the Day". *Aliran Monthly* 25, no. 7 (2005).

Malaysiakini. 17 and 18 June 2008.

Ooi Kee Beng. "Lost in Transition: Malaysia under Abdullah". Strategic Information and Research Development Centre, Petaling Jaya, and Institute of Southeast Asian Studies, Singapore, 2008.

Syed Husin Ali. "Looking at the Malay Problem". Speech delivered at the launch of his book, *The Malays: Their Problems and Future*, held on 14 June 2008 in Petaling Jaya.

Toh Kin Woon. "The State in Economic Development: A Case Study of Malaysia's New Economic Policy". Ph.D. thesis submitted to the University of Malaya, Kuala Lumpur, 1982.

Yeoh, Tricia. "Can Anwar Replace the NEP?". *The Edge*, 3 April 2008.

8

THE OLD AND NEW MALAYSIAN CHINESE LANGUAGE PRESS, WITH SPECIAL REFERENCE TO THE 12TH GENERAL ELECTION

Khor Yoke Lim, Beh Chun Chee and Lim Lai Hoon

INTRODUCTION

As mentioned by several authors of this book, one of the factors that contributed to the unexpected opposition win during the 12th Malaysian general election was the role of the mass media (Weiss 2008; Welsh 2008). The new communication technology, through online news sites, sociopolitical blogs, and emails, is said to have played a significant role in disseminating plural and dissenting views in a highly controlled media environment. Although the new media made their beginning during the 1999 general election, their impact was most felt during the 2008 general election. Then Deputy Prime Minister Datuk Seri Najib Abdul Razak acknowledged that the new communication technology was "one of the factors that led [to] us having a worse than expected performance" (*New Straits Times*, 28 May 2008). In an election post-mortem, Welsh said that people were disillusioned with the usual biased reporting of the mainstream media, preferring instead to search the Internet for alternative views (*Malaysiakini*, 12 March 2008). This chapter will compare the news coverage of the 12th general election by both the Chinese mainstream and online press to show the inclusion and exclusion of certain groups and individuals, reflecting the power structures within which the media operate. To contextualize the study, the chapter will analyse the Malaysian Chinese newspapers taking into account increasing state control and media concentration as well as the emergence of online news websites in response to the repressive media situation and social demand for greater political openness.

DIRECT STATE INTERVENTION

After Independence, two events that have had major impacts on the contemporary structure of the mass media are the separation of Singapore from Malaysia, and the May 13 riots in 1969. In 1965, with the separation of Singapore from Malaysia, the Malaysian authorities decreed that all foreign publications had to obtain prior permission before being circulated in Malaysia. This cumbersome arrangement affected all the major newspapers that were based in Singapore, namely, the *Straits Times*, *Berita Harian*, *Nanyang Siang Pau*, *Sin Chew Jit Poh*, and *Shin Min Daily*. These papers had no choice but to set up new entities in Malaysia, a move which laid the groundwork for direct state control of the newspapers.

After the May 13 riots in 1969, a national emergency was declared and Constitution suspended. All administration power was in the hands of the National Operations Council, headed by Deputy Prime Minister Tun Abdul Razak. When parliament reconvened in February 1971, several laws were amended to "remove sensitive issues from the realm of public discussions so as to allow the smooth functioning of parliamentary democracy" (Means 1991, p. 14). Article 10 of the Constitution was amended to prohibit the questioning of issues pertaining to citizenship, the national language, Malay rights, and the sovereignty of the Malay rulers. This was followed by the amendment to the Sedition Act, which provided that any publication or speech would be considered seditious if it touched on the issues protected under Article 10 of the Constitution.

In line with the Sedition Act, the Printing Presses and Publications Act (PPPA) was also amended in 1971 to prevent the publication of materials that may harm public order. In 1974, the PPPA was further amended to forbid foreign ownership of any printing press and newspaper by non-citizens. The amendment provided the opportunity for the state to assume direct control of the newspapers through the acquisition of shares. This, in turn, enabled the state to place its nominees on the newspapers' board of directors and in top management positions. To comply with the PPPA local ownership requirements, several Singapore-registered Chinese newspapers, such as *Nanyang Siang Pau*, *Sin Chew Jit Poh*, and *Shin Min Daily*, were restructured. When *Nanyang Siang Pau*, the leading Chinese newspaper, offered 51 per cent of its shares to the public, 30 per cent were bought by the government investment company, PERNAS, making it the largest shareholder. Prior to that, Tengku Razaleigh, as UMNO treasurer, had formed a company called Fleet Holdings to acquire 80 per cent of the *Straits Times* in Malaysia from its Singapore owners (Gomez 1990). Pressure to acquire the newspaper company, renamed New Straits Times Press (NSTP), came from UMNO Youth due to the paper's "alleged pro-Singapore stance" (M.G.G. Pillai 1972). Apart from the English language daily, Fleet Holdings also owns the Malay daily, *Berita Harian*, and an English tabloid, the *Malay Mail*. Prior to this, UMNO had in 1961 acquired another Malay daily, *Utusan Melayu*, using the newspaper's workers strike to justify government intervention.

Taking the cue from UMNO, the MCA, through its investment company, Huaren, also acquired the English-language tabloid, *The Star*, in 1979 and the MIC acquired the *Tamil Nesan*. In 1981, Huaren Holdings acquired *Malayan Thung Bao* from the Chiew family. The acquisition of the paper, renamed *Tung Bao*, was a failure. Its circulation continued to decline, apparently because the new management made too many changes until the paper became "too directly identified with a political party" (*Asiaweek*, 4 November 1983).

MEDIA CONCENTRATION IN AN ERA OF PRIVATIZATION

The 1980s was a turbulent period for the Chinese press, which had to face increasingly repressive laws, economic recession as well as media corporatization. Seven days before Mahathir became prime minister in July 1981, he delivered a scathing speech against the press. The thrust of his criticism was that the press was too powerful an institution to be left in the hands of journalists who were selected not for "their ability to judge correctly and dispassionately" but for "their ability to write" (*New Straits Times*, 9 July 1981). He further argued in the same article, that the elected government had the right to control an irresponsible press to preserve democracy. Similar ideas were again reiterated during the World Press Convention in 1985. Mahathir argued that just as individuals had rights, as did society and "it is the task of the democratically elected government to decide on the balancing of the two rights" (*The Star*, 20 September 1985). Given Mahathir's distrust of the media, it is not surprising that the laws were further tightened to curb criticisms and dissent. The PPPA was further amended in 1984 to disallow an applicant, who was refused a printing licence, to appeal to the king. The law further allows the minister for Home Affairs and "senior authorized officers" to search premises without a warrant and arrest persons suspected of committing an offence.

In the midst of various scandals that occurred in the mid-1980s, the laws were again tightened. The Official Secrets Act (OSA) was amended to empower any official in charge to OSA certify any government document an official secret. The decision to classify a document as an official secret cannot be challenged in a court of law. The law also stipulates the one-year mandatory jail term for any person convicted. In spite of widespread protests from journalists, lawyers, civil rights movements, and the public, the bill was passed on 5 December 1986.

By mid-1980, Chinese newspapers were not only facing increasingly repressive laws but also financial difficulties due to the increasing cost of newsprints, lack of advertising, and declining readership. In addition, several newspapers were also burdened by their parent companies losses during the economic recession. There were at least eight Chinese dailies and several weeklies competing for the combined daily sales of about half a million copies. Several newspapers finally ceased operations or changed ownership during the economic recession. In July 1985, *Shin Min Daily*, owned by Tan Koon Swan, the former president of MCA, was acquired by *The New Straits Times* Group. This was followed by the *China Press*, which ceased operations in November 1985 when its sales dropped to only 10,000 copies. A rescue attempt organized by the Chinese educationist, Lim Fong Seng, failed to revive the company. Later, Life Publishers, the magazine arm of Nanyang Press, took over the newspaper and it hit the street again in May 1986. The third casualty was *Kin Kwok Daily*, a regional newspaper based in Ipoh. It closed down in July 1986 when the assets of its parent company, Koperasi Belia Bersatu (KOSATU), were frozen and it was considered insolvent. As pointed out by Harry Toh, managing director of *Nanyang Siang Pau*, "the main problem with the industry today is too many newspapers chasing after too small a source of revenue". He explained that the total advertising spent on the Chinese press was RM31 million, with 57 per cent going to *Nanyang Siang Pau*, 20 per cent to *Sin Chew Jit Poh*, and the rest to the other six Chinese newspapers (*The Star*, 29 October 1986).

In 1986, another Chinese newspaper, *Sin Pin Jih Pao* was placed on receivership as a result of debt accumulation by its parent company. The owner, Lim Kheng Kim, a Penang-based property developer had bought both *Sin Pin* and *Sin Chew Jit Poh* from the Aw Par Brothers in 1982.

Alarmed at the plight of Chinese newspapers, the Penang Chinese Town Hall spearheaded a "Defence of *Sin Pin Jih Pao* Action Committee" in an attempt to prevent the demise of yet another newspaper. It was eventually bought over by Kemayan Oil Palm in 1987 and renamed *Guang Ming Ribao*.

In 1987, Anwar Ibrahim, then minister for Education, announced the appointment of non-Mandarin-speaking teachers as headmasters in national-type Chinese schools. This move was vehemently opposed by the Chinese community as they see it as an attempt by the government to control and change the nature of Chinese schools. The future of Chinese-language schools is of primary concern to the Chinese community and there was therefore tremendous coverage of the issue in all the Chinese newspapers. The Chinese dailies carried more than 400 articles over the six weeks of controversy, compared with about fifty articles in the Malay-language newspapers (Khor and Ng 2006). While the Chinese newspapers framed the articles in terms of the survival of Chinese schools, the Malay newspapers defined it as a normal teacher promotion issue that had been politicized by the Chinese political parties. Moreover, the cooperation between the Chinese-based opposition (DAP) and the ruling political parties (MCA and Gerakan), incensed UMNO which perceived this act as challenging the government and the ruling coalition. Ethnic tension reached a critical stage when mass rallies were organized by both the Chinese coalition groups, as well as UMNO. In October 1987, the government reacted by launching "Operation Lallang" which led to the arrest of 119 people and the suspension of three newspapers, including *Sin Chew Jit Poh*. The five-month suspension took a severe financial toll on the newspaper. *Sin Chew Jit Poh* (renamed *Sin Chew Daily*) was eventually sold to Pemandangan Sinar, a subsidiary of Rimbunan Hijau, which is a Sarawak-based timber conglomerate owned by Tiong Hiew King. In 1992, Tiong was able to add to his stable of newspapers by buying over the loss-making *Guang Ming* from Kemayan Oil Palm.

By the 1990s, the relationship between Mahathir and the Chinese community had begun to improve. The latter was able to obtain greater business opportunities in Mahathir's liberal economic policy which focused on market expansion and corporatization, rather than direct government intervention (Lee 2004; Loh 2002). Trade with China and Taiwan expanded, with Mahathir himself leading several trade missions. In 1996, laws pertaining to higher education were amended to allow for the setting up of private colleges and universities and local campuses of foreign universities. This move was well received by the Chinese community as it would expand higher education opportunities to Chinese students who were denied places in public universities. More Chinese television channels were made available, beginning with setting up of the first private television station, TV3, in 1984, followed by ASTRO satellite television in 1996, and NTV7 two years later.

As observed by Lee (2004, p. 184), "It was this positive Chinese sentiment that Dr Mahathir drew upon to ride through the most turbulent challenge to his power during the period of 1998–1999 involving his conflict with Anwar Ibrahim who was expelled from UMNO in 1998." During the 1999 general election, UMNO faced serious challenges from the opposition coalition, Barisan Alternatif (Alternative Front), comprising the Democratic Action Party (DAP), Parti Islam SeMalaysia (PAS), and Anwar Ibrahim's *reformasi* (reform) movement that gave birth to Parti Keadilan Rakyat or KEADILAN. The Chinese demonstrated their support for Mahathir's policies by helping the BN to win thirty-five parliamentary seats during the 1999 general election. In fact, the Chinese votes were crucial for UMNO candidates in many keenly contested Malay consituencies (Ong 2004). Given this scenario where ethnic relations were probably never better, it was surprising when UMNO leaders (see *Utusan Malaysia*, 14 August 2000, front page headline, "Abolish Malay privileges") condemned the *Suqiu* (literally translated as "appeal") for purportedly questioning Malay rights and supremacy. As a backgrounder, on 16 August 1999, eleven Chinese organizations, led by the Kuala Lumpur and Selangor Chinese Assembly Hall (KLSCAH) and the United Chinese School Committees Association, and United Chinese School Teachers Association, Dongjiaozong, launched the 17-point election appeal or Suqiu, which among other things, urged all parties to promote national unity, democracy, a fair and equitable economic policy, liberal and progressive education policy, and to curb corruption. In view that *Suqiu* was endorsed by more than 2,000 Chinese organizations, the MCA and Gerakan also threw in their support. Mahathir and the Malay newspapers, condemned Suqiu as an election "blackmail" (*Berita Harian*, 21 September 1999). However because of the impending general elections, the Cabinet delayed discussion by requesting the MCA to study the issue further.

A year later, the *Utusan Malaysia* highlighted the issue based on an interview given by a *Suqiu* committee member to the *Far Eastern Economic Review* (20 August 2000). The newspaper's headline "Abolish Malay Privileges" triggered a train of reactions from various Malay-based groups and individuals. Mahathir, in his Merdeka speech, likened the *Suqiu* to communists and militant Al-Ma'unah extremists. He also singled out the Chinese media for inciting racial feelings. This was given front-page coverage in *Kwong Wah Jit Poh* (1 September 2000) in comparison to *Nanyang Siang*

Pau's tame report that the *Suqiu* committee would seek a meeting with the prime minister. While the Malay newspapers translated the term *Suqiu* as *tuntutan* (demand), the Chinese used it to mean appeals or aspirations. While the Chinese newspapers viewed Suqiu as a set of appeals for all races and political parties, the Malay newspapers represented it as a host of chauvinistic Chinese demands.

The Chinese community registered its protest against the government over the Suqiu issue during the Lunas by-election on 29 November 2000, which was won by Anwar's KEADILAN candidate. As noted by Chandra (2000), "Mahathir's callous comment on Aug 31 evoked so much anger within the Chinese community — anger which expressed itself through the ballot box in Lunas." Mahathir admitted that Cabinet initially accepted Suqiu to avoid losing Chinese support for the 1999 general election (*Sin Chew Daily*, 12 December 2000). Obviously unhappy with the by-election results, Mahathir again lashed out at the Suqiu saying that "special Malay rights will be maintained" (*Nanyang Siang Pau*, 12 December, 2000) as being "detrimental to national interests and stability (*Sin Chew Daily*, 16 December, 2000) and said "the government will take action against those who raise sensitive issues" (*Nanyang Siang Pau*, 24 December 2000).

Since the sacking of Anwar Ibrahim, pressure mounted on his ally, Quek Leng Chan, to give up his share of the Nanyang Press, which publishes *Nanyang Siang Pau* and *China Press*. Quek had bought a strategic stake in Nanyang Press in 1991. By May 2001, Quek's shares were taken up by Huaren Holdings Sdn. Bhd. The takeover was widely opposed by the Chinese community as well as factions within the MCA. Fourteen Chinese organizations, including the Chinese education associations, signed a "yellow ribbon" campaign against the MCA's acquisition, protesting that as a member of the ruling coalition, it "should not directly or indirectly intervene in media operations" (*The Sun*, 25 May 2001). The Chinese community sees this as yet another attempt by the government to control the Chinese press and was concerned that the newspapers may suffer the same fate as *Tung Bao* and *Shin Min Daily*, which stopped publication after being taken over by the ruling coalition. During the takeover period, the circulation of *Nanyang Siang Pau* dropped substantially, from 177,824 in 1999 to 90,033 in 2000 (Media Guide 2003).

The Huaren takeover of the Nanyang Press also exacerbated factionalism within the MCA. Ling Liong Sik, the party president, defended his decision as a strategic political investment (*Nanyang Siang Pau*, 18 June 2001) whilst his rivals, Lim Ah Lek, Chua Jui Ming, Chan Kong Choy, and Ong Tee Keat, capitalized on this unpopular decision to criticize him (*Kwong Wah*

Yit Poh, 4 and 5 June 2001). Several divisions within the MCA, such as the Selangor MCA Youth, MCA Perak, and MCA Pahang branches also opposed the purchase (*Nanyang Siang Pau*, 7, 11, 17, 18 June 2001). In respond to appeals from several Chinese organizations to stop the sale, the prime minister replied that he would not interfere in this matter, which essentially meant that he supported the MCA's decision to purchase the newspapers (*Kwong Wah Yit Pao*, 3 June 2001). Even before the sale was completed, nine top management staff of the two newspapers, including the editors-in chief, deputy editors-in-chief, and general manager, were told to leave their posts. In protest, forty columnists and writers announced that they would not contribute articles to the two newspapers (*The Sun*, 27 May 2001). The Chinese community protests were hardly given any coverage in the *Sin Chew Daily*. With the MCA takeover, Sarawak timber entrepreneur Tiong, who is close to Ling Liong Sik, managed to obtain a 1.17 per cent share of Nanyang Press.

In protest against the MCA takeover, a Chinese newspaper, *Oriental Daily News*, was set up by former journalists of *Nanyang Siang Pau* and *China Press*, and financially backed by Tiong's business rival, KTS Sdn. Bhd. The latter is a Sarawak-based timber concessionaire owned by the Lau Hui Kang family, which owns several Chinese dailies in Sarawak. It is apparent that from the outset there were pressures to prevent it from obtaining the permit to operate. The newspaper claimed that it received "advice" from those in power, particularly the Ministry of Home Affairs, to withdraw its application. After several appeals and two years later, *Oriental Daily News* received its permit on the 24 December 2002. It is speculated that Mahathir finally allowed KTS Sdn Bhd to establish a rival newspaper to check Tiong's increasing influence of the Chinese media (Gomez 2004).

Oriental Daily's rivals were not about to take things quietly. Their next strategy was to block the distribution of the newspaper by threatening news vendors that they had to select between selling *Oriental Daily* or the other four dailies. This threat, real or a posture, proved to be a severe stumbling block as until this day readers still have difficulty getting the newspaper, especially those outside Kuala Lumpur and Ipoh. The *Oriental Daily* positions itself as an independent newspaper, not linked to any of the political parties, providing in-depth and analytical news. Its news reports are carried in its website, translated into the English language *The Sun*, as well as in AEC, an ASTRO Chinese channel. These strategies as well as the demand for alternative media during these turbulent times have led to a commendable rise in its sales, increasing from 80,000 in 2006 to 101,000 copies in 2008 (Audit Bureau of Circulation 2008).

The MCA takeover of Nanyang Press soon proved to be a major financial burden to the party. The newspaper's circulation declined until it currently ranks lowest compared with the other Chinese dailies (except *Oriental Daily News*). In 2006, having suffered a RM6.3-million loss, the MCA decided to sell the newspapers to Ezywood Options Sdn. Bhd., an unknown company owned by Tiong's family (*Malaysiakini*, 17 October 2006). With this purchase, Tiong now controls all the four major Chinese dailies, comprising about 85 per cent of the Chinese newspaper market (Wong 2007).

Tiong also owns *Ming Pao* and *Yazhou Zhoukan* in Hong Kong, as well as other newspapers in Cambodia and Papua New Guinea. On 23 April 2007, the Hong Kong-listed Ming Pao Enterprise Corporation Limited was merged with the two Malaysia-listed Sin Chew Media Corporation Limited and Nanyang Press Holdings Berhad, creating the largest Chinese media group outside China. Tiong's new media corporation comprises five daily newspapers with a combined circulation of over one million copies, and thirty-seven magazines (*New Straits Times*, 24 April 2007). The merger will materially benefit Tiong's plan to expand his business interests in China, especially through the vehicle of *Ming Pau*.

GROWTH OF ONLINE MEDIA — COUNTER HEGEMONY?

Against the backdrop of the increasing concentration of ownership of the mainstream newspapers, two Chinese web-based newspapers, *Malaysiakini* (Chinese version) and *Merdakareview* emerged, both being launched in 2005. *Malaysiakini* began as an English-language website and is now available in four languages. It was launched just prior to the 1999 general election, with a seed grant from the Southeast Asian Press Alliance (SEAPA). The organizers felt that there was a need for alternative sources of news, given the mainstream media's tame reporting of political events, especially after the controversial Anwar arrest.

According to *Merdekareview*'s editor, Chang Teck Peng, the initiative to set up the online news media was triggered by the sale of *Nanyang Siang Pau* to Tiong Hiew King. Chang observed that as a result of Tiong's close relationship with the MCA leadership, there was a climate of self-censorship, especially where the top MCA leadership was concerned. With financial backing from some Chinese businessmen, *Merdekareview* aims to provide an avenue for critical voices, specifically, news "that are not reported in the mainstream Chinese media" (interview with Chang).

Unlike the print media, the cyberspace media do not need a permit to operate. They are nevertheless subject to existing laws, namely, the Official Secrets Act, the Sedition Act, and the Internal Security Act, all of which have been used against these websites. On 20 January 2003, *Malaysiakini* was raided by the police and its journalists interrogated as a result of a report lodged by the UMNO Youth wing over a letter published on its website, which was deemed as "inciting racial hatred" (Tong 2004). In July 2007, Raja Petra Kamarudin, editor of the *Malaysia Today* news portal, was interrogated for eight hours by the police in Kuala Lumpur. In May 2008, Raja Petra was charged under the Sedition Act for allegedly implicating Najib Tun Abdul Razak and his wife in a murder case, and in September 2008, he was detained under the Internal Security Act for allegedly insulting Islam.

Another means by which the government tries to control the online news is to refuse issuance of the press accreditation card. Without a press card, journalists are denied entrance to ministerial and official functions. The justification given is that as the online media do have a printing permit, they are not recognized as "accredited media organizations". However, on most occasions, this is not a major hindrance as they are able to obtain government-released information from other blogs, websites, and other indirect sources. Moreover, for both these web-based media, presenting the official line is not normally considered as having "news value" to their readers. Realizing the popularity of these online sites, especially after the 2008 general election, the government decided that it was more prudent to engage them rather than to deny their existence. As a result ten web-based news sites including, *Malaysiakini* and *Merdekareview*, were recently issued with press cards (*New Straits Times*, 6 July 2008).

The popularity of *Malaysiakini* demonstrates that there is a demand for alternative news as readers become critical of mainstream newspapers. Together with blogs and other socio-political sites, online newspapers have thus far been able to enlarge the space for critical discussions and pluralistic viewpoints. These political websites emerged in significant numbers in 1998 after the controversial sacking of Anwar Ibrahim. The number of Internet subscribers has increased from about a quarter of a million in 1998 to about "11 million and with 10 million voters" largely in the urban areas (*The Star*, 5 August 2007). The impact of the news portal is many times more than its subscriber base as users tend to spread information that are not widely available through SMS, email, and fax to many more people.

As a result of the impact of the Internet, mainstream media realized that they need to be more transparent and representative of diverse viewpoints, now that the public has access to multiple sources of information and news.

Whilst in the past it used to be the opposition parties and activists urging for the repeal of repressive laws, such as the Printing Presses and Publication Act, of late, it has been the mainstream journalists who have been actively seeking a freer media environment. In May 2000, on World Press Freedom Day, journalists sent a memorandum to the government to repeal the media laws. In May 2008, the National Union of Journalists Malaysia appealed for the review of media laws, notably the Official Secrets Act, and for it to be replaced by an Information Act. NUJ president, Norila Md Daud, urged media owners to allow journalists to report "without fear or favour". She claimed that journalists had to engage in self-censorship due to interference from "higher-ups" (*The Star*, 3 May 2008). Likewise the Bar Council called on the mainstream media to give fair and equal access to views which are different from the ruling group (*The Star*, 5 May 2008). The online news portal may be small organizations, but they have been more effective in pushing the boundary for more democratic space than the large mainstream media organizations that prefer to toe the political line in order to safeguard their business interests.

THE 12TH GENERAL ELECTION OF 8 MARCH 2008

Before discussing the news coverage of the 12th general election, it is relevant to examine the political climate prior to the election. In 2004, Abdullah Badawi was given a huge mandate to bring about political openness, transparency and change. Four years later, many doubted that Abdullah had the political will to fulfil his election promises, namely to battle corruption, reform the police and judiciary, promote human rights, and improve ethnic relations. On the contrary, there was increased ethnic and religious tensions, increased Islamization in the judiciary, a worsening crime situation, inflation, and corruption. The lack of policies also led to public frustration and open dissent. Two public demonstrations, in almost unprecedented numbers, occurred in Kuala Lumpur. On 10 November 2007, organized by Coalition for Clean and Fair Elections (BERSIH), an estimated 40,000 Malaysians of all races, showed up in support for electoral reforms. This was followed by another show of people's power when about 30,000 supporters of the Hindu Rights Action Force (HINDRAF) rallied on 25 November 2007. The HINDRAF protests succeeded in drawing international attention to the plights of the Indian poor. The use of tear gas and excessive force by police against the demonstrators as well as the arrest of five HINDRAF members under the Internal Security Act, brought Abdullah's popularity to a new low. Against these challenges, the 12th general election resulted in an unexpected and unprecedented victory for the opposition parties, which, after the election, formed the coalition, Pakatan Rakyat (People's Alliance).

To evaluate the role of the media during the campaign period from 22 February to 7 March 2008, we have carried out a content analysis to examine how Chinese print and online media covered the election campaigns. The mainstream newspapers selected were *Sin Chew Daily* and *Guang Ming*, as they are the highest-circulation Chinese dailies, whilst the news websites picked were *Merdekareview* (*MR*) and *Malaysiakini* (*MK*). A total of 166 news items in *Merdekareview* (*MR*) and 176 in *Malaysiakini* (*MK*) were analysed.

Table 8.1 shows that both *Guang Ming* (GM) and *Sin Chew* (SC) gave the highest coverage to the Barisan National (BN) component parties which received 42.7 per cent and 32.9 per cent respectively, compared with the opposition political parties (DAP, PKR and PAS) which only had 21.6 per cent (GM) and 15.3 per cent (SC). The amount of coverage dedicated

Table 8.1
Main Actors of Election Campaign News in
Guang Ming* and *Sin Chew Daily
(Percentage)

Main Actor	*Guang Ming Daily* N=347	*Sin Chew Daily* N=215
Prime Minister/Deputy	7.6	10.2
Ministers/Deputies	16.1	12.1
UMNO	2.7	6.0
MCA	14.9	5.6
MIC	1.5	2.3
Gerakan	11.5	3.7
Other BN component parties/BN in general	12.1	15.3
DAP	18.2	8.3
PKR	3.1	4.2
PAS	0.3	2.8
Chinese organizations	0.3	1.5
Police/judiciary	0.0	1.5
Election Committee	0.5	3.3
Others	11.2	23.3

Source: Data collected by the authors.

to the power holders increased to 66.7 per cent (GM) and 55.2 per cent (SC) when the reportage of cabinet ministers was included. Much of the news on the BN was information on who would be contesting in which constituency. The BN was portrayed as the coalition that ensures stability and prosperity and protects the rights of all races. The Chinese community was persuaded that the country would have a disaster if Anwar became the prime minister. The main themes emphasized by the MCA were (1) MCA is the protector of the Chinese community, (2) there is a need for more Chinese representatives in Parliament, (3) the Chinese should not split their vote so as to ensure a strong Chinese representation, (4) the Chinese should be united as its population is decreasing, (5) the MCA and Gerakan are concerned about Chinese education, and (6) Penang may lose its Chinese chief minister if the BN loses.

Sin Chew's coverage highlighted the internal squabble within the DAP, particularly on Fong Poh Kuan of Batu Gajah, who initially withdrew from the elections due to differences with the Perak DAP chairperson. Other articles on the DAP trivialized their campaign efforts, with headlines such as "Lim Kit Siang: I am not a superman" (28 February 2008), "Lim Kit Siang makes jokes when he reads MCA flyers" (4 March 2008), and "Jeff Ooi speaks in Chinese dialect" (28 February 2008). Issues brought up by the DAP pertained to the selection of Penang's chief minister, such as "Koh Tsu Koon cannot make up his mind on his successor", as well as the Motorola issue (3 March 2008), and "Penang government needed to invest RM10 billion to upgrade Motorola's technology to entice the company not to relocate elsewhere" (4, 6–7 March 2008).

Guang Ming gave more coverage to the DAP compared with *Sin Chew Daily*, such as criticisms of the Election Commission's refusal to use the indelible ink (5 and 6 March 2008), and Koh Tsu Koon's inability to name his successor (4 March 2008). The paper also monitored the huge turnouts for the DAP talks. Like *Sin Chew*, some of the headlines were trivial, as if the DAP had no issue to bring up, such as on Karpal Singh, "Karpal visits market on wheel chair" (1 March 2008), "I am old but still strong" (4 March 2008), and "Four volunteer drivers accompany Kit Siang" (6 March 2008).

During this election both newspapers gave little prominence to the Chinese organizations, apart from the Penang Chinese Town Hall, which expressed support for Teng Hock Nan as chief minister of Penang (GM, 4 March 2008), the Associated Chinese Chamber of Commerce, which urged the government to control inflation (SC, 27 February 2008), and an educational group on the main issues faced by Chinese education (SC, 29 February 2008).

Table 8.2 shows a very different picture of news coverage by the online news media. The opposition parties were given the more prominent coverage, with MR giving them 44.6 per cent of total coverage and MK giving them 42.9 per cent, which come close to half of all news, compared with the BN getting 14.4 per cent from MR and 32 per cent from MK.

Coverage of the DAP and PKR dominates the election news. The main spokespersons for the DAP were Lim Guan Eng, Lim Kit Siang, and Jeff Ooi. Lim lambasted the BN for "double corruption, cronyism and nepotism" and blackmailing voters (MR, 28 February 2008) (MK, 25 and 27 February 2008, 6–7 March 2008); Jeff Ooi challenged Koh Tsu Koon on issues such as the building of Chinese schools (MR, 6 March 2008; MK, 6 March 2008) and his promise to develop Penang on par with Singapore (MR, 28 February 2008; MK, 28 February 2008). There was also the regular monitoring of the turnout of opposition parties' talks and rallies, including the mammoth turnout on 6 March 2008 in Penang, with accompanying photographs (MR, 6 March 2008; MK, 7 March 2008).

Table 8.2
Main Actors of Election Campaign News in
Merdekareview and *Malaysiakini*
(Percentage)

Main Actor	*Merdekareview* N=166	*Malaysiakini* N=175
UMNO	3.6	5.1
MCA	2.4	10.9
MIC	0.0	2.3
Gerakan	4.2	8.6
Other BN component parties/BN in general	4.2	5.1
DAP	17.5	21.1
PKR	19.3	14.9
PAS	1.2	1.1
Opposition in general	6.0	5.1
Independent candidate	0.6	0.0
Hindraf	0.6	1.1
NGOs	17.5	9.1
Police/Judiciary	0.6	0.0
Election commission	0.0	2.3
Contributors/journalists	20.5	11.4
Others	1.8	1.7

Source: Data collected by the authors.

Like the DAP, the PKR was given wide coverage in the online media, with a 19.3 per cent (MR) and 14.9 per cent (MK) share of the number of articles. Anwar Ibrahim talked about his plans to reduce the price of petrol (MK, 25 February 2008), building of more Chinese schools (MK, 27 February 2008) and his lawsuits against Chandra Muzaffar and Khairy Jamaluddin (MR, 5 and 6 March 2008; MK, 5 March 2008). Other PKR voices include Syed Husin Ali, Jeyakumar Devaraj, and Sim Tze Tzin from Penang who focused mainly on the bridge toll and the second Penang bridge issues.

In *Merdekareview*, there were twenty-four news items on the Barisan Nasional, seven of which were on Koh Tsu Koon, with four items unfavourable to him. Koh refused to comment on the Motorola issue which alleged that the previous Penang government invested RM10 billion to entice the company to remain in Penang (MR, 29 February 2008, 3 March 2008). Koh finally admitted to the issue (MR, 4 March 2008). *Malaysiakini* gave fairly balanced coverage to the Barisan Nasional with twenty-five articles favourable, seventeen neutral and fourteen negative. Most of the news items were on the MCA, with nineteen items, and Gerakan fifteen items. Ong Kah Chuan warned the voters not to vote for the DAP in Perak, as otherwise growth would be sluggish and Ipoh would become a city for the retired (MK, 28 February 2008). Abdullah Badawi warned the Chinese not to vote for the opposition — if they wanted to have strong representation in the government (MK, 7 March 2008). MK's commentaries claimed that previous BN election promises were largely unfulfilled (MK, 27 and 29 February 2008).

The online newspapers also gave considerable space for the non-governmental organizations with 17.5 per cent (MR) and 9.1 per cent (MK) of total coverage. Many of these organizations, such as the Group of Concerned Citizens (GCC), Transparency International, Coalition for Free and Fair Elections (BERSIH), and Youth for Change (Y4C), were usually ignored by the mainstream media. The topics raised by the non-governmental organizations touched on fair electoral system, the abolishment of the ISA, the existence of phantom voters, and cancellation of the use of indelible ink.

The content analysis of election news shows that there is clear distinction between the mainstream press and the online news websites. Predictably, the mainstream newspapers faithfully reported views from the BN and whatever minimal coverage about the opposition tended to be negative and trivial. It is thus left to the online media to provide alternative views and information not covered by the mainstream media such as the news *leak* about the monetary enticement for Motorola to remain in Penang.

The election results which showed the rejection among Chinese voters of candidates from the BN Chinese-based parties, namely the MCA and Gerakan, in favour of the DAP and Keadilan, also caused the Chinese newspapers to rethink their editorial policy. Apparently, several Cabinet ministers were upset that after the general election, newspapers were more critical of the government and had proposed the setting up of a media advisory council to monitor press performance (*The Malaysian Insider*, 8 September 2008). A content analysis of the same newspapers and online news, from 9–22 May 2008, showed a shift, at least for a while, in the coverage of the non-BN parties and organizations by *Guang Ming* whose base is in the Pakatan-controlled Penang state. Over 56 per cent of *Guang Ming*'s coverage was devoted to the opposition coalition (DAP, PKR and PAS) compared to 24.3 per cent for the BN. However, much of the news about the DAP state government was about day-to-day administrative matters such as crime prevention, distribution of rice to the needy, and land matters. The other mainstream newspaper, SC, continues to faithfully provide prominent coverage to the BN parties (24 per cent), the government (28.2 per cent), and voices of the top leadership (9.8 per cent). The coverage of non-government organizations was mainly focused on the traditional Chinese-based associations and organizations, such as the Associated Chinese Chamber of Commerce and the Malaysia-China Chamber of Commerce, with little news from the national-level multiracial organizations.

Both *Malaysiakini* and *Merdekareview* provided more balanced coverage to both the ruling and opposition coalition parties. In fact, after the general election, UMNO and MCA received substantially more prominent coverage because of Mahathir's criticisms of UMNO and Prime Minister Abdullah Badawi which culminated in Mahathir's resignation from the party on 20 May 2008 and the controversy on the MCA president's alleged "snoop squad" on rival members in the party. Predictably, the MCA issue was not given prominent coverage in the Chinese press. The third controversy which was highlighted in the online media was the Penang *Syariah* Court ruling to allow a non-practising Muslim to revert to Buddhism.

In summary, the overall coverage of *Sin Chew Daily* after the general election, remains politically conservative, keeping to a strategy of safe reporting by focusing on "official" voices from cabinet ministers, politicians and top bureaucrats. The shift in *Guang Ming*'s coverage does not necessarily reflect a change in editorial policy but rather a pragmatic decision as the opposition-led state is a critical news source and the decision of the state affects the interest of the local society. Hence, its routinized procedure of focusing on government spokespersons led to more coverage of the opposition parties. While both *Merdekareview* and *Malaysiakini* provide alternative views not covered in the mainstream media, the latter provides space to more diverse groups including the ruling coalition, opposition parties, government and non-government organizations. *Merdekareview* tends to focus on marginalized individuals and groups in order to counter the hegemony of the mainstream media.

CONCLUSION

Over the past thirty years, the ownership pattern of Chinese newspapers in Malaysia has shifted from personal ownership, where control was in the hands of the founding family or group, to state control in the 1980s, and finally to concentration in the hands of a conglomerate with strong connections to the power centre. Since Independence, the power holders have created an increasingly controlled media environment through a combination of repressive laws, shareholdings, direct nominees, and close political relationships.

As much as the power holders prefer to have direct controlling stakes in the media companies, the setback is that this requires substantial financial outlay, especially when the media company is not self-financing. For this reason, the MCA had to hive off its loss-making Nanyang Press to a supportive conglomerate. Given its high investment cost and the conglomerate's vision to expand into the regional market, it is unlikely that its priority would be to ensure plurality of ideas and press freedom. Rather, it prefers a more pragmatic strategy that would not jeopardize its business interests, that is, to focus on official and "accredited sources", which would provide "privilege access to those in power" (Hall et al. 1978). As a result, the Chinese newspapers' news sources became increasingly limited and dominated by the leaders in the ruling political parties, government, and business.

There are limits to focusing on the political and economic structures in analysing the role of the Chinese press, which is a site where conflicting forces and aspirations are being fought, especially on contentious issues pertaining to Chinese rights, culture, and education. Three key ethnic situations examined show that the role of the Chinese press depends on the interaction between the Chinese community, the Chinese-based political parties, and the state. At the time of the controversy in 1987 over the appointment of non-Mandarin-speaking headmaster to Chinese schools, the Chinese organizations, dominant political parties, opposition political parties, and business associations acted unanimously against the decision which they deemed as a threat to Chinese education. The Chinese press acted in tandem with the Chinese community and Chinese-based political parties to oppose the controversial decision. Thirteen years later, when the *Suqiu* issue took place, the status of Chinese political parties had weakened considerably within the ruling coalition. In a critique of the role of the MCA, Khoo pointed out that the party "today virtually serves as UMNO's 'Chinese adjunct'. With limited authority, MCA watches over Chinese welfare and make small redresses of Chinese grievances" (Khoo 2000, p. 5). In addition to the weakened political status of Chinese political parties, the Suqiu issue did not command the sense of urgency among the Chinese community the way the 1987 Chinese schools controversy did. The coverage of Suqiu in the Chinese newspapers was decisively dominated by the vitriolic attacks of UMNO, Malay-based organizations, and Mahathir, against which were framed the responses by the Suqiu organizers, the MCA and Gerakan, to "explain" that the appeals were universal and not ethnic concerns. Finally, the Suqiu committee had to withdraw some of the topics that pertained to Malay rights (*Nanyang Siang Pau*, 6 January 2001). In this context, the role of the Chinese press was limited, given the weak support from the Chinese community and Chinese political parties against a strong state.

Analysis of the 2008 general election shows biased coverage of Chinese newspapers towards the dominant ruling coalition, which recycled the same old messages of fear, that only Barisan Nasional could protect the rights of all races and the Chinese must be united to ensure a strong voice in the government. This is not surprising, given the highly controlled media environment, strong newspaper owner-state linkage, as well as a pragmatic culture of reporting that focuses on official lines. In fact by focusing on these official and dominant sources, the Chinese mainstream press was unable to reflect the views and dissatisfactions of the Chinese community. The public, especially the young voters, was disillusioned with the worsening sociopolitical situation, such as increasing corruption, inefficient administration, deterioration of religious freedom and human rights, rather than with narrow ethnic concerns. Most of these issues were raised by the opposition parties and non-governmental organizations, which were neglected by the mainstream press, but were at least discussed in the cyberspace blogs and news sites.

The diverse reporting of the online websites during the general election has forced mainstream media journalists to rethink their narrow pro-establishment stance in order to stay relevant to their readers. The convergence of the various media, whereby information is downloaded from the Internet and disseminated through traditional and new media, is a challenge to the state. Like it or not, the Internet will be a force to reckon as the number of users increases exponentially. In 1998 when the Internet made inroads into the Malaysian political sphere as a result of Mahathir's sacking of Anwar Ibrahim, the number of Internet users was a mere 6.8 per cent of the population compared to the current 62.8 per cent (Internet World Statistics 2008). However, analysis of the technology needs to avoid the trap of technology determinism. As mentioned by George (2005), "communication technologies are not 'independent variables' appearing from out of the blue, and that their forms and functions are shaped by the societies that absorb them". The technology does not operate independently of the societal context in which they are located. One important element is the legal environment. The Malaysian Government's pledge of a no-censorship policy for the Internet in order to attract investors from high-tech industries provided the opportunity for the emergence of online journalists and bloggers. They do not need to apply for a licence to publish but they are still subjected to the existing seditious and defamatory laws. Another factor to consider is the social-political environment that provoked an escalation of online diverging news and views. While issues such as corruption, cronyism, discrimination and religious fundamentalism have been mentioned, an issue that outraged and aggrieved Chinese voters is the brandishing of the *keris* during the UMNO Youth Assemblies. The incident and racial rhetoric by other UMNO leaders reinforced the perception that MCA and Gerakan are too subservient to UMNO. A third important factor is the linkage between the online journalism and mainstream press. *Malaysiakini* and *Merdekareview* operate as professional journalistic sites, being started and run by former journalists who learnt their craft in mainstream media. As argued by Steele (2009), it is the "norms and values of independent journalism that have made *Malaysiakini* such a threat to government authorities". As a result of these ties too, the online media get "leaks" from journalists on stories that could not be published in the mainstream media. Finally the last decade or so witnessed the emergence of a number of organizations willing to contest the boundary of free speech, human rights and social justice, such as the *reformasi* movement, BERSIH, ALIRAN, a social justice organization, the Bar Council, and human rights group, SUARAM. The relatively less regulated Internet provided the platform for these groups to voice their views that were commonly denied by the mainstream media. Hence, while the Internet can facilitate openness, transparency and civic participation, the legal political, economic and social environments are important.

References

Audit Bureau of Circulation, 2008.

Chandra Muzaffar. "Lunas and Beyond". *Aliran Monthly* 20, no. 10 (2000).

George, Cherian. "The Internet's political impact and the penetration/participation paradox in Malaysia and Singapore". Media, Culture & Society, vol. 27, no. 6 (2005): 903–20.

Gomez, Edmund Terence. "Politics of the Media Business: The Press under Mahathir". In *Reflections: The Mahathir Years*, edited by Bridget Welsh. Washington, D.C.: Southeast Asia Studies Program, John Hopkins University, 2004.

————. *Politics in Business: UMNO's Corporate Investments*. Kuala Lumpur: Forum, 1990.

Gurmit Singh, ed. *No to Secrecy*. Petaling Jaya, Malaysia: Aliran, SGS, EPSM, DAP, MAE & CRC, 1987.

Hall, S., C. Critcher, T. Jefferson, J. Clarke, and T. Roberts. *Policing the Crisis*. London: Macmillan, 1978.

Ho Khai Leong. "Imagined Communion, Irreconcilable Differences? Perceptions and Responses of the Malaysian Chinese towards Malay Political Hegemony". In *Chinese Studies of the Malay World: A Comparative Approach*, edited by Ding Choo Ming and Ooi Kee Beng. Singapore: Eastern Universities Press, 2003.

Jomo, K.S. "Mahathir's Flawed Economic Policy". In *Reflections: The Mahathir Years*, edited by Bridget Welsh. Washington, D.C.: Southeast Asia Studies Program, John Hopkins University, 2004.

Khoo Boo Teik. "When the Quitting Gets Tough". *Aliran Monthly* 20, no. 4 (2000).

Khor Yoke Lim and Ng Miew Luan. "Chinese Newspapers, Ethnic Identity and the State: The Case of Malaysia". In *Media and the Chinese diaspora*, edited by Wanning Sun. London: Routledge, 2006

Lee Kam Hing. "Differing Perspectives on Integration and Nation-building in Malaysia". In *Ethnic Relations and Nation Building in Southeast Asia: The Case of Ethnic Chinese*, edited by Leo Suryadinata. Singapore: Institute of Southeast Asian Studies, 2004.

————. "Mahathir's administration and the Chinese". In *Reflections: The Mahathir Years*, edited by Bridget Welsh. Washington, D.C.: Southeast Asia Studies Program, John Hopkins University, 2004.

Loh, Francis. "Developmentalism and the Limits of Democratic Discourse". In *Democracy in Malaysia: Discourses and Practices*, edited by Francis Loh Kok Wah and Khoo Boo Teik. Richmond, Surrey: Curzon, 2002.

————. "Looking Beyond Developmentalism". *Aliran Monthly* 24, no. 10 (2004).

Means, Gordon P. *Malaysian Politics: The Second Generation.* Singapore: Oxford University Press, 1991.

Media Guide Malaysia 2003. Kuala Lumpur: Whiteknight Communications, 2003.

M.G.G. Pillai. "Malaysian Patterns". *Far Eastern Economic Review,* 4 November 1972.

Ong Kian Ming. "Chinese-in-a-Box? The Future of Chinese Parties in Peninsular Malaysia". In *Reflections: The Mahathir Years,* edited by Bridget Welsh. Washington, D.C.: Southeast Asia Studies Program, John Hopkins University, 2004.

Steele, Janet. "Professionalism online: How Malaysiakini challenges authoritarianism". *The International Journal of Press/Politics* 14, no. 1 (2009): 91–111.

Tong Yee Siong. "Malaysiakini: Threading the Tightrope of Political Pressure and Market Factors". In *Asian Cyberactivism: Freedom of Expression and Media Censorship,* edited by Steven Gan, James Gomez, and Uwe Johannen. Bangkok: Friedrich Naumann Foundation, 2004.

Weiss, L. Meredith. "Mahathir's Unintended Legacy: Civil Society". In *Reflections: The Mahathir Years,* edited by Bridget Welsh. Washington, D.C.: Southeast Asia Studies Program, John Hopkins University, 2004.

———. "Malaysia's 12th General Election: Causes and Consequences of the Opposition's Surge". *Asia Pacific Bulletin,* no. 12, 17 March 2008.

Welsh, Bridget. "Election Post-mortem: Top 10 Factors". *Malaysiakini,* 12 March 2008. <www.malaysiakini.com> (accessed 10 June 2008).

Wong Chin Huat. "Malaysian Media Mogul's Big China Bet". *Asia Times Online,* 15 February 2007. <http://www.atimes.com> (accessed 6 June 2008).

Newspapers

Berita Harian, 21 September 1999.

Guang Ming Ribao, 22 February–7 March 2008, 9–22 May 2008.

Kwong Wah Jit Poh, 19 August–2 September 2000, 12 December 2000–23 January 2001, 3–5 June 2001, 21–22 June 2001.

Nanyang Siang Pau, 16 August–24 September 2000, 12 December 2000–9 January 2001, 7, 11, 17, and 18 June 2001.

New Straits Times, 9 July 1981, 6 January 2001, 24 April 2007, 28 May 2008, 6 July 2008.

Sin Chew Daily, 12 December 2000, 16 December 2000, 22 February–7 March 2008, 9–22 May 2008.

The Star, 20 September 1985, 29 October 1986, 5 August 2007, 3 and 5 May 2008.

The Sun, 27 May 2001.

Utusan Malaysia, 14 August 2000.

Websites

Malaysiakini, 17 October 2006, 12 March 2008 (accessed 7 June 2008); 22 February–
    7 March 2008, 9–22 May 2008.
Merdekareview, 22 February–7 March 2008, 9–22 May 2008.
The Malaysian Insider, 8 September 2008 (accessed 8 September 2008).

Magazines

Asiaweek. "Fighting for a Shrinking Market", 4 November 1983.
Far Eastern Economic Review, 20 August 2000.

9

EDUCATION OF THE CHINESE IN MALAYSIA¹

Lee Hock Guan

This chapter will look at the subject of the education of Malaysian Chinese rather than on Chinese education which focuses mainly on mother-tongue education. Two aspects of education which have preoccupied the Chinese community are mother-tongue education and education opportunities. The Chinese are concerned with these two aspects because of the centrality of education to them as a stepping stone to socio-economic success and a means to transmit and preserve their language and culture. During the colonial period, as an immigrant community, the Chinese saw their educational needs largely ignored by the British so they had to mobilize their own resources to establish mother-tongue schools to educate their young. Later, in the post-colonial period their education was subjected to the UMNO-Malay dominated state ambition to create a centralized education system to facilitate the construction of a Malay-centric nation and, after 1970, expand Malay enrolment at the higher education level. As a result, language and education became fiercely contested issues in independent Malaysia where the Chinese community struggled against the UMNO-Malay dominated state to protect and advance their community's education opportunities and mother-tongue education.

In colonial Malaya, there were limited education opportunities in the colony as the British were reluctant to finance an extensive public school system. For the Malays, the colonial state built a small number of Malay-medium schools mainly to teach them their language, culture, and religion, and to be "better" farmers and fishermen (Stevenson 1975). In a number of urban centres, English schools were founded, in part, to supply English-educated Malays, Chinese, and Indians to man the colonial service and British businesses.[2] Malay and English schools in effect constituted the colonial "public" school system. While the indigenous Malays were provided with Malay schools, the British regarded the Chinese as foreigners and did not feel morally obliged to provide schools for them. Chinese individuals, groups, and associations thus mobilized to build mother-tongue schools to educate their children and, up to the first two decades of the twentieth century, these schools were largely funded and administered by the community.[3] But, beginning in the 1920s, the colonial state, feeling threatened by the rising nationalism among the Malayan Chinese, tried to offer financial assistance to Chinese schools in exchange for political control; however, few Chinese schools accepted this bargain.[4]

Unsurprisingly, in colonial Malaya illiteracy rates were high across all the three major ethnic groups: Malays, Chinese, and Indians. The small fraction of Malays, Chinese, and Indians who obtained an education were usually educated in their respective mother-tongue schools. For the Chinese, the majority of whom resided in rural and semi-urban areas, usually only Chinese schools were available. Also, mother-tongue education was highly valued because Chinese parents were concerned that their children would lose their language, culture, and identity in a foreign land. In the urban centres, an increasing number of Chinese were enrolled in English-medium schools because of the better quality education these offered and because acquiring an English education was seen as a means to better employment opportunities in the colonial civil service and British firms.[5] Needless to say, for education beyond secondary school level, the opportunities were very limited and indeed the first university was established in Malaya only in 1949[6] in Singapore.

Unlike the British colonial state's half-hearted and *laissez faire* approach to education, the post-colonial state played an active and interventionist role in the provision of education. After political independence in 1957, the state proceeded to pursue its plan to achieve universal literacy in the country through free, mass public education. The segmented colonial education system was nationalized and transformed into a centralized system with a common administrative system and a standard curriculum and examination system. However, the UMNO-Malay dominated state sought to use education as a means to facilitate the national integration of the different ethnic groups in the context of nation building, envisioned in largely monolingual and monocultural terms. Thus state policies pursued, aggressively, to homogenize the population linguistically and culturally. Chinese primary schools, even though granted official recognition and included in the national educational system, were treated as subordinate to Malay-medium schools. The discrimination of mother-tongue education led many Chinese to harbour the suspicion that the Malay-dominated state retained an ulterior "final objective" to eliminate Chinese schools.[7] Hence, mother-tongue education has remained a perennial controversial and contested issue in Malaysia.

Since 1971, the state has implemented a comprehensive ethnic quota policy to advance Malay educational qualifications which has adversely impacted the education opportunities of Indian and Chinese students. Policies to expand Malay education opportunities were translated into a wide range of means such as: Malay-only residential schools, a matriculation examination system, ethnic quota for Malay admission into public tertiary institutions, and for scholarships and loans, and so on. As a result, the Chinese students' higher education opportunities in the country were reduced considerably until the liberalization of the higher education sector. The privatization of higher education and the intensive expansion of the public higher education sector indeed improved the higher education opportunities of all ethnic groups. However, as the Malay-dominated state continues to pursue its ethnic preferential policies, the privatization of higher education has the unintended consequence of ethnically segmenting that sector.

The first section of this chapter will look at selected indicators of the education profile of Malaysian Chinese. Section two examines the mother-tongue education problem that has continued to generate passionate debates from both sides of the divide. The privatization of higher education and its consequences for the education opportunities of Chinese students, and the pattern of ethnic enrolment in higher education, will be the focus in section three. Section four will address what the increasing ethnic segmentation of the Malaysian education system would mean for ethnic relations and social cohesion. This will be followed by a discussion on access to, and equity in education, with special focus on the education opportunities for poor Chinese. Since the 1998 political crisis, a "new politics" has emerged in the Malaysian political landscape and it appears that the results of the 12th general election on 8 March 2008 have consolidated the "new politics". The last section will explore the initial impact of the emergence of the "new politics" on the education of the Chinese in Malaysia

MALAYSIAN CHINESE EDUCATIONAL PROFILE

Since political independence in 1957, successive UMNO-dominated administrations have allocated sizeable public funds to build up the national education system. During the NEP period (1971–90), education expenditure averaged nearly 17 per cent of the total state expenditure, or 5 per cent of the Gross Domestic Product. The sizeable financial investments in education, coupled with the construction of a mass public education system, enabled the state to reduce illiteracy across all ethnic groups successfully. Thus by 1990 universal primary education enrolment was largely attained and the adult literacy rates have increased from 52 per cent in 1957 to 80 per cent in 1994 and 91.2 per cent in 2007. At the higher education level, the upward trend of gains made by the different ethnic groups was differentially impacted by the ethnic quota policy and the privatization of the sector. For Malaysian Chinese women, changing societal attitudes and expanding education opportunities have contributed to the gradual expansion of their participation at all education levels.

The Malaysian Chinese have become more educated, with a greater proportion of the community attaining secondary education and, increasingly, tertiary education as well (see Table 9.1). In 1980, about 21 per cent of the Chinese had no schooling but, by 2000, the proportion with no schooling has been pared down to 8 per cent. While in 1980 about 45.9 per cent of the Chinese attained primary school-level education, by 2000 nearly 46 per cent of the community had attained secondary school-level education. From the 1990s, the great expansion of tertiary education, rising Chinese family incomes, and the demand for higher skilled workers, all contributed to the almost tenfold increase in the proportion of Chinese who attained tertiary education, rising from 1.5 per cent in 1980 to 12 per cent in 2000. Consequently a greater proportion of the Chinese younger generation today will have higher levels of education compared with those of the older generation when they were in the same age group (see Table 9.3).

Table 9.1
Highest Education Level Attained by Chinese Malaysians
(Aged 6 Years and Above) (in Per Cent)

Educational Attainment	1980	1991	2000
No schooling#	20.9	13	8
Primary	45.9	39	30
Secondary	31.5	41	46
Tertiary	1.5	7	12

Note: # includes pre-schooling
Source: Calculated from the 1980, 1991, and 2000 Population Census.

Table 9.2 shows the gains and discrepancies in education attainment among members of the different ethnic groups, aged fifteen years and above, in 1991 and 2000.

Educational level attainment has improved for all ethnic groups so much so that by 2000[8] more than 90 per cent of Malaysians aged fifteen years and above have obtained at least a primary school education. Also by 2000, more than 50 per cent of Malays, Other *Bumiputra*, Chinese, and Indians had attained a secondary school education with Malays and Other *Bumiputra* achieving the biggest gains, from 33.8 per cent and 34.1 per cent in 1991, to 59.7 per cent and 57.1 per cent in 2000 respectively. The increasing percentage of Malaysians acquiring at least a secondary school education is reflective of the fact that primary and lower secondary education enrolments have become more widespread. Also, since automatic promotion up to Form 5 was instituted in 1996, in part, to reduce the high dropout rates after Form 3, most Malaysians can now expect to attain at least eleven years of free public education.

In 1991, one in ten Malays obtained tertiary education, while the proportion for Other *Bumiputra* was one in thirty (see Table 9.2). Thus the proportion of Malays who obtained tertiary education was higher than that for the Chinese (8.9 per cent) and Indians (7.4 per cent) by 1991. This was a consequence of two decades of using an ethnic quota admission policy from 1970 to 1990 for public tertiary institutions that disproportionately benefited the Malays. Before the 1990s, qualified Chinese and Indian students, who were denied admission into public tertiary institutions, had limited higher education opportunities within Malaysia. But with the rapid expansion of the private higher education sector, especially since the 1990s, the Chinese and Indians students' opportunities to obtain tertiary education have expanded.

Table 9.2
Highest Education Level Attained by Members of Ethnic Groups
(Aged 15 Years and Above) (in Per Cent)

Educational Attainments	Malays		Other Bumiputra[9]		Chinese		Indians	
	1991	2000	1991	2000	1991	2000	1991	2000
Primary	28.3	21.7	24.9	29.6	30.6	23.6	30.3	23.9
Secondary	33.8	59.7	34.1	57.1	45.4	55.0	48.0	59.2
Tertiary	10.2	17.0	3.5	8.8	8.9	16.4	7.4	12.9

Source: Calculated from the 1991 and 2000 Population Census.

The Chinese and Indians thus recorded significant gains in the percentage of their adult population (aged fifteen years and above) who obtained tertiary education — from 8.9 per cent and 7.4 per cent in 1991 to 16.4 per cent and 12.9 per cent in 2000 respectively.

How the ethnic quota admission policy and the expansion of the private tertiary education have differentially impacted the different ethnic communities is best shown by contrasting higher educational experiences of the 20–24 and 40–44 years old cohort across the different ethnic groups (see Table 9.3). With the ethnic quota admission policy in operation, the percentage of Malays, Chinese, and Indians in the 20–24 years cohort who obtained tertiary education was 6.2 per cent, 5.3 per cent and 3.1 per cent respectively in 1991; and after the rapid privatization of tertiary education, the figures for Malays, Chinese and Indians were 16.5 per cent, 20.9 per cent, and 13.7 per cent in 2000 respectively. In contrast, the figures for Malays, Chinese and Indians in the age group, 40-44 years, who entered public higher education before the full impact of the ethnic quota policy, were 4.4 per cent, 5.2 per cent, and 4.8 per cent in 1991. But, by 2000, after the implementation of the Malay preferential policy, the percentage of 40–44 year-old Malays with higher education was 10.5 per cent, which is higher than their Chinese (9.6 per cent) and Indian (6.9 per cent) counterparts. In short, while the ethnic quota policy disproportionately benefited Malay tertiary students, the rapid privatization of the higher education sector predictably benefited the Chinese more and, to a certain extent, the Indian students.

In the past, there was much resistance to educating daughters in Chinese families, largely due to the persistence of conservative patriarchal Confucian

Table 9.3
Percentage of Members of Age Groups, 20–24 Years and 40–44 Years, Who Attained Certificate/Diploma/Degree Qualifications by Ethnicity (1991 and 2000)

Ethnicity/Aged Group	1991		2000	
	20–24	40–44	20–24	40–44
Malays	6.2	4.4	16.5	10.5
Other *Bumiputra*	2.1	3.6	6.4	4.3
Chinese	5.3	5.2	20.9	9.6
Indians	3.1	4.8	13.7	6.9

Source: Calculated from 1991 and 2000 Population Censuses.

ideology. Traditional Confucian attitudes, however, have changed over the years such that there is a general acceptance of Chinese women being given equal access to education opportunities. With the change in attitudes with the regards to the expansion of education opportunities in society, Chinese women in Malaysia have made impressive gains in education. For example, the education attainment gap between Chinese men and women has narrowed substantially over the years. In 1991, the percentage of Chinese men and women aged seventy-five years and above who had never attended school was 54 per cent and 87 per cent respectively; for the age goup, 50–54 years, the figures were 12.4 per cent and 38 per cent; for the age group, 30–34 years, 2.6 per cent and 5.0 per cent; and for the 10–14 age group, 0.5 per cent and 0.5 per cent. Similarly, the education attainment gap between Chinese men and women has narrowed over the years (see Table 9.4). Discrimination against Chinese women in education remains a major factor in the generally lower education attainment of Chinese women compared with men in 1980; 69.3 per cent of women with at least primary school education, to 87 per cent for men. And only 1.3 per cent of Chinese women obtained tertiary education compared with 3 per cent for Chinese men, confirming the prejudice against Chinese women acquiring higher education. By 2000, gender parity in education for Chinese men and women had already been achieved up to tertiary education, with the figure for men at 13.6 per cent and women at 12.3 per cent.

The substantial progress made by both Chinese men and women in obtaining tertiary education is best illustrated by the increase in percentage across all the three age groups from 1991 to 2000, for both men and women. For the 20–24 years age group, the figures for men and women in 1991 and 2000 were 5.7 per cent and 5.0 per cent, and 20.1 per cent and 21.6 per cent,

Table 9.4
Highest Qualification Attained by Chinese Men and Women
(Aged 15 Years and Over)

Qualification Attained	Male		Female	
	1980	2000	1980	2000
Primary	42.8	22.5	36.7	24.9
Secondary	42.2	59.2	31.3	57.7
Tertiary	3.0	13.6	1.3	12.3

Source: Calculated from 1980 and 2000 Population Censuses.

Table 9.5
Percentage Distribution of Chinese Men and Women with Certificate/
Diploma/Degree by Age Groups, 20–24, 30–34 and 40–44 Years
(1991 and 2000)

	20–24 Years		30–34 Years		45–49 Years	
	1991	2000	1991	2000	1991	2000
Men	5.7	20.1	9.0	15.1	6.1	10.0
Women	5.0	21.6	5.5	12.7	3.0	5.1

Source: Calculated from 1991 and 2000 Population Censuses.

respectively (see Table 9.5). Indeed, Chinese women have not only caught up with their male counterparts at this level — by 2000 the percentage of Chinese women, aged 20–24 years, with tertiary qualifications has slightly exceeded that for Chinese men.

The Malaysian Chinese, both men and women, have made impressive gains in education. Illiteracy is almost negligible in the community and successive generations of Chinese have benefited from better educational opportunities. At the higher education level, the Chinese have benefited from the privatization of that sector, such that acquiring a tertiary education locally is today not much of a problem for any qualified Chinese student who can afford to pay for it. For Chinese women, while they have made gains in education attainment, there is still discrimination against them in terms of the fields of study.

MEDIUM OF INSTRUCTION

The history and politics of Chinese mother-tongue education in Malaysia have received much attention, both in the popular media and academic publications (Kua 1985; Tan 1997; Lee 2006). In the political compromise agreed upon by the Alliance ethnic leaders before Independence in 1957, mother-tongue education was officially accepted as part of the national education system, but only at the primary school level.[10] For Chinese secondary schools, the Malay-dominated state first insisted that they switched to the English medium in 1961, and then to the Malay medium since 1971, in exchange for financial assistance and official recognition. The Chinese secondary schools which accepted these terms became the "national-type secondary" schools, and in 2000 there were seventy-eight such schools. Around sixty schools which persisted in using Chinese as the medium of instruction became the Independent Chinese Secondary Schools (ICSS). Efforts by the Chinese community, especially the Chinese educationist movement, to establish a Chinese-medium tertiary institution, called Merdeka University, failed as the Malay-dominated state refused to grant it permission. However, since the privatization of education, and coupled with the changing state attitudes towards education and political developments, the state has permitted the establishment of Chinese private colleges and the upgrading of Tunku Abdul Rahman College into a fully fledged university.

It is widely acknowledged that the Malay-dominated state had pursued policies to promote Malay aggressively as the main medium of instruction, while discriminating against mother-tongue education. In spite of state marginalization of the Chinese primary schools, the latter have not only survived, but have also become the mainstay of the education of Chinese students at the primary school level. From 1957 to 1967, the enrolment in English and Chinese primary schools grew by 8.3 per cent and 1.4 per cent respectively. In contrast, from 1971 to 1978, while the enrolment in Chinese primary schools grew by 20.6 per cent, the enrolment in English primary schools decreased by 10.9 per cent. Reflective of the resurgence of Chinese parents' preference to send their children to Chinese schools, the enrolment of Chinese students in Chinese schools increased from 82.4 per cent in 1973 to 88.2 per cent in 1978, 89 per cent in 1995, and more than 90 per cent since 1998 (see Table 9.6). The enrolment pattern of Chinese students at the primary school level has stabilized at slightly

Table 9.6
Chinese Student Enrolment in Primary Schools, Selected Years
(in Per Cent)

Year	Chinese Students Enrolled in SRJK-C	Chinese Students Enrolled in SRK
1973	82.4	17.6
1978	88.2	11.8
1995	89	11
1998	90.6	9.4
1999	90.9	9.1
2005	94.7	5.3

Notes: SRJK-C: Government Chinese Primary School; SRK: Government Malay Primary School.
Sources: Various sources.

above 90 per cent in Chinese primary schools, and less than 10 per cent in national primary schools.[11]

At the secondary school level, a sizeable majority of Chinese parents are acquiescent about enrolling their children in national secondary schools, with a significant number enrolling their children in the national-type Chinese secondary schools. In 2005, the seventy-eight national-type Chinese secondary schools enrolled nearly 128,500 students. Only a small percentage of Chinese students, about 10 per cent, were enrolled in the sixty ICSS, where the total enrolment has since 1990 stabilized at between 54,000 and 60,000 students; in 2007, the total enrolment was nearly 55,800 students. About 70 per cent of Chinese secondary school students are enrolled in the national secondary schools. In the 1996 Education Act, while the national education system was redefined to include the ICSS, the state still refused to grant financial assistance to the schools or to recognize the ICSS's United Examinations Certificate (UEC). Thus qualified ICCS graduates remain unable to gain admission into local public tertiary institutions even though the UEC is recognized by many foreign universities, including universities in Singapore, Australia, the United States, and Britain.

Several factors have contributed to the Chinese parents' increasing preference to enrol their children in Chinese primary schools. A perennial reason is that they regard mother-tongue education as indispensable to the propagation and preservation of their language, culture, and identity; indeed, the survival of Chinese schools is equated with the survival of "Chineseness" in Malaysia. The Malay-dominated state policies that aggressively push to entrench *Ketuanan Melayu* created gradually an intolerable environment in the national primary schools where non-Malays felt discriminated and mistreated. Symbolic violence against things Chinese in the national schools was also made worse by the ethnocentric attitudes and behaviour of the largely Malay teaching and administrative staff. And since the 1990s, Chinese parents' negative perception of the national primary schools have further worsened with the increasing Islamization of the national schools. In short, a majority of Chinese parents have come to view the increasing Malayization and Islamization of the national primary schools as intolerant of and discriminating against Chinese students in the schools.[12]

The combination of more than 90 per cent of Chinese students enrolling in Chinese schools and the changing distribution of the Chinese population in Malaysia has created problems of either declining enrolment or overcrowding in different Chinese schools. Enrolments in rural and certain inner city areas have declined because of rural to urban Chinese migration and of the Chinese moving out from the inner city areas to new suburban areas. Inadequate numbers of schools and a fast growing Chinese population have resulted in overcrowding in Chinese primary schools in several new suburban neighborhoods; the problem is especially acute in the Klang Valley. The overcrowding problem is also a direct result of the government's refusal to either build new Chinese schools or relocate Chinese schools that are facing declining enrolment or becoming unsustainable to the neighbourhoods where overcrowding is a problem.

In 1957, there were 1,333 Chinese primary schools, but that number dropped to 1,295 and 1,283 in 1987 and 1998 respectively, and then rose to 1,286 and 1,289 in 2002 and 2007 respectively.

The number of students per school for Malay primary schools has increased from 330 in 1987 to 412 in 1998 and 415 in 2006. In contrast, the number of students per school for Chinese schools started at a high of 450 in 1987 and rose to 467 in 1998 and close to 500 in 2006. The number of new Chinese schools being added is clearly not keeping pace with the number of Chinese students enrolled in those schools, thus leading to problems of overcrowding.

This problem is made worse by the fact that Chinese schools have continued to receive much smaller state financial assistance than the national primary schools. For example, in the 9th Malaysian Plan (2006–10), although Chinese primary schools enrolment made up nearly 21.1 per cent of the total number of primary school students, they were allocated only 3.6 per cent of total government expenditure for all primary schools. Because of the meagre government financial allocation, Chinese schools are very much dependent on the Chinese community for additional funds. In addition, the government has also failed to train an adequate number of qualified teachers for the Chinese schools so that there is a perennial shortage of teachers, and between 2,000 and 3,000 temporary teachers are hired by Chinese schools every year.

Concerned that the increasing polarization of primary schools along ethnic lines would hinder ethnic and national integration in the society, the government has introduced an assortment of initiatives to address the polarization trend in education. To promote ethnic integration, attempts were made to house Chinese, Tamil, and Malay schools in the same compound through the "Integrated Schools" and "Vision Schools"[13] strategies in 1985 and 2001 respectively. Presently there are five "Vision Schools", namely: (i) Pekan Baru Vision School Complex, Parit Buntar, Perak, (ii) Taman Aman Vision School Complex, Alor Setar, Kedah, (iii) Tasik Permai Vision School Complex, Pulau Pinang, (iv) USJ 15 Vision School Complex, Subang Jaya,

Table 9.7
Enrolment in National and Chinese Primary Schools,
1987, 1998 and 2006

| | Year | | | | | | | | |
| | 1987 | | | 1998 | | | 2006 | | |
	No. of Students	No. of Schools	No. of Students per School	No. of Students	No. of Schools	No. of Students per School	No. of Students	No. of Schools	No. of Students per School
Chinese Primary	582,126	1,295	450	599,520	1,283	467	639,310	1,288	496
Malay Primary	1,604,408	4,856	330	2,175,831	5,283	412	2,400,089	5,774	415

Source: Ministry of Education.

Selangor, and (v) Pundut Vision School Complex, Seri Manjung, Perak. However, the implementation of the "Vision Schools" strategy was resisted vigorously by Chinese educationists who suspected that it was another government subterfuge to eliminate the Chinese primary schools. They also argued that the "Vision Schools" as conceived would result in the Chinese primary schools losing their autonomy and character.

In 2003, the government announced the stunning policy to re-introduce English as the medium of instruction for mathematics and science at all levels; the policy was to be implemented in staggered phases.[14] Interestingly, the state's decision to revive English as a medium of instruction prodded the Malay-language nationalists and Chinese educationists to collaborate to oppose this new policy — but for different reasons. While the former felt that this would dilute the status of Malay as the official and national language, the latter objected because they felt that it would dilute the use of some Chinese as the medium of instruction in the Chinese schools. Although there were some Chinese who supported this policy, many Chinese remain sceptical of the Malay-dominated state's real intention. The haphazard manner in which the policy was formulated and implemented did not inspire much confidence either.[15] Nevertheless, the conversion of national primary schools into bilingual-medium schools could potentially result in more Chinese parents sending their children to the national schools and thereby creating an ethnically less polarized education system.[16]

Generally speaking, although the vast majority of Chinese parents have opted out of the national primary schools for Chinese schools, at the secondary level, the pattern of enrolment is more diverse. Only about 10 per cent of Chinese students are enrolled in ICSS, with another slightly more than 20 per cent enrolled in national-type secondary schools, and some 70 per cent enrolled in the national secondary schools. That more than 90 per cent of Chinese students are enrolled in Chinese primary schools has raised a number of issues and challenges. Driven by a largely assimilationist conception of education, the Malay-dominated state has continued to marginalize Chinese mother-tongue education in terms of financial allocation, training of teachers, and the relocation and building of new Chinese primary schools.

PRIVATIZATION OF HIGHER EDUCATION

Since the mid-1980s, the increasing internationalization and privatization of higher education has influenced the Malaysian state to appropriate neoliberal ideas and pro-competition instruments to reform and restructure its higher education sector. The trend towards the privatization of this sector was in part driven by the sector's inability to meet the fast industrializing economy's growing demand for a higher educated and skilled labour force. The economic recession in the 1980s and the financial crisis in 1997[17] also crucially influenced the government to privatize higher education in order to relieve its overdependence on state financing and provision. A third reason was the government ambition to make Malaysia an education hub which could generate revenue by attracting foreign students to pursue their higher education in Malaysia. Thus the government relinquished its monopolistic control of the provision of higher education, as well as relaxed its obsession with promoting Malay as the main medium of instruction so English, the preferred medium of instruction, was allowed as the medium of instruction for the private tertiary sector.

During the NEP period, the total demand for higher education far exceeded what the public sector could supply. For Chinese students the problem of the already limited higher education opportunities was further aggravated by the imposition of the pro-Malay ethnic admission quota system since 1970. In 1970, enrolment in public tertiary education by ethnic groups was 49.7 per cent Malays, 42.7 per cent Chinese, and 5.1 per cent Indians. By 1980, after the implementation of the ethnic quota policy, the ethnic enrolment breakdown was 60.4 per cent Malays, 32.7 per cent Chinese, and 6.1 per cent Indians. Hence, in the 1970s and 1980s the scarcity of local higher education opportunities for Chinese students generated growing frustrations and tense ethnic relations.

By the 1990s, the Malay-dominated state had come around to recognizing that for the Malaysian economy to remain globally competitive, and to upgrade it to a knowledge-based economy, the country would need to increase its pool of better educated and higher skilled human capital. Several statutes were enacted in order to facilitate and regulate the expansion of the private higher education sector: the Education Act 1996, Private Higher Education Institution Act 1996, National Accreditation Board (LAN) Act 1996, University and University Colleges (Amendment) Act 1996, and National Higher Education Fund Corporation Act 1997.

In 1990, there were seven public polytechnics and seven public universities and by 2004 there were eleven and eighteen respectively. By 2007, the number of polytechnics has increased to twenty-two, and public universities to twenty. However, it was the dramatic expansion of the private provision of higher education that generated substantial gains in the supply of higher educated and skilled human labour in the country. This privatization of higher education in the 1990s was greatly assisted by the increasing internationalization of the sector as declining student populations and cut backs in public spending drove increasing numbers of tertiary institutions in the United Kingdom, Australia, New Zealand, the United States, and Canada to recruit more full-fees paying foreign students in order to generate more revenue. The growth of the private tertiary education sector was most impressive indeed: the number of private colleges increased from 280 in 1995 to 611 in 1999, local private universities and university colleges rose from none in 1995 to nineteen in 1999, and there were also four foreign university branch campuses in Malaysia by 1999. And by 2007, the private higher education make-up had changed to four foreign branch universities, eighteen private universities, fifteen university colleges, and 485 private colleges.

The privatization of higher education helped to expand greatly the access to higher education for Malaysian students. In 1990, the enrolment of students in the public and private higher institutions was 122,340 and 35,600 respectively. By 2000, the enrolment in the private higher institutions had surpassed the public higher institutions, 203,391 to 167,507 (see Table 9.8).[18] Total enrolment of students at the higher education level has more than doubled between 1990 and 2000, from 157,940 to about 370,898. Indeed, the enrolment growth since 2000 has been even more spectacular; the 2007 intake saw 167,788 students enrolling at public higher institutions, and 190,265 at private higher institutions, and in total there were 365,800 students enrolled in the public institutions, and 507,438 enrolled in their private sector counterparts.

For the Chinese community, the most important consequence of the privatization of higher education is that it expanded the opportunities for Chinese students to acquire higher education qualifications. Admission into

Table 9.8
Numbers of Enrolled Students in Public and Private Higher Institutions in Malaysia, 1985, 1990, 2000, and 2007

Type of Institutions	1985	1990	2000	2007
Public Institutions	86,300	122,340	167,507	365,800
Private Institutions	15,000	35,600	203,391	507,438
Total	101,330	157,940	370,898	873,238

Source: Various Malaysian Plans; Educational Statistics, Ministry of Education.

private higher education institutions varied widely in terms of academic standards and financial costs and depends on whether the admission is for certificate, diploma, or degree courses. As long as they meet the academic standards and can pay the fees, Chinese students will encounter little difficulty in gaining admission into a private higher education institution. After all, the majority of private higher education institutions are profit-making businesses and thus more students will mean more revenue for them.

Given the difficulties Chinese students encountered in getting admission into the public higher education institutions, even after the implementation of the supposedly merit admission system in 2002, they have no choice but to enrol in the private higher education sector. It is not surprising then that enrolment in the private higher education sector is overwhelmingly Chinese. For example, in 1999, the ethnic breakdown for the certificate and diploma courses at private higher institutions was Malays 44.5 per cent and non-Malays, 55.5 per cent, and for degree programmes the figures were 16.3 per cent and 83.7 per cent respectively. The relatively high percentage of Malays enrolled in private higher education institutions is a reflection of the government policy to increase the number of Malay-owned private higher institutions and helping these by funding Malay students to enrol with them.

The higher proportion of Malay enrolment in the private higher education institutions for diploma and certificate courses was not indicative of a more ethnically integrated private education sector because the majority of the Malays were enrolled in Malay-owned colleges while non-Malays were largely found in the non-Malay-owned colleges. Lastly, ethnic segmentation at the tertiary level is also reflected in the ethnic make-up of the people employed in the two sectors, mostly Malays in the public tertiary sector, and Chinese in the private tertiary sector.

Figure 9.1 shows the percentage of 25–29-year-old Malaysians who obtained higher education qualifications for 1980, 1991, and 2000. From 1980 to 1991, before the extensive privatization of higher education, the percentage of Malays aged 25–29 years who obtained higher education qualification increased from 4.8 per cent to 16.9 per cent while the rate of increase was slower for the Chinese: from 6.4 per cent to 13.4 per cent. However, by 2000 a larger percentage of Chinese aged 25–29 years had obtained higher education qualifications, compared with their Malay counterparts: 18.8 per cent as opposed to 17.4 per cent. Obviously, the privatization of private higher education has enabled more Chinese to

Figure 9.1
Percentage of Persons 25–29 Years Old with Higher Education
(Certificate, Diploma, and Degrees)

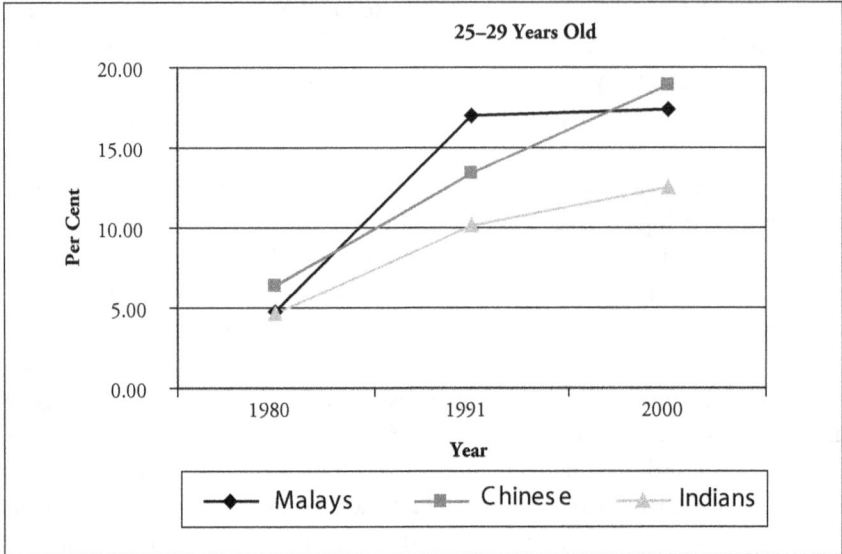

25–29 Years Old

Source: Calculated from the 1980, 1991 and 2000 Population Census.

graduate with higher education qualifications.[19] The privatization of the Malaysian higher education has clearly expanded the opportunities of Malaysian students, especially Indian and Chinese students, to acquire higher education qualifications, if they can afford it.

EDUCATIONAL INEQUITIES

How have the Malay-dominated state discriminating education policies towards mother-tongue education and Chinese students' admission into local public tertiary institutions impacted the different Chinese income groups?[20] Because of the unequal state financial allocation for Chinese schools and because the ICSS continues not to receive state financial assistance, it means that the Chinese community has to help shoulder the Chinese schools' financial burden substantially. In tertiary education, the privatization of higher education may have expanded the education opportunities for Chinese students, but it also comes with a higher price tag which makes it out of reach for Chinese students from lower-income background. Generally then, the state marginalization of mother-tongue education and Malay preferential policies have perpetuated, if not generated, educational inequalities in the Chinese community, especially for the Chinese in the New Villages.

In a study commissioned by the Malaysian Chinese Association (MCA) in 2005, a survey followed about 99,000 UPSR Chinese school students who went on to Forms Four and Five between 1997 and 2002. (UPSR is Malay for Primary School Education Test.) A surprising finding of this survey was that an estimated 25 per cent of the Chinese students dropped out and quit studying before they were eighteen years old; that is, when they were due to sit for the Form Five examination, the Sijil Pelajaran Malaysia (SPM) (Chow 2008). This estimate puts the annual dropout figure for Chinese students at over 120,000. Unlike their Malay counterparts who have more opportunities to enrol in various state-sponsored skills training centres and programmes, the Chinese dropouts received little state support and were thus left to fend for themselves. While some dropouts would acquire skills by attending training centres established by the MCA or working as apprentices in various trade and craft businesses, there is growing concern that a significant number of dropouts have ended up in menial jobs, or are turning to illicit activities, such as peddling pirated DVDs, joining gangs, and committing petty crimes.

As expected, the majority of the dropouts come from the lower-income Chinese families both in the urban and rural areas. A number of factors have contributed to students dropping out of school: families unable to pay for their children's education; students forced to quit school in order to work to supplement family incomes; and where parents operate their own businesses, such as hawkers, students forced to stop their schooling to assist their parents in running businesses. However, a major contributing factor is also attributed to the fact that many Chinese students encounter difficulties in making the transition from Chinese to the Malay medium of instruction. Chinese school students generally have a poorer command of the Malay language because it is taught only as a subject in their schools. While Chinese school students are required to enrol in "Remove" classes in order to raise their Malay proficiency, anecdotal evidence suggests the "Remove" classes have been rather ineffective in what they are supposed to do. It is not surprising that the majority of Chinese students having difficulties in making the transition come from the lower-income groups. This means they have to depend on the "Remove" classes to improve their Malay language skills as their parents are not be able to provide them with private Malay tuition, which the middle- and upper-income Chinese families usually give their children.

Glaring inequalities also exist across the Chinese primary and independent Chinese secondary schools. Even though Chinese schools enrol about 20 per cent of the total primary school students, they receive only about 10 per cent of the expenditure allocated for primary education. The underfunding of Chinese schools is further compounded by the fact that 50 per cent of Chinese schools are partially aided schools. For the ICSS, since they do not receive any form of state funding, they are entirely dependent on donations from the various Chinese groups. Fund raising has thus become a perennial activity for the majority of Chinese primary schools and ICSS, with the donors usually being Chinese associations, boards of governors, parent-teacher associations, and others, especially Chinese businessmen. Well known and popular Chinese primary and independent Chinese secondary schools[21] are usually located in better off neighbourhoods and they receive generous financial support from various sources, especially from their alumni and students' families. On the other hand, Chinese primary schools and ICSS in the rural or poor urban areas are frequently in dire conditions precisely because they have a hard time raising funds.

While the privatization of higher education has expanded the education opportunities for Chinese students to gain higher educational qualifications, it has also widened the educational disparities within the Chinese community. Since private education in Malaysia operates on a profit basis, it invariably charges much higher fees than their state-subsidized public counterparts. For example, in 2007 the cost of attending a private education institution for a first degree ranged from RM$24,000 for local students, to RM$36,000 for outstation students, compared with RM$9,000 and RM$16,000 for public higher institutions respectively (see Table 9.9). As a matter of fact, the majority of Chinese students who remain enrolled in the national secondary schools to sit for the Sijil Tinggi Persekolahan Malaysia (STPM) are usually from lower-income background as Chinese students from higher-income families will have switched to private higher education institutions. By and large then, the majority of Chinese students enrolled in the public higher institutions are from lower-income groups while those in the private higher education institutions are from middle- and upper-income groups. Middle- and upper-income Chinese groups have thus benefited the most from the privatization of education in several ways, precisely because they have the most resources to purchase educational services in a private market.[22] On another different level, this is another form of inter-ethnic wealth transfer from the Chinese to the Malay *Bumiputra*.

Table 9.9
Higher Education Costs for First Degree Per Academic Year (10 months), 2007
(in Malaysian Ringgit)

		Public		Private	
		Local Student	Outstation Student	Local Student	Outstation Student
Educational Expenses	Registration Fees	600	600	540	540
	Tuition	700	1,102	9,531	15,200
	Other Fees	196	196	740	940
	Books & other expenses	400	400	600	600
	Subtotal	1,896	2,298	11,411	17,280
Living expenses	Lodging	0	4,500	2,700	5,000
	Food	7,000	9,500	3,000	4,500
	Transportation			2,000	3,000
	Other personal expenses			5,000	6,000
	Subtotal	7,000	14,000	12,700	18,500
Total costs		8,896	16,298	24,111	35,780

Source: Author's own calculations.

The overall dire conditions of the Chinese residing in the New Villages have long been neglected by both government and civil society. In 2002, there were a total of 450 New Villages accounting for 1.3 million people, down from 1.7 million in 1995 due to rural to urban migration.[23] While the majority of New Villagers are still located in the rural areas, a small number of New Villages are now located in areas which have become urbanized. Chinese households in the New Villages generally belong to the lower- and middle-income groups. In 2002, 80 per cent of New Villages has primary schools within the villages while 20 per cent has primary schools outside. While Chinese primary education is easily accessible to most New Village Chinese students, because of declining enrolment an increasing number of Chinese primary schools are facing sustainability issues because of declining enrolment. The problem is further compounded by the fact that the lower- and middle-level income New Villagers have limited financial resources to support the neighbourhood Chinese primary schools. Hence, a significant number of Chinese primary schools found in New Villages are in dilapidated conditions, lack adequate facilities, and are under utilized because of declining enrolment.

While New Villagers have convenient access to primary schools, the situation is very different when it comes to secondary schools. In 2002, 13 per cent of New Villages have a secondary school within their villages while 89 per cent of New Villages have no secondary school. The majority of New Villagers thus depend on secondary schools outside the villages;[24] for 13 per cent of the New Villagers the nearest secondary schools were 10 km or more away, and for another 20 per cent, the nearest secondary schools were 5–10 km away. Because of the distance, New Villagers frequently encounter difficulties in sending their children to secondary schools; the parents' low incomes mean that they cannot afford to send all their children to secondary schools in towns as this would incur expenses beyond their affordability.

An additional problem encountered by New Villages students is that because they attended Chinese primary schools, their command of the Malay language is usually weak. Thus when they move on to secondary school after completing their primary education, many will drop out because they cannot cope with the lessons since the medium of instruction in the national secondary schools is Malay. The general pattern of the education attainment of the New Villagers is reflective of the education problems they have encountered. In 2000, the breakdown of the education attainment of the New Villagers is 37.4 per cent with primary education or less, 25.2 per cent with upper secondary education, and only 4.8 per cent with tertiary education, compared with the national figures of 29.5 per cent, 40.9 per cent, and 10.2 per cent respectively.

CONCLUSION

Although the fundamental principle of Malay dominance underpinning the Malaysian political regime — *Ketuanan Melayu* — is set to remain, the increasing differentiation, especially of class, of the Malay society has resulted in the increasing differentiation of interests and expectations among the Malays. Signs of the fragmentation of Malay support for UMNO have forced the party to rely more on non-Malay support. This not to say that ethnicity is no longer deeply embedded in the fabric of Malaysian politics, economics, and society, but rather that emerging class- and other non-ethnic-based issues have emerged to complicate the political culture in the 1990s. Thus, the new politics — first encapsulated by the *Reformasi* movement and later entrenched in Pakatan Rakyat coalition party — contributed to weakening the ethnicized polity. In a nutshell, this trend has strengthened the bargaining power of the Chinese community and this is demonstrated in the scaling back of ethnic preferences and the liberalization of the education and cultural/language policies that assuaged minority concerns.

Even before the 2008 general election, Selangor Menteri Besar Dr Mohamad Khir Toyo announced in December 2007 that the state government has decided to waive all quit rents, amounting to about RM500,000, of the Tamil and Chinese primary schools and Chinese private secondary schools (Duzhong). The 105 Chinese and 97 Tamil schools only need to pay RM1 as a token in future. On top of that, all quit rents in arrears were also written off by the state government.

After the stunning results of the 12th general election, the Pakatan Rakyat-controlled state governments have implemented various policies towards education that have pleasantly uplifted the Chinese community, including the Chinese educationists. The Penang, Kedah, Perak, and Selangor Pakatan Rakyat state governments have all announced that all the Chinese and Indian primary and private schools now only have to pay a nominal sum of RM1 for its quit rent.

The DAP-led Pakatan Rakyat Penang state government has established a committee in the State Executive Council to address Chinese education problems and issues specifically. In Perak, the state government has increased its financial support for the independent Chinese secondary schools in the state, with their annual grant increased from RM40,000 in 2006 to RM50,000 in 2008.

In a sense, the Pakatan Rakyat-controlled local governments' initiatives to assist with the various Chinese education problems and issues have pressured the BN to make various concessions also. For example, the Johor state government has also announced that the vernacular schools will now have to pay a nominal sum of RM1 for its quit rent. The deputy minister for Education, Dr Wee Ka Siong, has assured the Chinese community that the government will attempt to settle the problems encountered by the Chinese primary schools. Significantly, he has met up with representatives from the Chinese education movement to discuss the problems facing Chinese education. In April 2008, the deputy minister for Higher Education, Dr Hou Kok Chung, visited the New Era College, which was established and administered by the Chinese educationist movement. In fact, Chinese educationists are hoping that the government will finally give them permission to establish a Chinese-medium university in Malaysia.

Notes

1   The focus here will be on the Chinese in Peninsular Malaysia.
2   While a large number of the English schools were established by Christian missionaries, they eventually became government-assisted schools. To train the sons of the Malay aristocracy to serve in the colonial service, the British established the English-medium Malay College Kuala Kangsar (MCKK) in 1905. In later years, the MCKK started to admit sons of ordinary Malays also, but it retained its status as a Malay-only institution — and it has remained that way even after Independence.
3   The Chinese millionaire, Tan Kah Kee, played a key role in mobilizing the community to establish Chinese schools (Yong 1987).
4   Because few Chinese schools were willing to take up the offer, the British introduced other measures to exert control over them, such as requiring Chinese schools to register with the colonial state in order to operate.
5   In 1938, 91,534 (66,645 boys and 24,889 girls) were enrolled in Chinese schools, while only 18,522 boys and 8,452 girls were enrolled in English schools (Purcell 1948, p. 222).
6   The first medical college was established in 1905 and Raffles College was established in 1929. In 1949, the medical college and Raffles College merged into the University of Malaya.
7   Indeed, under Section 21(2) of the 1961 Education Act, under certain conditions, the education minister has the power to close down the Chinese and Tamil primary schools and convert them into Malay-medium schools. Although the 1996 Education Act eliminated Section 21(2), Chinese educationists remained sceptical of the government's "ultimate objective". In the latest 2006–2010 Education Development Blueprint, the Chinese educationists believe that the Malaysian state has not given its "ultimate objective" as Chapter 4, para 4.12 reiterates: "… the ultimate objective of educational policy in the country must

be to bring together the children of all races under a national educational system in which the national language is the main medium of instruction".

8   Even so, the percentage of Other *Bumiputra* with only primary education attainment increased from 24.9 per cent in 1991, to 29.6 per cent in 2000. This was due to the high dropout rates from primary schools for Orang Asli and non-Malay *Bumiputra* groups in Sabah and Sarawak in the 1990s; for example, in 1995 the Ministry of Education reported that their dropout rate was a staggering 62 per cent against the [national] average of 3.1 per cent.

9   Other *Bumiputra* include the Orang Asli, Kadazan, and Iban.

10   Except since 2003, when the government implemented the use of English as the medium of instruction for mathematics and science subjects. National primary schools, in principle, would have to teach Chinese or Tamil as subjects under the Pupils Own Language programme.

11   An important trend in recent years has been the rising numbers of non-Chinese Malaysians enrolling their children in Chinese schools; in 1998 there were 70,000 non-Chinese Malaysian pupils in Chinese-medium primary schools.

12   In addition, the implementation of Malay preferential policies in education and government jobs has also discouraged more Chinese parents from enrolling their children in the national primary schools. If learning English is regarded as a means to enhance educational and employment opportunities, the fact that is very difficult for non-Malays to get admission into local public universities or get a job in the civil service, has removed an important incentive to enrol in the national primary schools. In fact, learning Chinese has become more attractive with the re-emergence of China as a major economic power. Another pull factor is the perception that Chinese schools provide better quality education and school discipline compared with the national primary schools.

13   According to the Ministry of Education, the aims and objectives of "Vision Schools" are:

— To foster solidarity among pupils of different races and backgrounds.
— To instil the spirit of integration among pupils of different streams.
— To produce a generation that is tolerant and understanding so as to realize the goal of a united nation.
— To encourage maximum interaction among pupils through the sharing of school facilities and implementation of other activities in school.

14   In the 1990s, Mahathir was already convinced that Malays need to master the English language in order to upgrade their scientific and technical knowledge and skills, as well as for the community to stay relevant and competitive in the increasingly globalized knowledge economy. In December 1993, Mahathir announced that universities would be allowed to use English as a medium of instruction in courses related to science and technology. Two years later in 1995, the MOE issued an education guideline that permits public universities and higher institutions to determine the percentage of courses to be taught in

English and this should be in accordance with the relevance and need of the use of the language, as well as with the ability of these institutions to conduct academic courses in the language. Apart from this, a 100-per-cent usage of English is allowed if the courses concerned are taught by foreign lecturers, or if the courses are postgraduate ones which are attended by foreign students as well. The guideline also proposes that these institutions should increase the use of English in tutorials, seminars, assignments, etc. (Asmah 2003, p. 91).

The government thus gave the legal green light to [higher educational] institutions to seek official approval for the use of the English medium in science and technical subjects.

15   The status and function of English in the society has experienced a radical policy shift since 1990. Malay political and bureaucratic elite have come around to acknowledging that the switch to Malay as the main medium of instruction has not only not helped, but has retarded, the growth of scientific and technical knowledge and research in the country, especially for the Malays. English, they also recognize, continues to be the primary working language of business in Malaysia and that is an asset to have in the global economic marketplace. Anecdotal findings have also indicated that public universities graduates' poor command of the English language has negatively affected their employability in the private sector — and the majority of those affected were Malays.

16   However, the Najib administration has announced reverting to Malay as the medium of instruction for mathematics and science subjects from 2012 onward.

17   Financially, the country was losing a huge sum of money by having tens of thousands of Malaysian students studying overseas. This problem became especially painful during the 1997 financial crisis. Also, the state came to see the business potential in education and thus proceeded with plans to make Malaysia an education hub in the region. An additional factor was that the brain drain of young non-Malay Malaysians — bound for Australia, Britain, Canada, New Zealand, Singapore and the United States — was depriving the local economy of the skilled human resource the country badly needs for its objective to be a knowledge economy.

18   A number of factors had contributed to the declining number of students studying overseas; from 73,000 in 1990 to 50,600 in 1995 and, especially after the 1997 financial crisis, to 13,000 in 2000. Various quarters have raised concerns over the privatization of higher education in the country and its consequences, such as, it excludes students from poor families, the quality of instruction and facilities, commodification of education, and so on.

19   Lastly, the privatization of higher education has also led to the establishment of Chinese-medium colleges in Malaysia. In 2007, there were three Chinese-medium colleges, namely: Southern College (est. 1990) in Johor, New Era College (est. 1998) in Selangor, and the Han Jiang International College (est.

1999) in Penang. This means that for Chinese students, especially graduates of the ICSS, there are now opportunities to have Chinese-medium instruction all the way up to certificate and diploma levels locally. In addition, they can also further their studies in an increasing number of Taiwanese and Chinese universities that are recognized by the Malaysian Government.

[20]   In 2003, the average Chinese household income was 1.8 times that of the average *Bumiputra* household income. Since this is an average figure, it does not tell us how income is distributed within the Chinese community. It would thus be wrong to assume that the "average" Chinese earns 1.8 times the "average" *Bumiputra*. Also, since the majority of the Chinese reside in the urban areas, it would mean that they are subject to higher costs of living. In 2004, for the peninsula, the Chinese recorded the second highest income inequality, after the *Bumiputra*; with a Gini coefficient of 0.446. In the urban areas, there are still lower-income Chinese neighbourhoods and squatter areas. Another sizeable group of poor Chinese are the New Villagers.

[21]   Examples are the Independent Chinese secondary schools, Foon Yew (Johor Bharu), Chung Hwa and Kuen Cheng (Klang Valley), and Han Chiang (Penang), and primary school Puay Chai.

[22]   Amid the 1997 financial crisis, the government established the National Higher Education Fund Corporation (NHEFC) to provide subsidized loans to students studying in the private higher education institutions. By 2000, the loans were also extended to students enrolled in the public universities and, in 2010, students with UEC (United Examinations Certificate) qualifications could also apply for the loans as long as they registered in an accredited course in a private higher education institution. From 1995 to 2005, the NHEFC disbursed more than RM15.1 billion to more than 800,000 students (World Bank 2007). Chinese students, especially those from lower-incomes families, have also benefited from this extensive student loan programme.

[23]   In 2000, the Chinese constituted 82 per cent of the total New Village population followed by Malays 13 per cent and Indians 4 per cent.

[24]   This phenomenon is the result of the fact that New Villages had not reached the minimum population requirement of 15,000, out of which at least 10 per cent were of school-going children, in order for a secondary school to be provided.

References

Abd. Rahim Abd. Rashid. *Education and Nation Formation in Malaysia: A Structural Analysis*. Kuala Lumpur: University of Malaya Press, 2002.

Asmah Haji Omar. *Language and Language Situation in Southeast Asia: With Focus on Malaysia*. Kuala Lumpur: Hakcipta Akademi Pengajian Malay, 2003.

Chow Kum Hor. "Battle to Save Malaysia's Chinese Dropouts". *Straits Times*, 31 January 2008.

Faaland, Just, et al. *Growth and Ethnic Inequality: Malaysia's New Economic Policy.* Kuala Lumpur: Dewan Bahasa dan Pustaka, 1990.

Kua Kia Soong. *The Chinese Schools in Malaysia: A Protean Saga.* Kuala Lumpur: United Chinese School Committees Association of Malaysia, 1985.

Lee Ting Hui. *Chinese Schools in British Malaya: Policies and Politics.* Singapore: South Seas Society, 2006.

Malaysia. Government. *Ninth Malaysian Plan.* Kuala Lumpur: National Printing Press, 2000.

———. Ministry of Education. *Educational Statistics of Malaysia 1980.* Kuala Lumpur: National Printing Press, 1980.

———. *Educational Statistics of Malaysia 1990.* Kuala Lumpur: National Printing Press, 1990.

———. *Educational Statistics of Malaysia 1995.* Kuala Lumpur: National Printing Press, 1995.

———. *Educational Statistics of Malaysia 1999.* Kuala Lumpur: National Printing Press, 1999.

———. *Educational Statistics of Malaysia 2000.* Kuala Lumpur: National Printing Press, 2000.

Stevenson, Rex. *Cultivators and Administrators: British Educational Policy towards the Malays, 1875–1906.* London: Oxford University Press, 1975.

Tan Ai Mei. *Malaysian Private Higher Education: Globalisation, Privatisation, Transformation and Marketplaces.* London: Asean Academic Press, 2002.

Tan Liok Ee. *The Politics Of Chinese Education in Malaya, 1945–1961.* Kuala Lumpur: Oxford University Press, 1997.

Yong, C.F. *Tan Kah-kee: The Making of an Overseas Chinese Legend.* Singapore: Oxford University Press, 1987.

INDEX

Straits Chinese, 8
Straits Times, 145
SUARAM, 61, 162
Sulaiman Abdul Rahman Taib, 111, 122n11
Sun, The, 151
SUPP (Sarawak United People's Party), xxiv–xxv, xxvi, 62, 96–97, 109, 110–15
Suqiu, 61, 90, 149–50, 161
Syariah Court, 51, 95, 159
Syed Husin Ali, 158

T
Taiwan, 148, 191n19
Taman Aman Vision School Complex, 176
Tamil language, 189n10
Tamil Nesan, 146
Tan Chee-Beng, xvi–xviii, 1–23, 42n15
Tan Kah Kee, 188n3
Tan Koon Swan, 147
Tan Siew Sin, 49
Tasik Permai Vision School Complex, 176
Teng Hock Nan, 156
Teochews, 114
Terengganu, xvii, 10, 11, 13, 22n12, 57
Thailand, 55
Tiong Hiew King, xxix, 148, 151, 152
Toh, Harry, 147
Toh Kin Woon, xxvii
Transparency International, 158
Tung Bao, 146, 150
Tunku Abdul Rahman College, 53, 174
TV3, 149
20-Point Agreement, xxv, 118–19
2008 election
    allegations of fraud in, 76
    politics of fear and, 2, 20
    potential consequences, xviii

rejection of racial politics in, 18
results, xv
role of media and, 144–62
seats won, 71

U
UMNO (United Malays National Organization). See also BN (Barisan Nasional)
    Chinese community and, xxi, xxii, 121
    democracy and, 5–6
    distrust of IMP, 19
    dominance of BN, 45–46, 129
    in East Malaysia, 120, 122, 123n25
    education policies, 167, 168–69
    Islamization policy, xvii
    leadership struggle, 56
    Malay nationalist agenda, xvi–xviii, 18, 82–83, 90
    Malay voters and, 19, 87, 129, 187
    media coverage of, 159
    NOC and, 21n5
    non-Malay parties and, 49, 83, 148, 162
    PAS and, xx, 10, 48, 87, 90, 105
    politics of fear, 2, 18, 93, 138
    rentier class and, xxvii
    sacking of lord president and, 12
    split in 1987–88, 89
    2008 election and, 13
    younger generation and, 57–58
UMNO Youth, 45, 50, 93, 146, 153, 162
United Chinese School Committees Association, 149
United Chinese School Teachers Association, 89, 94, 149
United Kingdom, 180, 190n17
United States, 180, 190n17
University and University Colleges (Amendment) Act, 179